- describing characters
- describing pictures

Let's go!

1 02

Tipp

Wenn Sie ein Wort nicht kennen, dann fragen Sie: What's ... in German, please?

Liebe Schülerinnen und Schüler,

mit **Keep Going 4th edition** halten Sie ein neues Englischbuch in den Händen, mit dem Sie auf dem richtigen Weg sind, sich sprachlich für den mittleren Schulabschluss und die Berufswelt von morgen zu rüsten. Das Buch enthält folgende Teile:

Let's go!	Hier können Sie Ihre Grundkenntnisse wiederholen und auffrischen. Übrigens: Es geht um Computerspiele – trockene Grammatikübungen werden Sie hier nicht finden.
Units 1–15	Hier gibt es alle Themen, die Sie benötigen, um sich das nötige Englisch für Alltag und Beruf anzueignen. Der Einstieg wird Ihnen mit dem *Warm-up* leicht gemacht. In den nachfolgenden Texten und Übungen dreht sich alles um die Welt von heute. Wie denkt ein Soldat über einen Auslandseinsatz? Was bewegt einen Fahrradkurier in Moskau? Warum graben junge „guerilla gardeners“ nachts fremde Grundstücke um? Wie funktioniert eine Karaokeanlage? Wenn Sie sich den Anfang einer Unit anschauen, werden Sie neben dem Titel ein paar Hinweise darauf finden, was Sie in der Unit lernen. Etwa „describing pictures", „making appointments", „applying for a job" oder „taking part in a discussion". Diese Inhalte vermitteln Ihnen das Rüstzeug, um in Alltag und Beruf auf Englisch kommunizieren zu können. Und um das Lernen effektiver zu machen, finden Sie in jeder Unit eine *Skills*-Box, in der Ihnen Tipps zum effektiven Lernen gegeben werden.
Do you remember?	Nach den Units 3, 7, 11 und 15 können Sie Ihren Fortschritt anhand eines kurzen Tests überprüfen. Die Lösungen stehen hinten im Buch, aber schlagen Sie sie erst nach, wenn Sie die Aufgaben fertig bearbeitet haben, sonst wissen Sie nicht, was Sie wirklich behalten haben.
Files	Dieser Teil enthält Materialien für Partner- und Gruppenarbeit. Im Verlauf des Buches wird mehrmals darauf verwiesen.
Grammatikübersicht	Zum Nachschlagen: Hier sind alle Regeln und Formen übersichtlich zusammengefasst.
Grundwortschatz	Hier finden sich diejenigen Wörter, die in **Keep Going** vorausgesetzt werden. Gehen Sie ab und zu mal eine Spalte durch, um sich zu vergewissern, dass die Grundlagen sitzen.
Chronologisches Wörterverzeichnis	Dieses Wörterverzeichnis enthält alle neu im Buch eingeführten Vokabeln. Die mittlere Spalte enthält Hilfen zum Lernen – meist ein Beispielsatz. Es hilft, eine der drei Spalten zuzuhalten und anhand der anderen beiden zu erschließen. Decken Sie am besten nicht immer dieselbe Spalte zu.
Alphabetisches Wörterverzeichnis	Zum Nachschlagen sind alle Wörter noch einmal alphabetisch aufgeführt.
Unregelmäßige Verben	Eine Liste wichtiger unregelmäßiger Verben und ihrer Stammformen.

Und nun:
Viel Erfolg bei der Arbeit mit **Keep Going!**

Die Autoren und der Verlag

Inhalt

1 Describing characters

a Copy the table and complete it with information about the characters.

name	*place*	*age*	*favourite tool(s)*	*magic*	*strength factor*	*intelligence factor*
Aquarius					36	64
Blaze					24	76
Dr Stink					85	15
Massive Man					7	93
Silver Queen					63	37
Voltage					79	21

b **Work with a partner. Use the information from your table to ask and answer questions about the characters.**

Where's (he/she/it) from?
How old is (he/she/it)?
What's (his/her/its) favourite tool?
Is (he/she/it) strong?
Is (he/she/it) intelligent?
Where's their home?

What's her name?

Her name is Silver Queen.

Question words

how?	*wie?*
what?	*was?*
when?	*wann?*
where?	*wo?*
who?	*wer?*
why?	*warum?*

2 Speaking: asking questions

a **Partner A: ask your partner questions. Partner B: introduce yourself as one of the characters.**

Partner A	Partner B
What's your name?	I'm (Silver Queen).
Where ... you from?	I'm from (Lower Earth).
How old ...?	I'm (38) years old.
What ... your favourite tool?	My favourite tool is (my magic wand).
... you strong?	Yes, I am / No, I'm not.
... you intelligent?	Yes, I am / No, I'm not.

b **Now Partner B asks the questions and Partner A answers as a different character.**

3 Translating

How do you say it in English?

1 Ich heiße BrownBearSpirit. Wie heißt du?
2 Ich komme aus Azeroth. Wo bist du her?
3 Trajuwu, das ist meine Freundin, Vadaa-Dar. Sie ist ein Elf.
4 Meine Lieblingsstadt ist Orcville.

4 Translating *sie* and *ihr*

a Change 'sie' to *she* or *they*, and say who it is.

EXAMPLES:	'Sie' are from Upper Earth.	They are from Upper Earth. It's Massive Man, Voltage and Blaze.
	'Sie' is a dragon.	She is a dragon. It's Blaze.

1 'Sie' is beautiful and intelligent.
2 'Sie' are from Lower Earth.
3 'Sie' are from a city.
4 'Sie' can breathe fire.
5 'Sie' is very big.
6 'Sie' are very old.

b Now do the same with 'ihr' (*her* or *their*).

1 'Ihr' magic is the energy of fire.
2 'Ihre' bodies are large.
3 'Ihr' favourite tool is 'ihr' magic wand.
4 'Ihre' faces are green.

5 *Is, isn't, are,* or *aren't*?

Complete with *is, isn't, are* or *aren't*.

1 His favourite video game ... Live For Speed. It's Need For Speed.
2 She ... a bad player, she's very good.
3 My friend loves video games. They ... his hobby.
4 I don't think video games ... much fun.
5 Mario and Luigi ... cousins, they're brothers.
6 Pac Man ... a popular game anymore. It's old now.
7 He ... winning because he's the best player.
8 You ... a video game designer yet, but you will be someday.

6 What does *'s* mean?

Is *'s* here the short form of *is*, or is it the genitive?

EXAMPLES:	Tomb Raider's a fun video game.	's = is
	Laura Croft's hair is brown.	's = genitive

1 Final Fantasy's a very popular game.
2 This video game's story is complicated.
3 Grand Theft Auto's characters are criminals.
4 She's a character in an adventure game.
5 This game's designer is very talented.
6 He's very small but extremely clever.

Grammar

***to be* and possessive adjectives**

	to be	possessive adjectives
I	am	my
you	are	your
he/she/it	is	his/her/its
we	are	our
they	are	their

Do you want to be a video games designer?

1 03

The video games industry has a big future. In 2007, people spent $42 billion on video games, and this number gets larger every year.

As the industry grows, our company, Creative Software, also grows. We make computer games, gaming consoles, mobile telephones and smartphones. Our technology can be used for fun or for practical things, so we also make 'games' which teach people to do things like repair cars.

Do you want a piece of the action? We are looking for game designers who can make the games fun. We also need artists and salespeople. What we need most are people who can program the games. To be a programmer, you should know a programming language like C++ or Java. You should also speak very good English.

(135 words)

7 Reading for detail

Read the text above and say whether these statements are true or false. Correct the false statements.

1 This text is an advertisement for a video game.
2 The company Creative Software made $42 billion in 2007.
3 Creative Software makes products for professional training.
4 Creative Software needs salespeople more than it needs designers, artists or programmers.
5 C++ and Java are video games programmers need to know.

8 Prepositions of place

Complete the sentences with the words from the box.

behind | between | in front of | near | ~~next to~~ | opposite

EXAMPLE:

The ball is *next to* the two boxes.

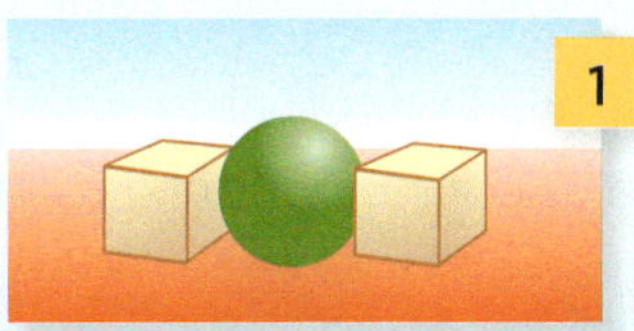

The ball is ... the two boxes.

The ball is ... the two boxes.

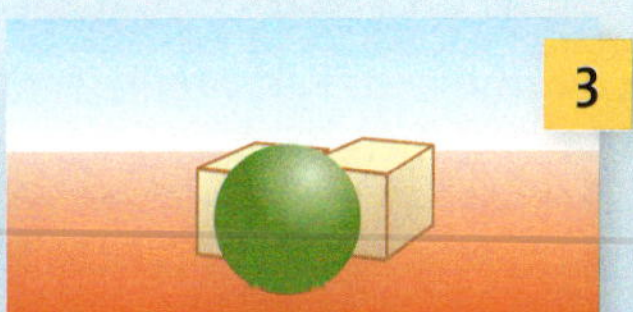

The ball is ... the two boxes.

The ball is ... the two boxes.

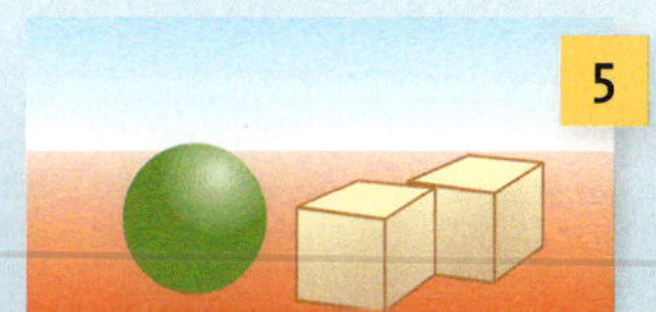

The ball is ... the two boxes.

9 Plural endings of nouns

Copy the table below and put the plural forms of the following words into the correct categories.

1 ~~glass~~	2 man	3 box	4 woman	5 boy	6 bus
7 baby	8 game	9 day	10 child	11 story	12 church

+ *-s*	+ *-es*	*-y* → *-ies*	*irregular*
	glass – glasses		

10 Hidden object games

Complete the gaps with the plural forms of the nouns in brackets.

'Hidden object' *(versteckter Gegenstand)* video games are very popular with *children*[1] (child). Some are designed especially for ...[2] (boy), but this one is for ...[3] (girl). But even adult ...[4] (man) and ...[5] (woman) like to play these ...[6] (game) sometimes. On the right, there is a list of ...[7] (object) the player has to find in the picture. The player collects ...[8] (point) when he or she clicks on one of the ...[9] (word) and then on the object it describes. Some of these ...[10] (game) have ...[11] (story), for example when the player visits different ...[12] (city) to find objects. These ...[13] (game) are one of the popular ...[14] (trend) in modern gaming because they do not cost very much money. ...[15] (Person) are often allowed to download them and use them for free for 30 ...[16] (day).

11 *There is/isn't, there are/aren't*

Look at the picture of the video game. Complete the sentences below with *there is, there isn't, there are,* or *there aren't*.

EXAMPLE: ... a beach chair in the middle of the picture.
There is a beach chair in the middle of the picture.

1 ... four people in the background.
2 ... 20 men playing football.
3 ... a herd of elephants.
4 ... three beach balls at the bottom of the picture.
5 ... a hotel at the top of the picture.
6 ... palm trees in the background.
7 ... a list of objects on the right-hand side.
8 ... a time display in the top right-hand corner.

Grammar

there is/are

There is an airplane, but **there isn't** an airport.
There are some women, but **there aren't** any men.

12 Building skills: describing pictures

Find the following things in the hidden object game and make sentences with *there* and the phrases from the box.

EXAMPLE: flamingo *(Flamingo)*

There are two flamingos on the right-hand side of the picture.

1 bus *(Bus)*
2 airplane *(Flugzeug)*
3 beach umbrella *(Sonnenschirm)*
4 glass *(Glas)*
5 woman *(Frau)*
6 sandal *(Sandale)*
7 gift box *(Geschenkkarton)*
8 strawberry *(Erdbeere)*

Skill

Bilder beschreiben

in the top left-hand corner
at the top of the picture
in the top right-hand corner
in the background
on the left
on the right
in the middle
on the left-hand side of the picture
on the right-hand side of the picture
in the foreground
in the bottom left-hand corner
at the bottom of the picture
in the bottom right-hand corner

13 Writing: *how much / how many?*

Write four questions with *How much* ... and four with *How many* ... on a piece of paper.

Then, give the eight questions to your partner.

Finally, give your partner an answer to one of the questions and he/she has to say which question you mean.

How much does a video game console cost?

150 euros.

How many people are there in the classroom?

21.

14 *Much, many, a lot of*

Complete the sentences with *much*, *many* or *a lot of*. Use *a lot of* only once in each number.

1 There are ... objects in the picture.
There isn't ... grey in the picture.
Hidden object games don't cost ... money.
They make ... work for the artists.

2 Ralph has ... games on his computer.
He says, "I have ... fun with the games."
"I don't have ... time for other things."
"There aren't ... other things for me to do."

Grammar

much, many, a lot of

Welches Wort man benutzt, hängt davon ab, ob das Substantiv zählbar oder nicht zählbar ist.
Bei nicht zählbaren Substantiven in einem Aussagesatz verwendet man normalerweise nicht *much*, sondern *a lot of*.

	zählbares Substantiv, z. B. *object*	nicht zählbares Substantiv, z. B. *money*
Aussagesatz	There are **many** objects. There are **a lot of** objects.	~~This costs **much** money.~~ This costs **a lot of** money.
Verneinung	There aren't **many** objects. There aren't **a lot of** objects.	This doesn't cost **much** money. This doesn't cost **a lot of** money.

15 Object pronouns

a Complete the text with object pronouns.

Grandma: What are you guys doing?
Joanne: We're playing an auto-racing game.
Grandma: Can I play with ...[1] (you)?
Bill: Sure. Wait, we'll start the game again.
Grandma: So, how do we play ...[2] (it)?
Bill: We play against each other. Each of ...[3] (we) has a car. Can you see ...[4] (they)?
Grandma: Of course I can see ...[5] (they). I'm not blind, you know.
Bill: Sorry, Grandma. You're the red car. You try to drive faster than Joanne and ...[6] (I).
Grandma: That sounds easy.
Bill: Ha! Just wait, Grandma. Joanne is really good at this game. She always wins. At least I always lose against ...[7] (she).
Joanne: Don't listen to ...[8] (he), Grandma. He beats ...[9] (I) sometimes.
Bill: OK, the race is starting. Three ... two ... one ... go!
Grandma: Hey, this is fun.
Joanne: You're playing well, Grandma! Hey, you hit ...[10] (I) off the road!
Bill Grandma, don't hit ...[11] (we) off the road! You play dirty!
Grandma: Ha! I told ...[12] (you) this would be easy.

b Say whether the statements are true or false.

1 Grandma has played the game before.
2 The game is a car race.
3 Joanne often beats Bill at the game.
4 Grandma likes the game.
5 Grandma loses the game.

16 Reflexive pronouns

Complete the sentences with reflexive pronouns.

EXAMPLE: *I hurt myself when I fell over.*

1 My brother can't stop ... from playing video games. He's addicted.
2 We gave ... a Wii console for Christmas last year.
3 People always talk to ... when they play video games.
4 My aunt surprised ... when she beat me at Trespasser.
5 I didn't have a partner so I had to play against ... .
6 This video game company calls ... the leader in adventure games.

Grammar

personal pronouns

subject pronouns	object pronouns	reflexive pronouns
I	me	myself
you	you	yourself
he/she/it	him/her/it	himself/herself/itself
we	us	ourselves
you	you	yourselves
they	them	themselves

- talking about sports
- talking about daily routines
- making appointments

Fitness and sport 1

WARM-UP

1 *Play, do or go?*

a What sports do these people do?

EXAMPLE: *Lucy plays tennis.*

b What other sports do you know in English?

EXAMPLE: *go skateboarding*

2 Speaking about sports

Work with a partner. Ask/Answer questions about sports.

EXAMPLE:

A: *Do you go skateboarding?*

B: *No, I don't. I'm bad at it.*

It's fun/healthy/good for you.
It's boring/too hard/dangerous/expensive.
I'm good/bad at it.

Unit 1

3 Reading for gist

Skim the text below, then choose the best place (1–4) for these headings.

a What the player needs

b Young, talented – and homeless

c A dream becomes reality

d Football – but not as we know it

1 04

Weekly Review | SPORT | Sunday 13 September

Changing lives through football

1 ...

Patrick Allen is a brilliant football player. In fact, he is so good that he plays for his country. Sometimes over 100,000 people watch him and his team play. Patrick is a bright young man. He is mad about football. 'It's my life,' he says. But Patrick is a football player with a difference. He isn't rich and he doesn't have a sports car or a smart home. In fact, his home is a cardboard box under a bridge. Patrick is a member of England's team for the Homeless World Cup.

2 ...

The Homeless World Cup lasts seven days. During this time, there are 200 games. The games follow the rules for street soccer: each team has four players on the court. They play for seven minutes, then there is a one-minute break, then they play for another seven minutes. That means that a match only lasts 15 minutes in total. The match starts when the referee throws the ball into the court. The ball is a normal soccer ball.

3 ...

To play in the Homeless World Cup you have to be 16 or over. You can be a man or a woman: teams can be all male, all female or mixed. You have to be homeless, of course.

4 ...

For the players, it is a 'dream come true' to play for their country and travel around the world. Each player leaves the Homeless World Cup with a medal. They also get the chance to change their lives.

The Homeless World Cup means more than just 15 minutes of fame. Most players have better lives after the competition. They may find a home, go back to school or get a job. They may give up drugs and alcohol. Many players improve their relationships with friends and family. Several players each year become professional footballers. Others become coaches or sports instructors.

(311 words)

4 Reading for detail

Read the text carefully, then correct these false sentences about it.

EXAMPLE: Patrick Allen is a bad football player.
Patrick Allen is a very good football player.

1 Patrick has a lot of money.
2 Patrick plays football for Germany.
3 In a street soccer game, there are ten players in total.
4 Only men can play in the Homeless World Cup.
5 Only the best team gets a medal at the Homeless World Cup.
6 Most players become professional footballers.

5 Speaking: a team for the Homeless World Cup

Work in a small group.

- Choose your Homeless World Cup team from the players below. You need four players: a goalkeeper, a defender, a captain and a striker.
- Discuss your choice in the group. Use these useful phrases:

I think In my opinion, If you ask me,	we need *(Name)* *(Name)* is a good/bad (striker)	because	he/she is/isn't ...

- Write down your team list.
- Read out your team list to the class. Explain why you want those players.

6 Internet research project

Find out about the Homeless World Cup. Find answers to these questions. Report back to the class.

- Which country holds the current Homeless World Cup trophy?
- How many countries take part in the Homeless World Cup?
- What are the names of the German team players?
- Where does next year's Homeless World Cup take place?
- When does it take place?
- How can we support the team?

7 Speaking: Patrick's daily routine

After the Homeless World Cup, businesswoman Clare Wilson gets in touch with Patrick Allen.

She gives him a job as a trainee fitness instructor at her leisure centre.

Patrick draws up a timetable to help him to remember what to do and when.

Work with a partner. Take turns to describe Patrick's daily routine.

EXAMPLE:

On Mondays he works at the leisure centre from six o'clock to half past eleven.

	a.m	p.m
Mon	Leisure centre 6.00–11.30 a.m.	
Tues	Leisure centre 6.30–11.45 a.m.	Football training 6.50–8.50 p.m.
Wed		Leisure centre 12.45–6.15 p.m
Thurs	College 9.00 a.m. – 4.30 p.m.	
Fri	Leisure centre 6.30 a.m.–2.30 p.m	Football training 7.10–9.10 p.m.
Sat	Football for college team 8.30–11.30. a.m.	Leisure centre 2.45 p.m.–8.00 p.m.

Useful phrases: *talking about clock times*

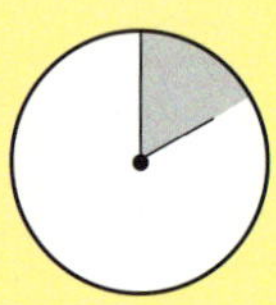

two o'clock

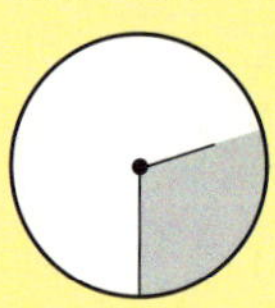

half past two

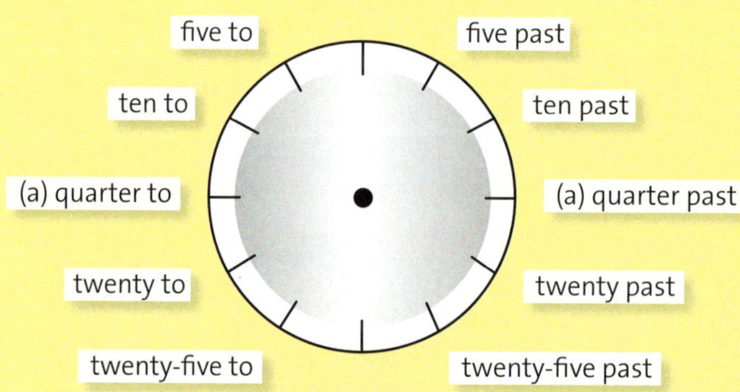

He starts work at six o'clock.
He works from six o'clock to half past eleven.
He works until half past two.

8 Reading: staff at the leisure centre

1 05 Read the texts. Work out who the people in the pictures are.

EXAMPLE: 1 *Clare*

My name's Andy.
I maintain all the equipment in the gym and make sure that it is safe to use. When something breaks down, I fix it. I also do odd jobs around the centre, like putting up signs and so on.

My name's Josh.
I'm responsible for the safety of pool users. You need certificates in first aid and lifesaving to do my job. A lot of the time I just sit around!

Hello, I'm Ramesh.
I work in the office. I send out emails and newsletters to keep our members informed about classes at the centre. I also assist Clare with office work.

Hi, I'm Emma.
When users arrive at the leisure centre, I give them information about classes. I also check their membership cards or take their money if they are non-members.

I'm Clare.
I'm responsible for running the leisure centre. I hire staff and supervise their work. I also decide what classes to run and what equipment to buy.

Good morning, I'm Barbara.
There's always a lot of cleaning to do around here – that's my job. I have to vacuum the carpets, mop and polish the floors and empty the bins. I start early in the morning, before the centre opens.

9 Building skills: learning useful expressions

a Match the parts of the expressions together. They are all in the texts above. Write them in your exercise book with the German meaning next to them. If there is more than one possibility, check in the texts.

EXAMPLE: 1 d *to assist someone with a task*
jemandem bei einer Aufgabe behilflich sein

1	to assist	a	emails/newsletters
2	to be responsible for	b	equipment
3	to do	c	odd jobs
4	to empty	d	someone with a task
5	to maintain	e	someone's safety
6	to send out	f	someone's work
7	to supervise	g	the bins
8	to vacuum	h	the carpet

b Think of other expressions using the verbs on the left.

Skill

Vokabeln im Zusammenhang lernen

Anstatt Vokabeln einzeln zu lernen, ist es wirksamer, sie im Zusammenhang (als Teil einer Redewendung oder eines ganzen Satzes) zu lernen. So merken Sie sich nicht nur die Bedeutung der Vokabel, sondern auch, wie sie im Alltag gebraucht wird.

10 Working with words: tools of the trade

Identify the objects from the sports centre and say who they belong to. (Look at the texts on page 17 for clues.)

EXAMPLE: a *That's Andy's toolbox.*

h

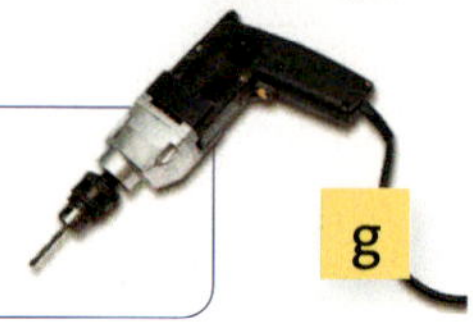
g

briefcase | cash register | drill | first aid box | smartphone | printer | toolbox | vacuum cleaner

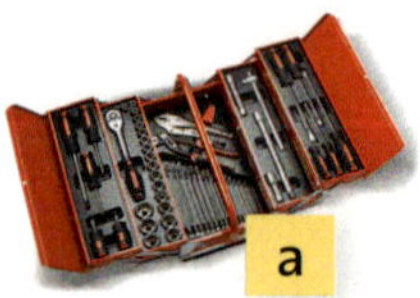
a

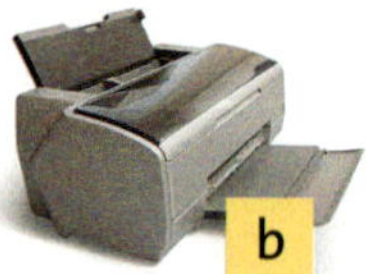
b

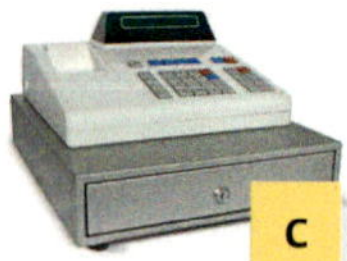
c

d

e

f

11 Listening: an appointment with Clare Wilson

Jack Smith wants to make an appointment with Clare Wilson to discuss his company's new exercise machines. He phones Clare's assistant, Ramesh Kumar.

a Complete the gaps (1–10) below with the useful phrases (a–j) from page 19.

EXAMPLE: 1 a

Ramesh:	Hello. Ramesh Kumar speaking. *How can I help you?*[1]
Jack:	Hi. It's Jack Smith here, of Power Train Ltd. ...[2]
Ramesh:	I'm afraid Mrs Wilson isn't in the office today. Can I help?
Jack:	Er, yes. I'd like to make an appointment to see her, please.
Ramesh:	I'll just look at her diary ... She could see you next Monday afternoon ...
Jack:	I'm afraid I can't make Monday. ...[3] Tuesday afternoon?
Ramesh:	She works from home on Tuesdays. She's free on Thursday morning at 10 o'clock, though. ...[4]
Jack:	Yes, it does. Thursday morning at 10 o'clock is fine.
Ramesh:	Good. ...[5]
Jack:	It's Jack Smith.
Ramesh:	Jack Smith ... And what was the name of your company?
Jack:	It's Power Train Ltd.
Ramesh:	Power Train Ltd. ...[6]
Jack:	...[7] 0407 297428.
Ramesh:	0407 297428.
Jack:	...[8]
Ramesh:	Is there anything else I can help you with?
Jack:	No, that's it. ...[9]
Ramesh:	...[10], Mr Smith. Goodbye.
Jack:	Goodbye.

1 06

b Now listen and check your answers.

12 Speaking: making an appointment

Work with a partner.

Partner **A:** You are John/Jenny Smith from Energy Drinks Ltd. You want to make an appointment with Dan Fraser, the café manager at the leisure centre.
Partner **B:** You are Dan Fraser's assistant, Sam Fryer. You start the conversation.

Before you start the role-play:

1 Read the instructions carefully. 2 Find phrases to help you in the box below.

A: Caller	B: Assistant
	Grüßen Sie mit Ihrem Vornamen. Fragen Sie, wie Sie behilflich sein können.
Stellen Sie sich mit Ihrem vollen Namen und Ihrem Firmennamen vor. Sie möchten Herrn Fraser sprechen.	
	Herr Fraser ist leider nicht da. Fragen Sie, ob Sie helfen können.
Ja. Sie möchten einen Termin mit Herrn Fraser vereinbaren.	
	Schlagen Sie einen Tag vor.
Dieser Tag ist für Sie leider nicht möglich. Schlagen Sie einen anderen Tag vor.	
	Herr Fraser arbeitet nicht an diesem Tag. Machen Sie noch einen Vorschlag.
Das passt Ihnen gut.	
	Fragen Sie nach dem Namen des Anrufers / der Anruferin.
Sagen Sie Ihren Namen.	
	Bitten Sie um die Telefonnummer.
Geben Sie eine Handynummer.	
	Wiederholen Sie die Nummer.
Bestätigen Sie, dass die Nummer richtig ist.	
	Gibt es sonst noch etwas, womit Sie helfen können?
Nein, das war's. Bedanken Sie sich.	
	Reagieren Sie auf den Dank. Verabschieden Sie sich.
Verabschieden Sie sich ebenfalls.	

Useful phrases: *telephoning*

a How can I help you?
b Can I speak to *(Name)*, please?
c What was your name again, please?
d That's right.
e Can I have your phone number, please?
f Yes, of course. It's *(Nummer)*.
g What about *(Tag/Uhrzeit)*?
h Does that suit you?
i Thanks for your help.
j You're welcome.

13 Writing about yourself

Write eight true things about yourself. You can use the ideas below or your own ideas.

EXAMPLE: *I speak three languages: Turkish, German and English.*

come to school (on the bus) | do (kickboxing) | enjoy school | get up early on (Sundays) | go (running) | live near here | pay attention in class | play (football) | speak (two) languages | work on (Saturdays)

14 Interviewing your partner

Work with a partner. Ask about the activities above. Answer your partner's questions with *Yes, I do* or *No, I don't*.

EXAMPLE:

A: Do you play football?

B: No, I don't. / Yes, I do.

15 Writing about your partner

Write down what you found out about your partner.

EXAMPLE: *She speaks three languages. She doesn't play football …*

Grammar

The simple present (Die einfache Gegenwart)

Aussage	Verneinung	Fragen	Kurzantworten	
I You We They work.	I You We They **don't** work.	**Do** I you we they work?	Yes, I you we they **do**.	No, I you we they **don't**.
He She It work**s**.	He She It **doesn't** work.	**Does** he she it work?	Yes, he she it **does**.	No, he she it **doesn't**.

- Bei *he, she, it* muss das ‚s' mit: *he/she/it work**s**, play**s**, live**s**.*
- Besonderheiten der -s-Endung:
  - auf Verbendung *-ch, -sh, -s, -x* folgt **-es**: *watch* → *watches, wash* → *washes, kiss* → *kisses, fax* → *faxes*
  - Konsonant + *-y* wird Konsonant + **-ies**: *try* → *tries, fly* → *flies*
  - Sonderformen: *do* → ***does**, go* → ***goes**, have* → ***has***
- Verneinung mit dem Hilfsverb *do: I **don't** work, he **doesn't** work.*
- Fragen mit dem Hilfsverb *do: **Do** you work? **Does** she work?*
- Kurzantworten mit dem Hilfsverb *do: Yes, … **do/does**. No, … **don't/doesn't**.*
- Die einfache Gegenwart beschreibt etwas, das immer, regelmäßig oder nie geschieht.
- Signalwörter: *always* (immer), *usually* (normalerweise), *often* (oft), *sometimes* (manchmal), *never* (nie), *on Mondays* (montags), *every (day, week, Tuesday, etc.)* usw.

- using an online forum
- socializing

English around the world 2

WARM-UP

1 A quiz

1

a Guess the correct answers.

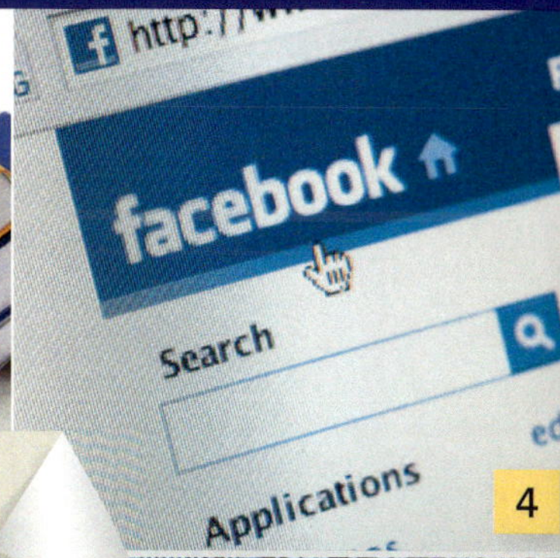

4

2

3

1 English has official or special status in at least … countries.
[a] 15 [b] 41 [c] 75

2 English is spoken as a first language by around … and as a second language by around … people in the world.
[a] 300 million; 300 million [b] 375 million; 375 million
[c] 450 million; 450 million

3 … people speak English as a foreign language.
[a] 400 million [b] 600 million [c] 750 million

4 Just over half of all ... are in English.
[a] school books [b] web pages [c] restaurant menus

5 There were … learners of English in 2000.
[a] 500,000,000 [b] 750,000,000 [c] over one billion

5

6

b English is the main language for many things. Look at the photos above and name them. Can you think of any other areas where English is used?

advertising | books | business | the Internet | music | newspapers | sport | technology | travel

2 Past or present?

Work with a partner. Say whether these verbs are in the past or present tense:

ARE was spoke taught try said could went SAW build need feel come were

3 Reading for gist

Before you read the discussion forum, look at the name of the website and the subject headings. What do you think this discussion is about?

4 Scanning a text for specific information

Now read the discussion forum quickly and find the following information:

1 Wer war ein Zivildienstleistender?
2 Wer ist ein Soldat?
3 Wer ist eine Sanitäterin?
4 Wer war ein Lehrer?
5 Wer hat mit einer Katastrophenschutz-Organisation gearbeitet?

1 07

http://www.

SmallWorld.com

Discussion forum | Travel | Working abroad | Homesickness

Meet cool people from all over the world.

subject: Homesickness
Tue, 16 January 11:54
BlueHelmet

I'm a peacekeeping soldier. I just came back from a nine-month NATO mission in Afghanistan. It was really different to where I'm from and I really felt homesick. I missed my friends, my family, the beach, etc. I'm sure some other people here have had this problem. How did you deal with it? What did you do to feel better? I need some advice before I go away again. Soon I'm going to Sudan with the United Nations.

Subject: Re: Homesickness
Tue, 16 January 15:16
KeepMoving

I know what you mean about homesickness, BlueHelmet. I did my community service abroad, in Brazil, with Brazilian farmers. Before I left, I didn't think I would have any problems with homesickness, but then I had terrible culture shock! What helped me the most was talking about it with the other foreign development workers. Luckily, they all spoke English.

Subject: Re: Homesickness
Wed, 17 January 8:04
Boots23

Hey BlueHelmet, I was in Afghanistan with you Italians and you were great soldiers. Yes, it's hard sometimes. I had a boyfriend back home and it wasn't easy being so far away from him. But I tried to think about the good aspects of the job. I'm a medic with the military, and I was able to help a lot of people in Afghanistan. Some of the poor people we helped there didn't know much English, but they could say "thank you", and that was always wonderful to hear.

Subject: Re: Homesickness
Thu, 18 January 19:22
TornadoTakeo

After the Tsunami in 2004, I went to Indonesia with a disaster-relief organization. For the first time in my life, I had no culture from home, not even Manga comics, haha! But it felt really good to give the people the help they needed. We built places for them to sleep and gave them food. Just remember that you will only be there a short time, so give your project your full attention, so that you have no time to be homesick.

Subject: Re: Homesickness
Fri, 19 January 12:29
free2Bme

BlueHelmet, I know how you feel. I taught English and health (HIV/AIDS) to teens in Russia, and I missed EVERYTHING from home – especially the food. I wrote about it in my blog. My advice is to write about your experiences, maybe not online, but privately.

(359 words)

5 Reading for detail

a Read the discussion forum again and answer these questions.

1 Each member of the forum mentions a problem he or she had. Which of the following problems do they *not* mention?
   a homesickness / culture shock
   b cold weather
   c unfriendly people

2 What advice do the other four members *not* give BlueHelmet?
   a Talk about the problem with colleagues
   b Focus on the good aspects of the job.
   c Focus on your work.
   d Get a lot of exercise.
   e Write about the problem.

b Say where each person is from and where they worked in the past.

EXAMPLE: *BlueHelmet is from Italy and he worked in Afghanistan.*

6 Building skills: learning vocabulary

Match the word on the right to its definition on the left.

1 something you tell a person to help them
2 belonging to another country
3 a soldier's assignment somewhere in the world
4 a non-military job you do for your country
5 mental and physical well-being
6 more than other things
7 mental focus
8 something you did

a foreign
b community service
c experience
d health
e especially
f mission
g advice
h attention

Skill

Vokabellernen mit Kärtchen

Um Vokabeln zu lernen, müssen Sie nicht stundenlang pauken. Hier ist eine Methode, die Sie während einer fünfminütigen Busfahrt anwenden können.

Schreiben Sie die Wörter auf Kärtchen oder Papierzettel. Auf die eine Seite schreiben Sie das englische Wort. Auf die andere Seite schreiben Sie die Übersetzung, Definition, oder einen Beispielsatz.

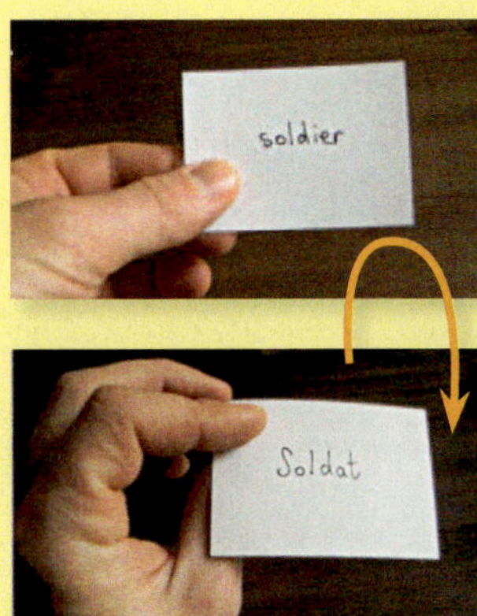

Wenn Sie Kärtchen beidseitig beschreiben, achten Sie darauf, dass Sie den Text auf der Rückseite auf dem Kopf schreiben, weil Sie das Kärtchen so mit nur einer Hand wenden und problemlos Vorder- und Rückseite lesen können.

Und so haben Sie immer noch Ihre zweite Hand, um sich während der Busfahrt ordentlich festzuhalten.

7 Looking at language

Look back at the discussion forum on page 22 and answer these questions.

1 Find this positive statement one of the forum members makes in the simple past. What form is the verb in?
Luckily, they all (**speak/spoke**) English.

2 Find this question with the word *did*. What form is the main verb in?
How **did** you (**deal/dealt**) with it?

3 Find this negative statement with the word *didn't*. What form is the main verb in?
I **didn't** (**think/thought**) I would have any problems ...

8 Stella and Senghor

Complete the sentences with *was/were*.

Stella ...[1] from Sweden and Senghor ...[2] from Senegal. They met while they ...[3] sailing the southern seas. It ...[4] love at first sight. Stella said, 'I ...[5] made for you, Senghor!' Senghor said, 'You ...[6] made for me, Stella!' Stella said, 'We ...[7] made for each other!' But Senghor ...[8] already married. There ...[9] six sons and a springer spaniel waiting for him in Senegal. Stella ...n't [10] sad about Senghor. Soon, there ...[11] a sexy señor from El Salvador.

Grammar

Was/were

I/he/she/it	was
you/we/they	were

9 A board game

In the 21st century, attractive foreigners are everywhere, at home and abroad. But your English has to be really good if you want to flirt with them. This game is for two players and a referee. Referee: Look at File 2 on page 134.

Players: When it's your turn, toss a coin. If it lands heads up, move one space. If it lands tails *(Zahl)* up, move two spaces. After you answer the question in the square, do what the referee tells you to do. If your English is good, you'll finish faster. Whoever finishes first is the winner.

An International *Love* Story

START

1
Your parents started letting you go on dates
a. as you were 16.
b. when you were 16.

2
A beautiful foreign exchange student came to your school.
a. Both ...
b. Neither ...
of you spoke good English.

3
You told the exchange student he/she was ...
a. smart
b. annoying

4
The student is in a hot brand. You ...
a. say, 'You look nice today.'
b. throw water on the student and save his/her life.

5
The student asked you out on a date. You said, ...
a. 'Are you paying?'
b. 'How about a movie?

3A
You tell the student, 'I got my driving licence ...
a. for a week.'
b. a week ago.'

3B
You ...
a. often
b. sometimes
c. never d. always
... did your English homework.

3C
The student heard you while you were being ...
a. polite
b. impolite
... to the teacher.

6
The student went back to his/her country, but you promised yourself you would love again.

7
A date brought you flowers. You said, …
a. 'I don't mind.'
b. 'What a surprise!'

8
You and a date ate a big …
a. menu
b. hamburger from McDonalds

9
Your English got so good that you became a travelling salesperson.

10
You invite an attractive customer to tea. You serve it in a …
a. pot.
b. can.

11
After the date, you make it clear to him/her that you are still …
a. curious.
b. strange.

12
The customer tells you he/she is …
a. engaged.
b. divorced.

13A
You stopped flirting with the customer, but you stayed in his/her city, only to be near him/her.

13B
The customer invited you to his/her wedding. You …
a. decline, because the wedding would make you too sad.
b. accept, because you can at least enjoy the buffet.

13C
The customer ran out of the church in the middle of the wedding. You …
a. stay in the church. b. follow him/her.

13
You gave the customer your …
a. handy
b. cell phone
c. mobile
… number.

14
The customer finally said it's you he/she loves. You become lovers.

15
You had to travel again for your job. You told your lover, 'See you …
a. bald.'
b. soon.'

16
While in Italy, you find a wonderful …
a. Roman b. CD

17A
You met an Italian …
a. artist
b. photograph

17
You had a lot in common with the Italian.
Both of you liked travelling and moonlit walks on the beach.

17B
You told your Italian you liked him/her because he/she was …
a. great b. gross
c. tall

17C
The Italian said, 'Thank you!' You answered, …
a. 'Please!'
b. 'You're welcome!'

18
The Italian was a vegetarian. You made him/her pizza with lots of …
a. pepperoni
b. peppers c. shrimps

FINISH

19
Your Italian liked your pizza so much that he/she asked to marry you. You lived happily ever after in the Tuscan countryside.

1 08

An internship abroad

Hi, I'm Barbara from Spain. I want to be an airplane technician, so I'm doing an internship at Airbus in Toulouse, France. I just helped them build this airplane!

It's an Airbus A380, the largest passenger airplane in the world. Its nickname is the 'Superjumbo'. Airbus began designing it in 2000, and the first one flew five years later.

Airbus is a European company. Government ministers from France, Germany and the United Kingdom founded the company in 1967. The company's language has always been English. The whole airline industry uses English so that everyone all over the world can communicate and work together.

The major parts of my plane came from France, Germany, Spain and the United Kingdom, but many smaller parts came from outside Europe. Every piece of the plane travelled to Toulouse, France, where we put it together.

(143 words)

10 Reading for detail

Read the text above and answer the questions:

1 Why did Barbara go to Toulouse, France? What happens there?

2 What happened in these years?

a 1967 b 2000 c 2005

3 What is special about the Airbus A380?

11 Speaking in the simple past

Look at the table and ask your partner where the different parts of Barbara's Airbus A380 came from.

EXAMPLE: *Where did the … come from?* *It/They came from …*
Did the … come from …? *No, it/they came from …*

part	*country*
wings *(Flügel)*	UK
cockpit *(Cockpit)*	France
fuselage *(Rumpf)*	Germany
tail *(Heck)*	Spain
wingtips *(Flügelspitzen)*	Australia

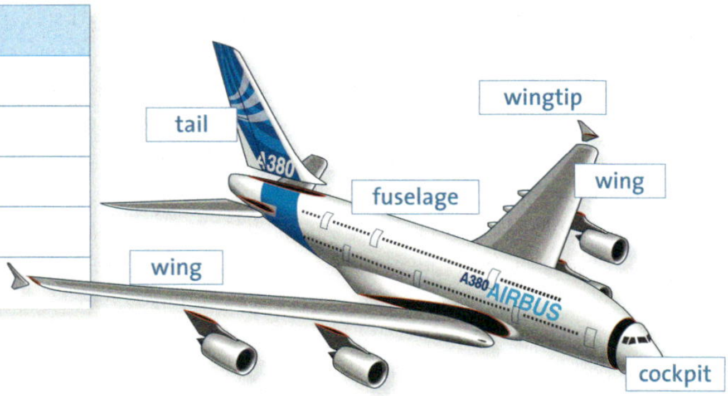

12 Talking about the past

a Play 'What I Did Yesterday' in groups of three. This is similar to the game *Ich packe einen Koffer*, but it goes like this:

Example: **1st person:** Yesterday I flew to Madagascar.
2nd person: Yesterday I flew to Madagascar and I built a house.

b Write down the events you thought of in part a.

13 Using the simple past

Put each verb in the past tense. You will have to insert *did* for negative statements and questions.

1 How ... (you know) that I speak English?
2 ... (you read) this book in German? – No, I ... (not find) a German translation.
3 He ... (get) the lyrics to the song online and ... (give) them to me.
4 She ... (not know) that so many Chinese learn English at school.
5 We ... (want) a newspaper but the shop ... (not have) any in German.
6 The chancellor ... (say) 'How do you do?' in English because she ... (not speak) Japanese.
7 ... (an English song win) the Eurovision Song Contest last year?
8 ... (your family have) a nice time in Poland?

14 Listening: what Anna did yesterday

1 09

Listen to the CD and make notes about what Anna did yesterday.

EXAMPLE: *First, she got up. Then she fed the cat. And then … And then finally, …*

drink | drive | feed | fly | get up | go | have | listen to | see

Grammar

The simple past (Die einfache Vergangenheit)

Aussage	Verneinung	Frage	Kurzantworten
a) regelmäßige Verben			
She listen**ed**. We work**ed**.	She **didn't** listen. We **didn't** work.	**Did** she listen? **Did** we work?	Yes, she **did**. / No, she **didn't**. Yes, we **did**. / No, we **didn't**.
b) unregelmäßige Verben			
I **flew**. They **came**.	I **didn't** fly. They **didn't** come.	**Did** I fly? **Did** they come?	Yes, I **did**. / No, I **didn't**. Yes, they **did**. / No, they **didn't**.

- Die Vergangenheitsform der Verben ist für alle Personen *(I, you, he/she/it, we, you, they)* gleich.
- Regelmäßige Verben: Endung *-(e)d*
- Unregelmäßige Verben: eigene Formen (s. Liste S. 206)
- Verneinung mit *didn't*. (Nach *didn't* steht die Grund-, nicht die Vergangenheitsform des Verbs!)
- Fragen und Kurzantworten mit *did*. (Auch nach *did* steht die Grundform des Verbs!)
- Die Vergangenheitsform verwenden wir, wenn wir sagen, was zu einem bestimmten Zeitpunkt oder in einem bestimmten Zeitraum der Vergangenheit abgeschlossen wurde.
- Signalwörter: *yesterday, last week/month, last Tuesday, (two years) ago.*

15 Who is saying which word?

a These people were photographed just as each of them was saying the simple past form of one of the following verbs. Who is saying which word?

~~come~~ | get | stand

b Which verbs have the same vowel sounds? Put the past tense of each verb into the same group: 'Tina', 'Rene' or Sam'.

eat | forget | give | lose | make | shoot | understand

c What do these words have in common?

buy | bring | catch | fight | seek | teach | think

16 Translating English film titles

a People all over the world know these Hollywood film titles, but sometimes they don't really understand them. What about you? Translate the titles into German.

Men in Black Speed Batman: The Dark Knight A Crime Pirates of the Caribbean

Star Wars Independence Day The Sixth Sense Ice Age

Mission: Impossible The Day After Tomorrow Pretty Woman

Tipp

Schauen Sie sich Filme auf Englisch an. So können Sie Ihr Englisch verbessern. Viele DVDs kann man auf Englisch mit deutschen Untertiteln schauen, damit man sie besser versteht.

b What films with English titles are currently in cinemas?

17 A word game

How many words can you make from the letters in the word 'Hollywood'?

EXAMPLE: *holly, wood, wool, …*

- talking about free-time activities
- applying for a job
- describing jobs

Free-time activities 3

WARM-UP

What can you do in your free time?

GO TO A FOOTBALL MATCH

LISTEN TO MUSIC

READ A MAGAZINE

DO VOLUNTARY WORK

GO TO THE CINEMA

PLAY A COMPUTER GAME

GO CLUBBING

TAKE PHOTOS

GO SHOPPING

1 Listening: free-time activities

1 10 Listen to the CD. What are the people doing?

EXAMPLE: *Person 1 is reading a magazine.*

2 A guessing game

Work with a partner. Choose something you do in your free time and mime it. Can your partner guess what you are doing?

http://www.

THE ABINGDON MUSIC FESTIVAL VOLUNTEERS WANTED!

The Abingdon Music Festival takes place over four days from Friday 24 June to Monday 27 June. Thousands of people come to see famous and not-so-famous musicians and bands. The different music styles include indie, techno, blues and folk.

We need volunteers for these areas and activities:

Festival Information: Where are the disabled toilets? Where can I get some cash? Where is my child? These are some of the questions that people ask every few minutes at the Festival Information Office. It's a great place for people who have good customer service skills.

Shop: The Festival Shop sells CDs, T-shirts, baseball caps, posters and souvenirs. You can get useful experience in retail sales here.

Surveys: Thousands of people come to the festival, but are they enjoying it? Your job is to find out.

Ticket Sales: You sell entry to the festival. You learn how to take credit card payments and handle cash. It's busy and time passes quickly.

Stewards: We need friendly and helpful people to direct cars in the car park, show people where to put up their tents on the campsite and generally help people find what they're looking for.

Catering: We need people to help with the Big Breakfast on Saturday, Sunday and Monday morning. Help us to cook bacon and eggs for 10,000 hungry people.

Volunteers get a free ticket to the festival (worth £120) and free meals and accommodation. They also get useful job skills and the chance to meet some great singers and bands. All this for just 10 hours of work!

(266 words)

3 Reading for detail

You're a volunteer at the Abingdon Music Festival. It's the day before the festival and you're answering questions on the telephone hotline.

Read the text above, then help these people with their questions.

1 'How long does the festival last?'
2 'Are there any famous bands?'
3 'Where should I go for information when I'm at the festival?'
4 'I want to buy a souvenir of the festival. Where can I do that?'
5 'Can I pay for my tickets by credit card?'
6 'Can I camp somewhere nearby?'
7 'How many people attend the festival?'
8 'I'm thinking of volunteering. Do I get anything for my hard work?'

4 Building skills: using a dictionary

a Decide which dictionary definition fits the situation in the text best.

1 volunteer (line 5)
- a *n* Freiwillige(r) m/f
- b *vi* sich freiwillig melden

2 disabled (line 6)
- a *adj* körperbehindert
- b *adj* Behinderten-

3 cash (line 6)
- a *n* (Bar)geld
- b *vt* einlösen

4 experience (line 11)
- a *n* Erfahrung
- b *n* Erlebnis
- c *vt* erleben

5 retail (line 11)
- a *n* Einzelhandel
- b *adj* Einzelhandels-
- c *vt* im Einzelhandel verkaufen

6 handle (line 15)
- a *n* Klinke
- b *n* Henkel
- c *vt* anfassen
- d *vt* umgehen mit

b Now use a dictionary to look up these words from the text. Write down the different meanings you find, then choose the one which fits the text best.

1	area	(line 5)	5	busy	(line 15)
2	great	(line 8)	6	direct	(line 16)
3	survey	(line 12)	7	job	(line 22)
4	entry	(line 14)	8	skill	(line 22)

Skill

Mit einem Wörterbuch umgehen

Wörterbücher sind nicht nur nützlich, um die Bedeutung eines Wortes zu überprüfen, sondern auch, um Hinweise für den Gebrauch des Wortes zu finden. Wenn Sie mit mehreren möglichen Übersetzungen konfrontiert werden, sollten Sie sich fragen: Welche Übersetzung passt am besten zum Text? Machen Sie sich mit den Abkürzungen und Symbolen Ihres Wörterbuchs vertraut, wie z. B. *n* = Nomen, *vt* = transitives Verb.

5 Project: designing a flyer

Work in a small group. Design a flyer for a music festival. Make sure that your flyer gives the following information:

- when
- where
- what kind(s) of music
- how much it costs
- where to get tickets
- where to get more information (website, phone, etc.)
- food and drink
- whether volunteers are needed
- how to get there

6 Reading: a CV

Tobias Schuster is looking for a working holiday in England to improve his English. He applies to be a volunteer at the Abingdon Music Festival. He sends his CV.

Read Tobias' CV and find the English for these German expressions.

1 Adresse	3 Grundschule	5 Gewerbliche Schule	7 Freiwilligentätigkeit
2 Geburtsdatum	4 Hauptschule	6 Praktikum	8 Erste-Hilfe-Zertifikat

CV

Name:	Tobias Schuster
Address:	Beethovengasse 19, 73708 Neudorf, Germany
Telephone:	+49 (0) 7051 556991
Date of birth:	17 June 1993

Education

1999–2003	Neudorf Primary School
2003–2007	Neudorf Secondary School
2007–	Altstadt Trade School

Work experience

2008	Work placement, LADI supermarket, Neudorf
Summer 2009	Holiday job, Restaurant Waldeck, Altstadt
Easter 2010	Voluntary work, 'Schloss-Rock' rock festival, Schloss Neudorf

Skills

Languages	English (fluent), French (basic)
IT	MS Office, MS Frontpage

Other

European First Aid Certificate

References available on request

7 Writing a CV in English

Write your own CV in English, using Tobias' CV as a model.

8 At the festival

Find the following people in the picture below.

EXAMPLE: **1 d**

1 roadies 2 security officers 3 DJ 4 caterers 5 event organizer

9 Reading: entertainment jobs

Read what the people say and work out what their jobs are. (They are all in exercise 8).

EXAMPLE: *Rob and Dean are roadies.*

1 11

'Hello. I'm Rob and this is Dean. At the moment we're unloading the sound equipment from this truck. We have to take the equipment to the stage, you see. When it's all on the stage, we set it up and test it. You have to be quite fit in this job – this stuff is heavy!'

'Hi, I'm Lara. Right now I'm choosing my music for tonight's techno trance session. I always check my equipment to make sure that the sound system and the lights are working correctly.'

'I'm Ann, this is Ben and that's Sam. We're cooking food for the performers and backstage crew. We've got curry, pies, burgers, kebabs and chips. Hundreds of people work backstage at a big event like this – and they're all hungry!'

'Hi, Leanne Smith, pleased to meet you. I'm supervising all the backstage people. It's my job to make sure that everything runs smoothly and to solve any problems. Excuse me, I need to make an urgent phone call ...'

'Hello, sir. I'm Sean and this is Eric. We're checking people's passes. Only performers and other authorized people can come in here. Sorry, you don't have a valid pass for the backstage area, so I must ask you to leave ...'

10 Do you remember?

a **Without looking back at page 33, say whether these statements about the picture are true or false.**

1 The dog is drinking water.
2 The two boys are climbing over the fence.
3 A girl in a red T-shirt is sitting on the ground.
4 The rock star is signing a photo.
5 The paramedic is helping an old lady.
6 A young man in a green T-shirt is waving to the rock star.
7 The roadies are carrying a piano.
8 The event organizer is using a mobile phone.

b **Now look back to check your answers. Are they correct?**

11 Writing: sentences in the present continuous

Correct the false sentences from exercise 10.

EXAMPLE: 1 *The dog isn't drinking water. It's eating a pie.*

12 Listening: in the canteen tent

1 / 12

Tobias meets a girl called Lexi at the festival.

Listen to the dialogue and choose the correct options (a, b or c) below.

1 Lexi is ...	a	a fan of a band called the Black Daisies.
	b	a member of a band called the Black Daisies.
	c	a roadie for a band called the Black Daisies.
2 The Black Daisies are ...	a	a punk band.
	b	an electronic rock band.
	c	an indie rock band.
3 They are playing ...	a	this afternoon.
	b	this evening.
	c	tomorrow evening.
4 Tobias is working ...	a	in the car park.
	b	at the campsite.
	c	in the Information Office.
5 Lexi invites Tobias to ...	a	have a drink with her.
	b	see the Black Daisies playing at the festival.
	c	meet the members of the Black Daisies backstage.

13 A survey

You are a volunteer at the festival. Your job is to chat with the festival goers, find out about them and find out their opinions about the festival.

Choose the correct form of the question for the situations on page 35.

Sie möchten wissen …

1 *… ob es ihm/ihr hier gefällt.*	a	Do you have a good time?
	b	Are you having a good time?
2 *… ob er/sie das warme Wetter heute genießt.*	a	Are you enjoying the warm weather today?
	b	Do you enjoy the warm weather today?
3 *… ob er/sie sonst viele Musikfestivals besucht.*	a	Do you go to a lot of music festivals?
	b	Are you going to a lot of music festivals?
4 *… welche Musikrichtung er/sie am liebsten mag.*	a	What sort of music do you like best?
	b	What sort of music are you liking best?
5 *… ob er/sie auf dem Campingplatz übernachtet.*	a	Are you staying at the campsite?
	b	Do you stay at the campsite?
6 *… wo er/sie herkommt.*	a	Where are you coming from?
	b	Where do you come from?
7 *… was er/sie beruflich macht.*	a	What do you do?
	b	What are you doing?

14 Writing answers

Write your own answers to the questions in exercise 13.

15 Speaking: small talk

Work with a partner. You meet each other for the first time at a music festival. Make small talk, using the questions and answers from exercises 13 and 14.

16 A project: jobs

Research one of the jobs from exercise 8. What does the person do? Write 6–8 sentences in the simple present (= things you do regularly). Read your text to the class.

EXAMPLE: *A roadie transports and sets up equipment for a band. He or she …*

Grammar

The present continuous (Die Verlaufsform der Gegenwart)

Aussage	Verneinung	Frage
I'm	I'm not	Am I
You're	You're not / You aren't	Are you
He's	He's not / He isn't	Is he
She's	She's not / She isn't	Is she
It's working.	It's not / It isn't working.	Is it working?
We're	We're not / We aren't	Are we
They're	You're not / You aren't	Are you
You're	They're not / They aren't	Are they

- Mit der Verlaufsform der Gegenwart sagen wir, dass etwas gerade jetzt geschieht und noch nicht abgeschlossen ist: I'**m standing** outside the cinema.
- Die einfache Gegenwart beschreibt etwas, das immer, regelmäßig oder nie geschieht: I **go** to the shops **every Saturday** / **on Saturdays**.

TEST 1 Do you remember?

1 **Sie unterhalten sich im Internet mit einem netten Australier. Er möchte gern wissen, wie ein typischer Schultag in Deutschland aussieht. Schreiben Sie auf Englisch, was Sie machen und wann Sie es machen (drei Sachen).**

Tipp: Da es um regelmäßige Handlungen geht, sollen Sie hier das *simple present* verwenden.

points 3

2 **It's your first day of work experience, and you have to take a phone call in English. What's a more polite way of saying these things?**

a 'What do you want?'
b 'Who are you?'
c 'Give me your phone number.'

Tipp: Telefonieren haben Sie in Unit 1 gemacht.

points 3

3 **Die nette englische Sprachassistentin möchte wissen, was Sie am Wochenende alles gemacht haben. Denken Sie sich drei interessante Aktivitäten aus – auf Englisch, versteht sich!**

Tipp: Nicht vergessen! Das *simple past* (S. 27) verwenden: *I saw, I went,* usw.

points 3

4 **What can you do in your free time? Think of ...**

a two things for a person who likes sports;
b two things for a person who likes music;
c two things for a person who likes to spend money.

Tipp: Freizeitaktivitäten haben Sie in Unit 3 gemacht.

points 3

5 **Ihre Freundin bewirbt sich um eine Stelle in England und braucht Ihre Hilfe mit ihrem Lebenslauf. Wie sagt man das auf Englisch?**

a Geburtsdatum b Grundschule c Praktikum

Tipp: Schauen Sie sich den Lebenslauf (S. 32) nochmals an, falls Sie Hilfe brauchen.

points 3

6 **Sie sind in der Stadt und warten auf Ihren britischen Austauschpartner, aber er kommt nicht. Rufen Sie ihn an und erklären Sie, ...**

a dass Sie vor dem Kino warten; b dass es regnet; c dass der Film gerade beginnt.

Tipp: Sie müssen dafür das *present continuous* (S. 35) nehmen.

points 3

How did you do?

15–18 points	Excellent. Keep up the good work!
10–14 points	Good. Keep working hard so that you can get even more points in the next test (Unit 7).
less than 10 points	Take another look at the tasks you found difficult. Ask your teacher for help if you need it.

(Lösungen auf Seite 207.)

- finding your way in the city
- working and ordering in a restaurant

Life in the big city 4

WARM-UP

1 Listening: buildings in a city

a Match the pictures and words.

1 cinema	4 library
2 block of flats	5 hospital
3 railway station	6 pharmacy

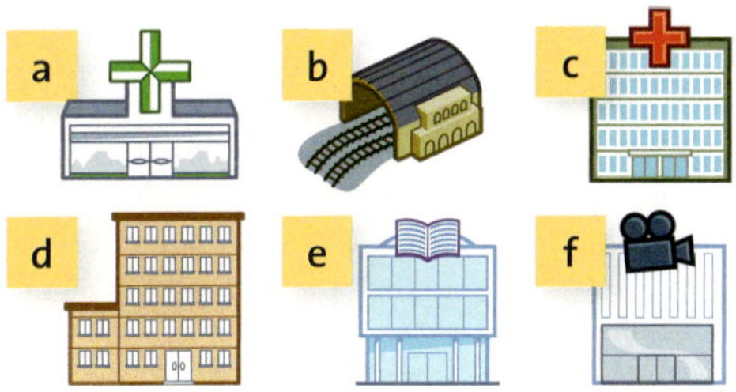

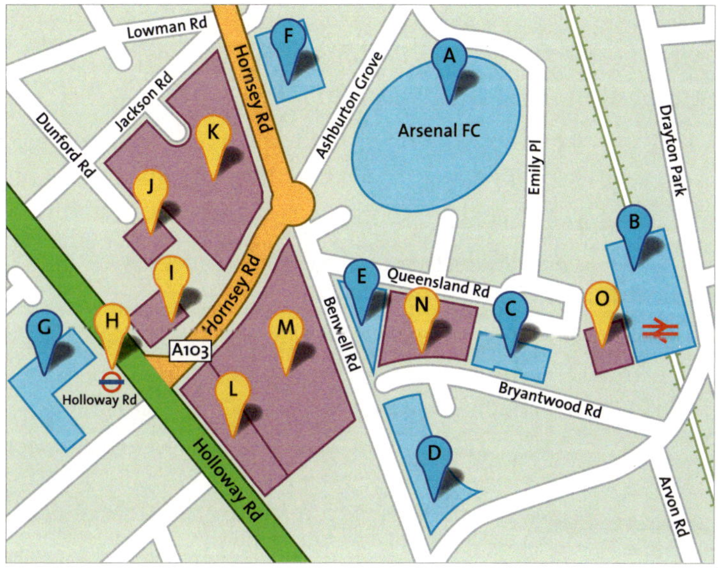

1 13

b Make a list A–O. Listen to find out what the blue buildings (A–G) are.

block of flats | bus station | car park | concert hall | cinema | hospital | hotel | library | pharmacy | post office | police station | railway station | shopping centre | sports stadium | underground station

2 Speaking: describing where something is

Partner A: look at this page. Partner B: turn to File 5 on page 136.

a Partner A: unscramble the sentences and answer your partner's questions.

1 The underground station is ... the / hotel / near
2 The shopping centre is ... of / Hornsey Road / Benwell Road / the corner / at / and
3 The police station is ... railway / behind / the / station
4 The post office is ... station / opposite / underground / the

b Now ask your partner where the following buildings are.

1 bus station 2 hospital 3 car park 4 pharmacy

c Now complete your list with the buildings H–O.

1
14

People on the move

1

Bicycle courier, Moscow

I love riding my bike. It's the best way to get around because it's good for the body and good for the earth. I've always liked looking at maps and getting to know the city. I know every street in the city centre now, and I know the fastest way to get everywhere. I have to be fast – it's my job! Even when I get a flat tyre, I have to fix it very quickly. It's really cool going to all the embassies and meeting all the people from different countries that live and work there.

2

Auto rickshaw driver, Bangkok

This must be the busiest and most chaotic city on Earth. I love that about Bangkok! Our economic situation is getting better, too. I drive a rickshaw because I like the activity in the streets and I like talking to the people I drive around. I drive a lot of tourists and tell them about the city. It's been very good for my English. Most tourists are very nice, but sometimes they have an old guidebook and they think my price is too high. Then they argue about it with me. That's the worst part of the job.

3

Bus driver, Johannesburg

Everyone has a hard time when they start driving a bus, because it's such a huge vehicle, but it's easy for me now. I think Johannesburg is the most interesting city in South Africa, but the people have to work very hard. Sometimes people get on the bus and I can see they are stressed out. I always smile and say hello and maybe even give them a compliment. You can really see they are more relaxed after I do this. I try to make a positive atmosphere on my bus. This way I can make lots of people happier every day. And when they leave my bus, they go and make even more people happier. What a great job!

(329 words)

3 Reading for detail

a **Match each person's photo to his or her text.**

b **Answer these questions on the text.**

1 What do these three people have in common?
2 What does each person like about his or her job? What is difficult about each job?
3 Who said what? The bicycle courier, the rickshaw driver, or the bus driver?
  a Hello! 8 rand and 50 cents please. That's a nice hat you're wearing!
  b Good afternoon. I have an important letter for Ambassador Liu.
  c Look! There's the palace where our king lives.
  d I'm sorry but the price has gone up since 1991.

4 Working with words: adjectives

Find the opposite of these adjectives forms in the text.

1 worst – *best*	4 worse	7 easy	10 relaxed
2 slowest	5 new	8 tiny	11 negative
3 most organized	6 low	9 most boring	12 sadder

5 Using comparatives and superlatives

Copy this table and complete it with the adjectives from the text. Give their comparative and superlative forms.

adjective	comparative	superlative
good	*better*	best
fast	*faster*	fastest
...	...	...

6 Speaking: making comparisons

Compare the three cities with a partner. Use the adjectives in the column on the right.

	 Moscow, Russia	 Bangkok, Thailand	 Johannesburg, South Africa	? your city/town/ village	
Population	10,400,000	5,700,000	3,900,000	...	big/large, small
Area	1,081 km^2	1,569 km^2	1,645 km^2	...	big/large, small
People per km^2	9,605	4,051	2,364	...	crowded
Founded in	1147	1782	1886	...	old, new
Average temperature	5°C	28°C	16°C	11°C	hot/warm, cold/cool
Number of billionaires	20	2	2	...	rich, poor
Price of a hamburger	€ 1.67	€ 1.67	€ 1.88	...	expensive, cheap
Number of traffic accidents	3,350	10,498	8,164	...	safe, dangerous

Is Johannesburg warmer ***than*** *Bangkok?*

No, it isn't. Bangkok is the warmest city.

Is where we live ***as*** *expensive* ***as*** *Moscow?*

Grammar

Comparative and superlative adjectives

eine Silbe	*-er, -est*	fast, **faster**, **fastest**
eine Silbe, die auf Vokal + Konsonant endet	*letzter Buchstabe wird gedoppelt -er, -est*	fit, **fitter**, **fittest**
endet mit y	*-ier, -iest*	happy, **happier**, **happiest**
zwei oder mehr Silben	*more, most*	interesting, **more interesting**, **most interesting**
unregelmäßig		good, **better**, **best** bad, **worse**, **worst**

Making comparisons:

A bus is bigger **than** a car.

I think Bangkok is **as** interesting **as** Moscow.

The bus is **not as** expensive **as** a taxi.

7 Building skills: reading and understanding a text

a Skim the text below. What is the subject of the text?

Das Thema eines Textes erfassen — Skill

Manchmal werden Sie aufgefordert, einen Text kurz zu überfliegen *(skim)*, um das Thema zu erfassen. Fangen Sie dann nicht an, Wort für Wort zu lesen – lesen Sie die Aufgabenstellung genau, schauen Sie sich die Abbildungen an, lesen Sie die Überschriften und halten Sie nach häufig wiederkehrenden Schlüsselwörtern Ausschau.

b Now read the text closely. In what ways will this invention be used?

1 15

A Map On Your Eye

A new way to find your way around a city

Computer monitors will soon become smaller – ***much*** smaller. Scientists at the University of Washington in the US are making screens on contact lenses. They will connect our eyes to our computers. Soon we will be able to read emails, watch movies and play video games with these tiny screens. How do they work? LEDs in the centre of the lens produce semi-transparent images. The circuits on the lenses are 1/1000 the width of a human hair. Technology on this very small scale is called nanotechnology. Another way these lenses could be used is to connect our vision to GPS navigation systems. Imagine you are on holiday in New York City. You look at the Empire State Building and – without opening a guide book – you can read when it was built, how tall it is, how many people work there, how far it is from where you're standing, etc. You turn and look in another direction and your lens shows you where the World Trade Center once stood. An arrow shows you the way to the nearest subway station.

Genaues Lesen – mit unbekannten Wörtern umgehen — Skill

Man stößt beim Lesen immer wieder auf Sätze, die man nicht versteht, egal wie sehr man sich konzentriert und wie viele Vokabeln man nachschlägt. Das ist ganz normal und passiert allen, die eine Fremdsprache lernen.

- Wenn Sie auf eine unbekannte Vokabel stoßen, überlegen Sie, ob Sie den Satz nicht auch ohne sie verstehen. Wenn es z. B. im Text heißt: *LEDs in the centre of the lens produce semi-transparent images,* kann man ahnen, dass es bei *semi-transparent* um eine Art von Abbildung geht – das reicht für ein grobes Verständnis. Wenn es z. B. im Text heißt: *You turn and look in another direction and your lens shows you ...* kann man den Satz komplett verstehen, ohne das Wort *turn* zu kennen.
- Im Englischen haben Nomen und Adjektive oft dieselbe Form – *look* bedeutet nicht nur „Blick“ oder „Look“, sondern auch „schauen“; *show* bedeutet nicht nur „Show“, sondern auch „zeigen“. So etwas kann auch den Sinn eines Satzes entstellen.
- Hakt es immer noch, lesen Sie einfach weiter. Vielleicht erschließt sich der Satz aus dem weiteren Textverlauf.

8 Over to you

What information would you like to see on these contact lens screens?

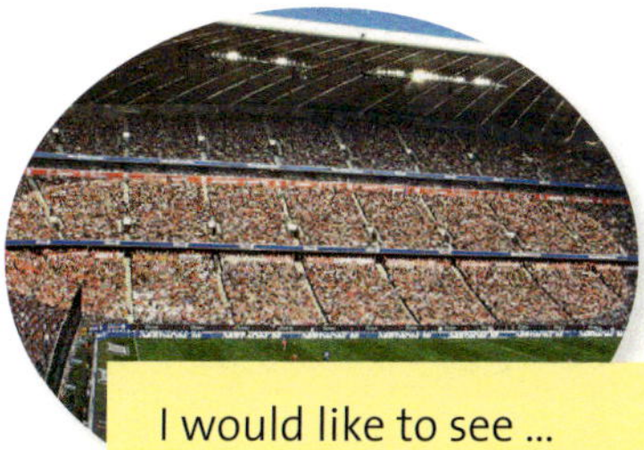

I would like to see ...
I would be interested in seeing ...
I think ... would be really useful.
It would be cool if it had ...

9 Listening: finding your way in a city

a Katja arrives in New York City at the Port Authority Bus Terminal. Where is it?

1 at the corner of Madison Avenue and 42nd Street
2 between 40th Street and 42nd Street

1 16

b Listen and find the answers to these questions.

1 Where does Katja want to go?
2 How will she get there? By train, by bus, or on foot?
3 Which important street is not named on the map?

c Katja repeats the directions to the helpful man. Complete her sentences.

1 When I leave the terminal, I ...
2 I ... 7th Avenue.
3 I turn ... Broadway.
4 I go ... Broadway until I ...
5 The Empire State building ... my right.
6 ... miss ...!

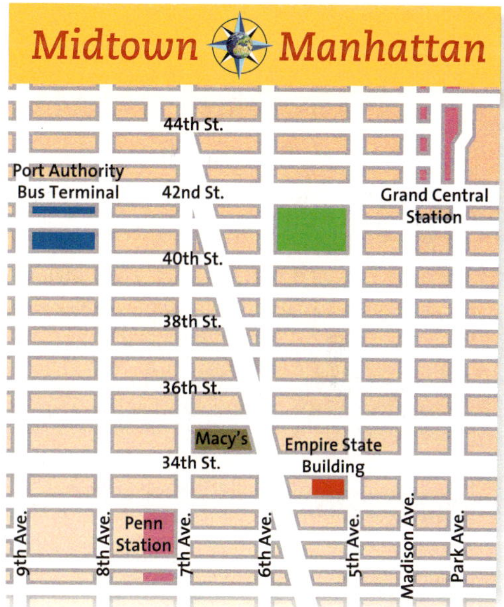

Tipp

in der Nähe von = near.
The library is ~~in the~~ **near** ~~of~~ Bryant Park.

10 Speaking: asking for and giving directions

a Ask your partner to use the map to give you directions.

EXAMPLE:

Can you tell me how to get from ... to ..., please?

b Ask your partner to give you directions to somewhere near your school.

Useful phrases: ***giving directions***

- When you leave the ...
- When you go out of the ...
- ... turn right/left (at ...)
- You'll pass ...
- Go along *(Name)* Street until you get to ...
- ... will be on your right/left.
- You can't miss it!

11 Making a mind map

In a group, make a mind map for one of the following courses. Think of several typical dishes and the ingredients you need for each one.

- appetizer
- main dish
- side dish
- dessert

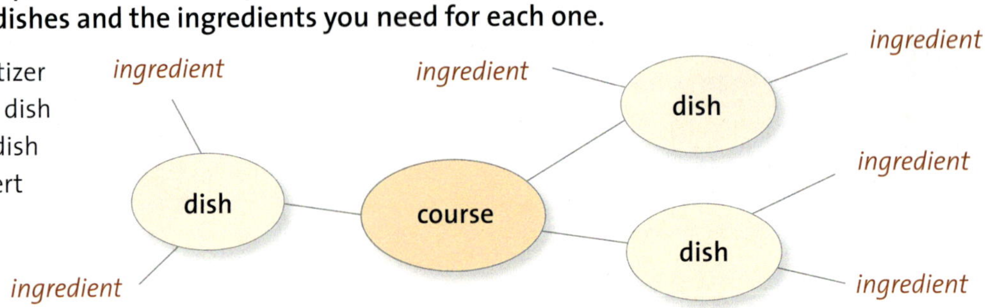

Meet the Kitchen Team

In a large, professional kitchen, the tasks are strictly divided between many people.

Prep cook
'Prep' means 'preparation'. After the ingredients are delivered, the prep cooks prepare them to be cooked. They peel vegetables and cut meat. Many trainees do this job, because here they can easily get to know all the ingredients and tools of the kitchen.

Main-dish chef
Cooks are only allowed to do this job after they have trained for at least two years. They have to cook very well, because they cook the meat, and if they overcook it, they have to throw it away, and this costs the restaurant money. Each piece of meat is different, so it's not always easy to know how to cook it.

Fish chef
The fish chef cooks everything that comes from the water: fish, crabs, lobsters and shellfish. Fish has to be timed exactly because when it is done, it has to be served immediately.

Side-dish chef
Side dishes can be vegetables, noodles or soups. These chefs generally work the hardest and get the least applause. One good thing about this job is that there is a lot of variety, but this also makes it difficult: the many vegetables have very different cooking times, so the side-dish chefs have to know a lot, and they are always moving.

Dessert chef
Many chefs don't like this job, because they get bored with sweet dishes. But dessert chefs can often cook very creatively.

Cold-dish chef
These chefs prepare the salads and appetizers.

Head chef
The boss of the kitchen doesn't normally cook very much, but instead represents the kitchen in the restaurant. He or she coordinates the jobs of the other cooks and checks the dishes carefully before they leave the kitchen.

Dishwasher
The mechanical dishwasher can clean dishes, but can't clean the pots and pans, so this person washes them.

(314 words)

12 Reading for detail

Read the text and answer the following questions.

1. What are the two meanings of the word *dish*? How would you translate them into German?
2. Why are only main-dish chefs allowed to cook meat?
3. Why is timing important when the fish is cooked?
4. What are the difficult aspects of the side-dish chef's job?

13 Working with words: wordfields

Complete the wordfields and their headings with the following words.

ingredients:	fish, meat, pepper, *salt*, vegetables
...:	knife, pan, pot
...:	chicken, lamb, pork, steak
seafood:	..., ..., fish, shellfish
side dishes:	noodles, soup, ...
tasks:	cook, coordinate, ..., ..., ..., peel, ..., wash

vegetables | cut | tools | check | clean | ~~salt~~ | meat | | lobster | prepare | crab

14 Using adverbs

Complete the sentences using adverbs instead of adjectives.

EXAMPLE: The chef was quick. — He cooked *quickly*.

1 The preparation was fast. — They prepared the food ...
2 This restaurant has polite waiters. — They speak to guests ...
3 It's early in the morning. — We have to start ...
4 The chef is careful. — He checks his work ...
5 Kitchen work is not easy. — It can't be done ...
6 It's hard work. — You have to work ...
7 The food here is very good. — They cook very ...
8 The Siemens dishwasher is automatic. — It washes the dishes ...

15 Writing a newspaper report

Translate the German words into English to complete this newspaper report.

Yesterday evening, a *berühmter* chef and his team cooked *wunderbar* for some *wichtige* guests. They *normalerweise* work in a *anderen* city, but for this event they *glücklicherweise* came here. They began *früh*, at 8:00 am. The guests arrived at *genau* 6:00 pm. The appetizer was *lecker*, the steak was cooked *perfekt*, and the dessert tasted even *besser* than it looked. After the meal the guests applauded the chefs *laut* and said they would never forget it.

EXAMPLE: *Yesterday evening, a famous chef ...*

Grammar

Adverbs (Adverbien)

Ein Adverb beschreibt ein Verb. Es sagt uns, wie etwas getan wird.

Bildung des Adverbs		
regelmäßig: + *-ly*	Fred is a **careful** cook.	He cooks **carefully**.
Es gibt aber wichtige Ausnahmen.		
y-Endung: + *ily* *ic*-Endung: + *ally*	Martha is a **happy** cook. Sue is a **fantastic** cook.	She cooks **happily**. She cooks **fantastically**.
ohne Änderung unregelmäßig	Esther is a **fast** cook. Jing is a **good** cook.	She cooks **fast**. She cooks **well**.

16 Working with words: in a restaurant

Match the words to the objects.

fork | knife | glass | napkin | plate | spoon

17 Speaking: ordering in a restaurant

a **What is the correct way to order lobster in a restaurant?**

1 I'll have the lobster. 2 I'd have the lobster. 3 I become the lobster.

b **Who says these things? The waiter or the guest?**

1 I think we need a couple more minutes to decide.
2 How would you like that cooked: rare, medium or well-done?
3 Would you like rice or potatoes with that?
4 I'm sorry. We're out of that at the moment.
5 Sure, I'll bring you one right away.
6 Yes, everything's fine, thank you.
7 No dessert, thank you. But I'll have an espresso.
8 Yes, we would. Can we have separate bills, please?

I become the lobster.

c **What could the other person say before each sentence? What could the other person say after each sentence?**

d **Role play restaurant dialogues with a partner or in a group. Change roles so that each person is the waiter/waitress at least once.**

Are you ready to order now?

Would you like something to drink?

Enjoy your meal.

Can I get you anything else?

- thinking about the future
- taking part in a discussion

The world in 2050 5

WARM-UP

1 A questionnaire

Complete the questionnaire. Then compare your results with a partner. Which of you is more optimistic?

Are you an optimist or a pessimist?

Complete the questionnaire to find out!

1 Is the glass ...

A half full; or

B half empty?

2 What does this photo make you think?

A He's an idiot – he'll probably lose his money.

B He's got the right attitude. You won't win if you don't take risks.

3 What clothes will you put on before you go out?

A A raincoat or a waterproof jacket. It might rain later.

B I'll go out in my jeans and T-shirt. It will probably be a nice day.

4 Which of these pictures best sums up your attitude to climate change?

A 

B 

5 You read a job advertisement for your dream job. You have almost all the qualifications and experience. What will you do?

A I'll apply for the job. I have a good chance.

B I won't apply for the job. Someone with better qualifications will get it.

6 Your favourite band is coming to play in a nearby town. You can't get tickets because they're sold out. What will you do?

A I'll stay at home and listen to my music player. There isn't any point in going to the concert without a ticket.

B I'll go anyway. Hopefully there will be some tickets on sale outside the concert.

How did you do? ▶ Turn to page 47 for the key.

Unit 5

The future – not what it used to be

by Ethan Jones

1 18

It was my 55th birthday yesterday and my little granddaughter Jazlyn came to visit. In a box in my bedroom she found an old exercise book with my name on it. 'Look, Grandad! What's this?' she asked.

In the book was an old school essay from 2010, when I was 15 years old. The title was 'The world in 2050'. Boy, I really got it wrong! Here are some of the predictions I made:

Prediction 1: 'There will be a United States of Europe.'

In those days, the countries of Europe were in the European Union. Now we have the World Government and there aren't any countries – so we don't need a European Union either. The idea of a United States of Europe seems very silly now, doesn't it?

Prediction 2: 'Everyone will speak English.'

Of course, we have the Universal Translator microchip in our heads these days, so we can understand every language. We don't have to learn foreign languages. In the old days, as a child, I had to learn French and German in school. Just imagine!

Prediction 3: 'Computer games will be as realistic as real life.'

Now we know that computer games are addictive and bad for our health. So they are illegal. It's a shame – I loved Grand Theft Auto and Streetfighter when I was a kid!

Prediction 4: 'Climate change will make many countries too hot to live in.'

There is no pollution now, so climate change is under control. So temperatures are only 1–2 °C warmer than in 2010. Phew!

Prediction 5: 'We will get all our energy from the sun and the wind.'

In 2040, scientists invented the Hadron Generator – clean, free, safe atomic power. Now we have as much free electricity as we need. We don't need solar power and we don't need wind farms.

Prediction 6: 'Humans will live on the Moon and Mars.'

What a silly idea that seems now! Who wants to live in a cold place without air? These days, humans don't travel into space because it is a waste of money.

Prediction 7: 'People will live longer.'

At least I got one thing right. On average, men live to 115 and women live to 120. Most 100-year-olds are fit and healthy, they play tennis, go skateboarding and enjoy life.

(396 words)

2 Summarizing the text

Read the first two paragraphs of the text on page 46. Choose the summary which fits the text best.

a It's the year 2050 and Jazlyn Jones is writing an essay about the year 2010, when her grandfather was at school.

b It's the year 2010 and Ethan Jones is dreaming about the world in 2050. His friend Jazlyn asks him to write an essay about it.

c It's the year 2050 and Ethan Jones is a grandfather. His granddaughter Jazlyn finds an essay he wrote in 2010 when he was at school.

3 Reading for detail

Read the text on page 46 again. Then decide whether the statements below are true or false. Correct the false statements.

EXAMPLE: **1** *False. In 2050 there won't be any countries.*

1 In 2050, there will be a United States of Europe.
2 In 2050, nobody will need to learn a foreign language.
3 Everybody will play computer games in 2050.
4 Climate change will be out of control in 2050.
5 The Hadron Generator is a type of solar power station.
6 Space travel won't be important in 2050.
7 In 2050 people won't live as long'.

4 Working with words: wordbuilding

Copy and complete the tables. The missing words are all in the text.

verb	*noun*
...	*speech*
...	*imagination*
...	*life*
...	*invention*

adjective	*noun*
...	*safety*
electric	...
healthy	...
wasteful	...
...	*fitness*

▶ Answer key, p. 45

How did you do?

5–6 'A's: You really are a pessimist! You expect things to turn out badly most of the time. Maybe you should try to be more positive about life. It will make you more self-confident and happier.

5–6 'B's: You are an optimist and a risk taker. You think that everything will turn out well. Maybe you should try to be more realistic, so that you don't take unnecessary risks.

2–4 'A's and 2–4 'B's: You are realistic about life. You know that things don't always turn out the way you want them to. That's probably a healthy attitude.

5 Using the *will* future

Which of these ideas from the text on page 46 will really happen in your lifetime? Use the phrases in the box to make sentences.

EXAMPLE: *There probably won't be dangerous climate change.*

There definitely will be	dangerous climate change.
There probably will be	free energy without pollution.
There probably won't be	cities on the Moon and Mars.
There definitely won't be	universal translator chips in our heads.
	fit and healthy 120-year-olds.

6 Taking part in a discussion

Work in a group of at least four. Use the expressions in the box and your ideas from exercise 5 to discuss this question: 'What will the world really be like in 2050?'

Useful phrases: ***taking part in a discussion***

Letting people know you want to speak
Can I just say something?
I'd like to say something at this point.

Expressing a point of view
In my view, ...
If you ask me, ...
What I think is this: ...

Agreeing/Disagreeing
I (don't) agree with you there.
I think you're right/wrong about that.

Inviting someone else to speak
What do you think, (Peter)?

7 Listening: population changes

1 19

Scientist Dr James Bader is being interviewed by a reporter for a documentary programme 'The future of Europe'.

a **Listen to the interview, then choose the two graphs which match what Dr Bader says.**

b **Listen again, then complete this summary of the interview.**

By 2050 there will be more than ... [1] million more Europeans ... [2] the age of 65, because people will ... [3] longer. At the same time, there will be ... [4] million fewer ... [5] people because ... [6] will have fewer ... [7].

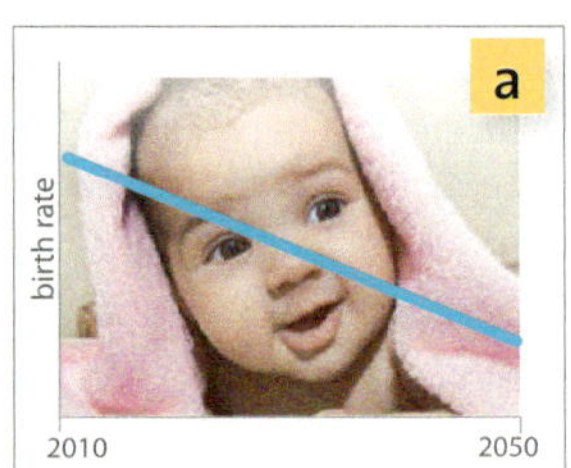

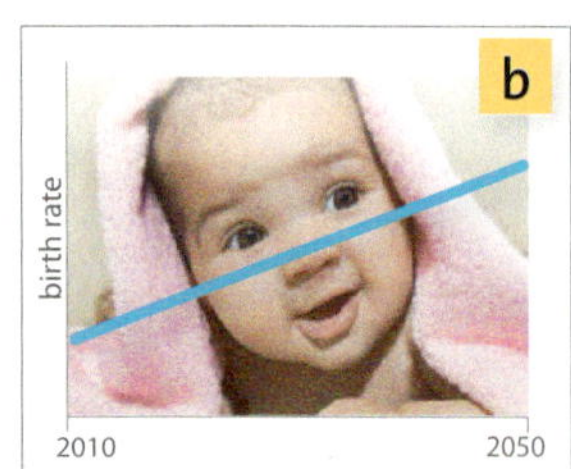

8 Building skills: describing a cartoon

Use the useful phrases to write about the cartoon.

Skill

Über einen Cartoon schreiben

Wenn Sie einen Cartoon beschreiben, sollten Sie diese drei Schritte befolgen:

1. **Beschreiben**
   Allgemein: Worum geht es?
   Im Einzelnen: Was ist im Bild zu sehen? Erwähnen Sie z. B. Gegenstände, Menschen, Handlungen, die im Gange sind *(present continuous!)*.
2. **Verstehen**
   Was ist die Aussage des Bildes? Hat es eine Botschaft oder will es ein bestimmtes Gefühl erwecken (z. B. Mitleid, Zorn, Heiterkeit)?
3. **eigene Meinung**
   Finden Sie das Bild gelungen? Warum (nicht)? Wie wirkt das Bild auf Sie?

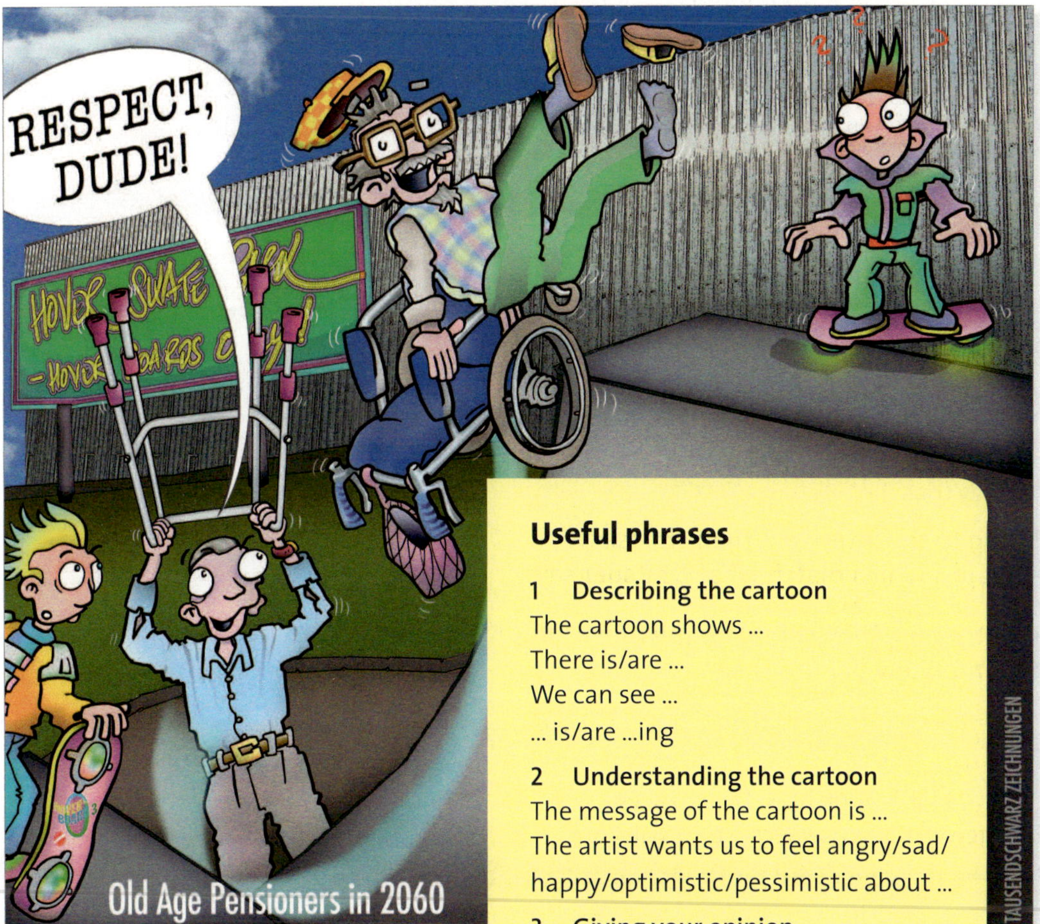

TAUSENDSCHWARZ ZEICHNUNGEN

Useful phrases

1 Describing the cartoon
The cartoon shows ...
There is/are ...
We can see ...
... is/are ...ing

2 Understanding the cartoon
The message of the cartoon is ...
The artist wants us to feel angry/sad/happy/optimistic/pessimistic about ...

3 Giving your opinion
I like/don't like the cartoon because ...
it's sad/funny/depressing/thought-provoking/clever/silly.

9 Reading: social jobs

Anna Spencer is looking for a new job. She finds the following jobs on a careers website. Read her profile and decide which job would be best for her. Note down your reasons, then compare ideas with a partner.

EXAMPLE:

A ... would be a good job for Anna because she ...

B Do you think so? What about ...?

1 20

Anna Spencer

I am a caring person with good communication skills. I want to make a difference to the world – particularly to people in countries which are less wealthy than our own. My strengths include creativity, imagination and the ability to organize people.

http://www.

Young careers

Home | About us | Jobs | Registration | Services | Contact

Search jobs

Care assistant

We need trainee care assistants to work in our nursing homes for the elderly. You will need to be caring, patient and physically fit.

Your duties will include: getting to know residents and finding out about their special interests and social needs; helping residents to wash, dress and feed themselves; helping to organize activities (games, etc.); going with residents on day trips.

» APPLY NOW

Social work assistant

Could you work with families under stress and children at risk? Then the Borough of Eastham needs you. This is an area with high unemployment and serious social problems.

We need a responsible, caring person who can carry out routine home visits to monitor clients' welfare and follow a social worker's care plan. You will work with other health and care professionals.

» APPLY NOW

Charity fundraiser

As a fundraiser for Feed the World, you will be responsible for raising as much money as possible. Can you think of new and imaginative ways to create new income and advertise our work?

You will assist in creating press, television, radio and poster advertisements to attract donors. You will also organize door-to-door collections and recruit and manage a team of volunteers.

» APPLY NOW

10 Questions about the future

Make a list of eight questions about the future. They must all be in the *will* future and require a yes/no answer.

EXAMPLES: *Will I be famous one day? Will my team win the Bundesliga this year? Will I get a good job? Will I live in Germany?*

11 Speaking: at the fortune teller

Work with a partner.
Partner A: Ask your partner the questions you wrote in exercise 10. Partner B: You are the fortune teller. Toss a coin to find out the answer. Heads *(Kopf)* = yes; Tails *(Zahl)* = no.

EXAMPLES:

A: *Will I be famous one day?*

B: (Wirft Kopf). *Yes, you will.*

A: *Will my team win the Bundesliga this year?*

B: (Wirft Zahl). *No, it won't.*

12 Writing about the future

Write down what you found out in exercise 11.

EXAMPLE: *I will be famous one day. My team won't win the Bundesliga this year.*

Grammar

The *will* future (Die Zukunft mit *will*)

Aussage	Verneinung
I/... **will be here** tomorrow.	I/... **won't be** here in the year 2050.
Frage	**Kurzantwort**
Will I/... get the job?	Yes, I/...**will**. / No, I/... **won't**.

- Die Zukunft mit *will*: *will* + Grundform des Verbs – für alle Personen gleich
- Verneinung: *won't (= will not)* + Grundform des Verbs – für alle Personen gleich
- Mit *will/won't* sagen wir, was in der Zukunft sein oder nicht sein wird.
  - In 2050 there **will be** free power.
  - There **won't be** as many young people.
  - **Will** the world **be** a more dangerous place? – Yes, it **will**. / No, it **won't**.
- Wir verwenden *will/won't* auch bei spontanen Entscheidungen, Versprechen und Angeboten.
  - What does this mean? – **I'll explain** it to you.

13 Listening: a new job

1 21

Anna Spencer is starting her new job. Fiona Rowntree, the personnel officer, is showing her around the building.

a Listen once. Which of the jobs in exercise 9 has she chosen?

b Listen again. Which of the expressions from Useful phrases do you hear?

EXAMPLE: 8 *This is your workstation.*

Useful phrases: *introducing a new employee*

Introductions

1 (Eric), this is (Anna Spencer). (She's) the new trainee.
2 (Anna), this is Eric Myer. (He's) our (senior fundraiser).
3 Pleased to meet you.
4 ... will help you with ...
5 Welcome to *(Firma/Abteilung)*.
6 I'm sure you'll enjoy working here.

Showing the new person around

7 This is the ... office.
8 This is your workstation/desk.
9 I'll show you where the ... is.
10 Let's have a look at the ... .
11 Can you tell me where the ... is, please?
12 Of course. I'll take you there.

14 Speaking: first day at work

Work in a group of three and role play the situation. A new trainee has arrived at the company.

A Manager

- Zeigen Sie B sein/ihr Büro und seinen/ihren Schreibtisch.
- Stellen Sie B und C gegenseitig vor.
- Versprechen Sie B, dass C sich um ihn/sie kümmern wird *(look after you)*.
- Verabschieden Sie sich fürs Erste.

B Trainee

- Sagen Sie, dass es Ihnen gefällt.
- Grüßen Sie C.
- Bedanken Sie sich bei C.
- Verabschieden Sie sich von A.
- Reagieren Sie höflich.

C Experienced worker

- Grüßen Sie B zurück und heißen Sie ihn/sie willkommen in der Firma.
- Bestätigen Sie dies.
- Bieten Sie B an, ihm/ihr den Kaffeeautomaten zu zeigen.

- talking about communications media
- writing an email

Social networks 6

WARM-UP

1 Communications

Match the communications media to the photos.

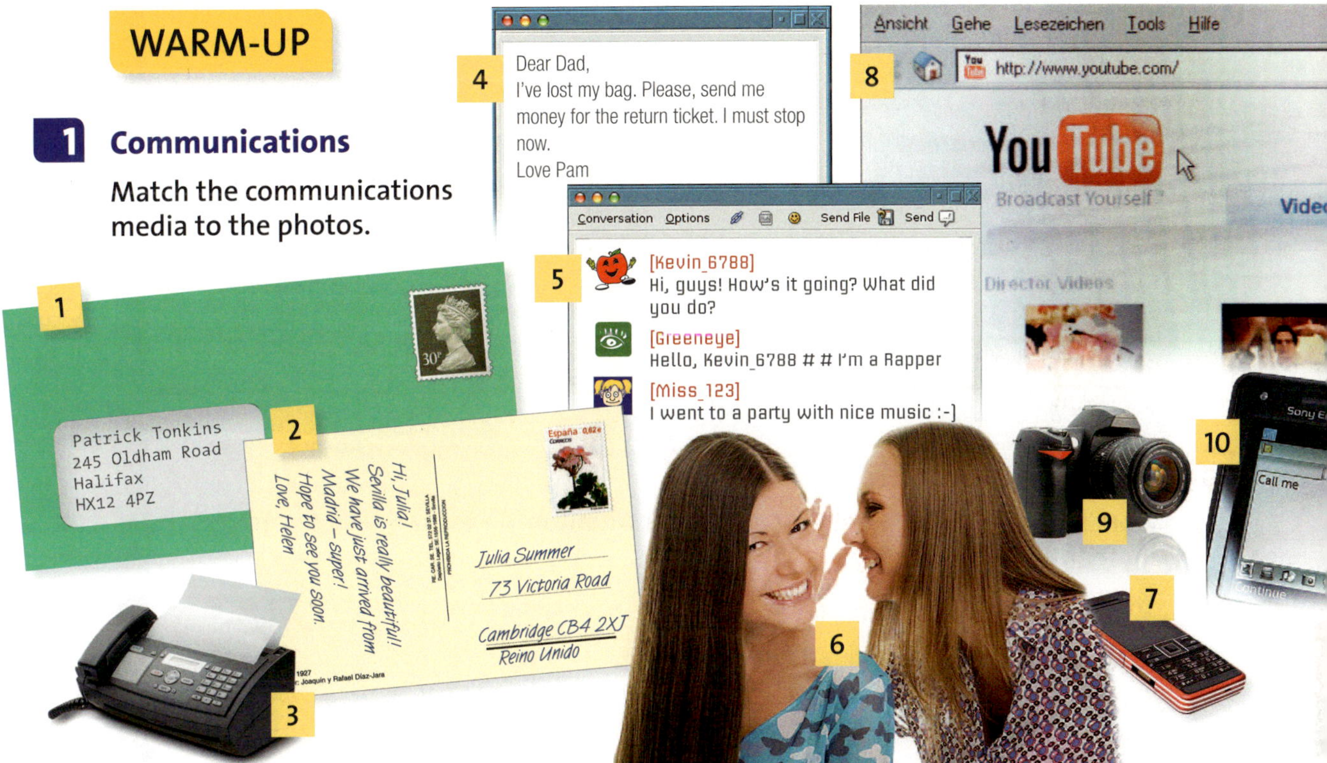

email | face-to-face | fax | forum post | letter | photo | postcard | (mobile) phone | text message | video

2 Matching the medium to the message

Which communications medium would you use for these messages? You can choose more than one.

1. a job application
2. inviting someone on a date
3. an invitation to a party
4. telling your parents that you're going to be home late
5. saying sorry for hurting someone's feelings
6. letting people know that you want to sell something
7. telling your friends about your holiday
8. chatting with a friend in America
9. ordering clothes from a mail-order company
10. booking a flight to Mallorca

http://www.

Confessions -online embarrassment

I have embarrassed myself online a few times.
I worked in a pizza restaurant for a while. It was fun but nobody liked the boss. One time I made some rude comments about him in a forum for restaurant staff. I didn't give his name, but it was clear who he was – and who I was.
Well, it turned out that my boss read the same forum! The next day at work he didn't say anything, but he stuck a printout of the forum post on my locker. For a month he gave me all the worst jobs. I had to clean the toilets, sweep the floor and empty the bins every night.
I have now learned to keep my thoughts about employers and colleagues to myself!

Jamie, waiter, Melbourne, Australia

I haven't often done stupid things online. But there was this one time …
There was this girl at school – I really liked her. My friends all knew it, because I talked about her all the time. But I was too shy to ask her out on a date. Then one day I received an email from her – she said that she really liked me and wanted to go out with me! But first she wanted to know what I thought about her.
Well, I wrote back to her. I told her how great she was. I told her how much I liked her. Then I clicked on 'send'. And THEN I thought: 'How did she get my email address?' It turned out that the email wasn't from her at all, it was a hoax from my brother!
He showed the message to all his friends. I was so embarrassed. In the end, Mum found out and she made him delete the message. After that he wasn't allowed to use his computer for a week. Ha!

Zack, college student, London, UK

I have occasionally sent emails to the wrong person.
In my last job, I was in customer service. I got a lot of emails from one particular customer. He was really annoying and I wasn't able to help him with his complaints, so I forwarded the emails to my colleague in another department. One time I added the message: 'Please can you help this idiot? He's driving me crazy!' I sent the message – but I accidentally clicked on 'reply' instead of 'forward' …
Well, of course he complained to my boss. I nearly lost my job and I had to apologize to the customer. Worse still, everyone in the office heard about my stupid mistake.

Suzie, website designer, Toronto, Canada

(433 words)

3 Reading for detail

Read the text opposite and write the correct name.

EXAMPLE: 1 *Jamie*

Who ...

1 posted rude comments in a forum?
2 replied to a message by mistake?
3 received a hoax email?
4 nearly lost his/her job?
5 sent a hoax email?
6 received annoying emails?
7 made his/her boss angry?
8 wrote an embarrassing email?

4 Working with words

Find the English equivalents of the German terms in the text. They are in the same order.

EXAMPLE: 1 *Ausdruck – printout*

1 Ausdruck
2 Forumsbeitrag
3 erhalten
4 klicken auf
5 E-Mail-Adresse
6 Scherz, Jux
7 Nachricht, Mitteilung
8 löschen
9 weiterleiten
10 antworten

5 Words in context

a Complete the sentences with suitable words from exercise 4.

1 Don't ... that hyperlink – it might download a virus to your computer.
2 Have you got Lucy's ... ? I want to send her this photo.
3 Who is this ... from? I don't recognize the sender.
4 The email wasn't really from my teacher – it was a ... .
5 This joke is really funny! Do you think I should ... it to my cousin?
6 Can you do a ... of the webpage, please? I'll stick it on the noticeboard.
7 I've found an interesting ... about online dictionaries – you should read it.
8 If you ... spam emails, you should just ... them.

b There is one word you don't need. Make up a sentence which uses the word and shows its meaning clearly.

6 Brainstorming: oops!

Work in a group. Brainstorm ideas to deal with this problem. You have just written an email criticizing your teacher. Unfortunately, you sent it to your teacher instead of your friend! What will you do?

Tipp

1 Sammeln Sie zwei Minuten lang Ideen. Ein Mitglied der Gruppe notiert alles.
2 Schauen Sie sich Ihre Liste noch einmal an. Streichen Sie die Ideen, die wenig sinnvoll sind.
3 Einigen Sie sich auf die beste Idee.

7 Listening: rules for online behaviour

a Complete the rules for 'netiquette' (online behaviour) with items from the box. (There are more items than you need.)

address book | capital letters | computer screen | emoticons or smileys | face-to-face | forward | Internet connection | send | spam | spell checker | upset or angry

Netiquette – rules for sending email and posting messages to forums

When you're sitting in front of your ...[1], it's easy to forget that you're communicating with people – people with feelings much like your own. If you follow these rules, it's less likely that you will offend somebody.

1 Ask yourself 'Would I say this in a ...[2] conversation?' If the answer is no, change the message.
2 Before you click on '...[3]', read what you have written. Does it make sense?
3 Don't send a message when you are ...[4]. Wait until you have cooled down.
4 Don't write the whole message in ...[5]. It looks like you're SHOUTING.
5 Use ...[6] – like :-) and :-(– in informal messages to show your tone of voice, but don't overdo it.
6 Respect people's time. You don't have to ...[7] that funny joke to everyone in your ...[8].
7 Respect people's connection speed. Not everyone has a super-fast ...[9]. Do they really want to wait five minutes for that video of your cat to download?

1 23 **b** Now listen to check your answers.

8 Mistakes in messages

Which rule do these messages break?

1

Conversation Options Send

@ ozkid
Of course Wolfmother are the greatest band alive, you stupid loser! Get a life, idiot!
Posted by: sunnyboy 3 minutes ago

2

new email

MR DAVIES
PLEASE SEND YOUR PAYMENT BY FRIDAY 6 JUNE. THANKS.
J CHAN (ACCOUNTS)

3

Hi Emma :D my name's Luke :-)
I love <3 <3 computer games too :-P

4

new email

Dear Mr Merton
I just got your email. I'm very angry about your criticism and I QUIT!!!
Caroline Coombes

5

new email

To: Kim Park, Jacky Allum ... *(50 other recipients)*

Subject: FW: Jokes that will make you laugh!

9 Network your career

You probably use a social network like Facebook or MySpace to keep in touch with friends and meet new people online. Could you also use a social network to get a job?

Match the explanations to the pictures to show how the social network XING works.

EXAMPLE: 1 *f*

Why network? A crash course in networking

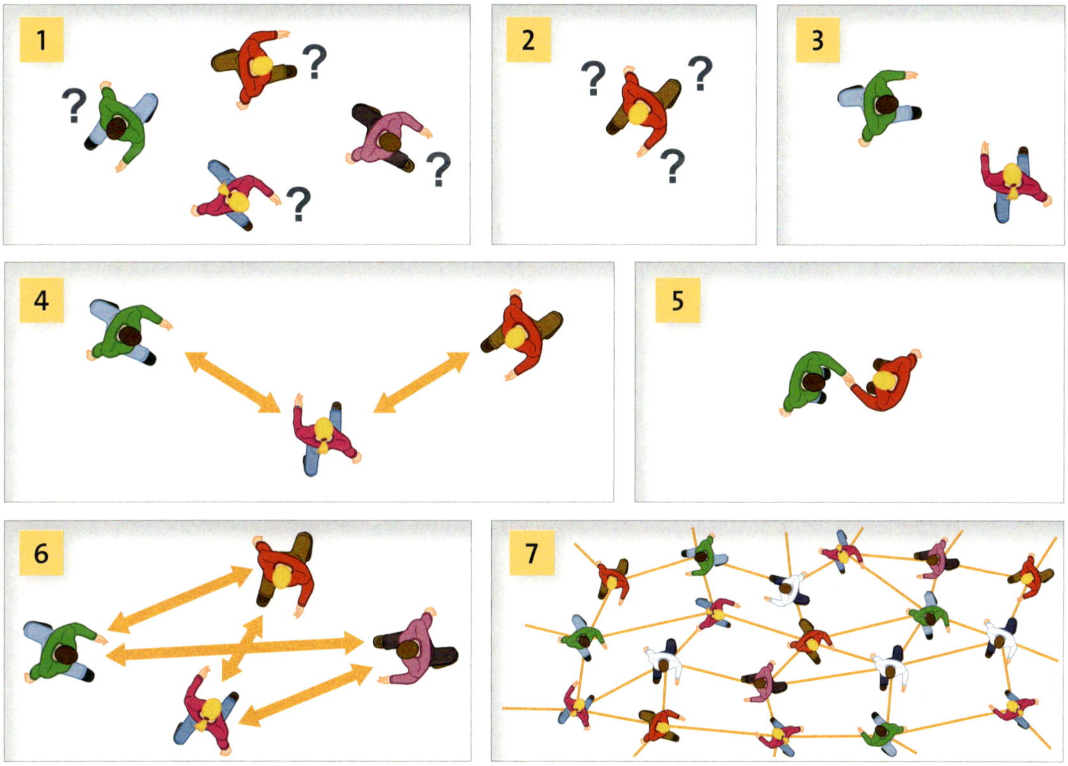

a This way Bill and Steve can start doing business.
b More than 7 million networkers have the potential to help you in your professional life.
c And that is Marissa. Her friend Steve is a graphic designer.
d Let's take Bill. He wants a graphic designer.
e Bill knows Marissa and Marissa knows Steve.
f XING brings people together who can help each other – they just need to know that the other person exists ...
g XING makes connections between people visible – so that searchers become finders.

10 Speaking: social networks

Discuss these questions in a group.

- Which social networks do you use?
- Why do you use them?
- What do you use them for?
- How often do you use them?

- I find ... really easy to use.
- ... has excellent features.
- All my friends use ...
- I use ... to chat to people all over the world.
- ... helps me to keep in touch with my friends.
- I log into ... every day / twice a week.

11 Building skills: translation

Your Canadian contact Katie sells snowboards on eBay. She has a lot of customers in Germany, so she wants to have a message in German on her eBay page.

Translate the message into German for Katie.

new email

Dear Sven

Here's the message for my eBay shop. Please can you translate it into German for me? Of course, I don't expect you to do it for nothing: I can send you €20 or give you $30 credit in my eBay shop. Just let me know which you prefer.

I look forward to hearing from you.

Yours Katie

> ***Welcome to our snowboard shop on eBay.***
>
> Snow Gear sells snowboards and snowboard equipment. We have new and second-hand snowboards and snowboard clothing at low prices. You can find top brands like Gnu, Lib Tech and Roxy in our eBay shop.
>
> Click here to sign up for our newsletter.
>
> Please add us to your list of eBay sellers.
>
> Come back soon!

Skill

Wie man einen Text übersetzt

1 Lesen Sie den englischen Text genau durch.
2 Schlagen Sie Wörter nach, die Sie nicht verstehen.
3 Schreiben Sie einen ersten Entwurf.
4 Korrigieren Sie den Entwurf.
5 Überprüfen Sie den Entwurf.
- Haben Sie wirklich alles übersetzt?
- Ergibt Ihr Entwurf einen Sinn?
- Ist er grammatisch korrekt und in ganzen Sätzen?

6 Machen Sie eine Reinschrift.

12 Writing an email

Write a reply to Katie's email.

- Thank her for her email.
- Say you've translated the message and attached it as a Word file.
- Say which payment you prefer.
- End with a polite phrase.

Useful phrases: *writing an email*

Dear Mr Smith / Ms Jones / Dear Bob / Hi Bob

Thank you for your email.
I hope this is of some help to you.
I look forward to hearing from you.
Please let me know if you have any questions.

Yours *(Ihr Name)*

13 Writing: Suzie's 'to do' list

Suzie writes a 'to do' list every morning and ticks off the tasks when she has done them.

Look at the list, then write about what Suzie has and hasn't done.

EXAMPLES: **1** *She has made coffee for the whole office.*
2 *She hasn't checked her voicemail messages yet.*

1 *make coffee for the whole office* ✓
2 *check my voicemail messages*
3 *read my email messages* ✓
4 *reply to any messages marked 'urgent'* ✓
5 *discuss the new project with Ben* ✓
6 *show the new trainee around the building*
7 *phone Mrs Smith about the new project* ✓
8 *help Gary to update the company website*
9 *tell Accounts about the mistake in the budget*
10 *order 100 blue pens from Office World*

14 Using the present perfect

Suzie's boss wants to know what she has done. Look at Suzie's list, then complete the dialogue. Use the question and short answer forms in the present perfect.

Boss: Hi, Suzie. *Have you read* your email inbox messages?
Suzie: *Yes, I have.*
Boss: Good. … [1] to any messages marked 'urgent'?
Suzie: … [2]
Boss: Great. … [3] the new project with Ben?
Suzie: … [4]
Boss: Sounds like you're keeping on top of things. Well done. … [5] the new trainee around?
Suzie: … [6]
Boss: Well, don't leave her waiting too long. … [7] Mrs Smith about the new project?
Suzie: … [8]
Boss: Excellent. … [9] Gary to update the company website?
Suzie: … [10] . We're just about to do that now.

Grammar

The present perfect (Das Perfekt)

Aussage			**Verneinung**		
I/You/We/They	**have**	started.	I/You/We/They	**haven't** (have not)	finished.
He/She/It	**has**	gone.	He/She/It	**hasn't** (has not)	gone.
Frage			**Kurzantworten**		
Have	I/you/we/they	started?	Yes, / No,	I/you/we/they	**have**. / **haven't**.
Has	he/she/it	gone?	Yes, / No,	he/she/it	**has**. / **hasn't**.

- Present Perfect: *have/has (not)* + **Partizip Perfekt** (3. Form des Verbs)
- Partizip Perfekt: regelmäßige Verben: Endung *-(e)d*; unregelmäßige Verben: eigene Formen (s. Liste S. 206)
- Wir verwenden das Present Perfect, wenn wir sagen wollen, dass etwas irgendwann in der Zeit bis jetzt geschehen ist.
- Signalwörter: *just, ever, never, already, so far, yet, before.*

15 You've been SNARKed!

The hacker 'SNARK' has broken into a social network website. As well as replacing people's photos with silly pictures, he has replaced some words with his nickname.

a Can you help the programmers to fix the website? All the words you need are in the box. There are three words you don't need.

advise | art | browser | busy | customers | designer | employee | faults | fix | network | phone | printers | programming | skills | tasks | type

http://www.

who-knows-who

email: nickname: Login

Rick Byrne

About me

I'm an IT support worker. I work in after-sales service for SNARK[1] of a big computer store. I have worked here for three years. I help customers to identify computer SNARK[2] and SNARK[3] them about how to SNARK[4] common problems with their computers. Most of my work is done over the SNARK[5]. I use fault-finding software to identify the problems and to advise the customer what to do.

Chin Ho Park

About me

I've been in my current job as a computer service technician for 18 months. I work as a member of an IT support team in an insurance company. There are about 120 computers on our SNARK[6], so this is a SNARK[7] place to work. My day-to-day SNARK[8] include upgrading hardware and software for the users in different departments, testing systems to make sure they are working properly and servicing SNARK[9] and scanners.

Kate Ellis

About me

I've always been interested in creative subjects like SNARK[10], but also technical subjects like computer SNARK[11]. Web design is a way to combine my creative and my technical sides. I've developed both creative and technical SNARK[12] on my college course, and now I'm looking for my first job as a web SNARK[13].

1 24 **b** Now listen and check your answers.

- talking about careers
- preparing for a job interview
- organizing a team

Future jobs and training 7

WARM-UP

1 Job-seeker's questionnaire

What sort of job suits you? Here are some of the questions from the UK government's careers website to help you find out.

a Write down your score for each question and total score for each section.

- strongly agree (4 points)
- agree (3 points)
- disagree (2 points)
- strongly disagree (1 point)

b Look at your partner's scores for each section and suggest what career(s) he/she could go into.

http://www.

Skills

PEOPLE

1 I like helping people.
2 I tell people when they do things well.
3 I listen carefully to what people say.
4 I am good at organizing people.
5 I can help people to learn.

DATA

6 I can sort through information or facts to find answers.
7 I like finding out what makes something succeed or fail.
8 I can look at a situation and work out what is good and bad.
9 When I read I can identify important facts.
10 I know how to manage money.

THINGS

11 I can use hand tools and power tools.
12 I am good at putting things together or building.
13 I like to repair things.
14 I am good at computer games that need quick reactions.
15 I am strong and keep myself fit.

IDEAS

16 I like drawing and painting.
17 I play a musical instrument.
18 I enjoy writing a diary or a weblog (blog).
19 I can tell what colours will go together well.
20 I can take a material (wood, fabric, paper etc) and make something creative.

Your highest score is in 'people' (1–5).
People skills are needed in many jobs, but here are some examples: teaching and training, nursing, retail sales, security services, sport, leisure and tourism.

Your highest score is in 'data' (6–10).
You enjoy working with facts and figures. You might be interested in finance and banking, IT, marketing or advertising.

Your highest score is in 'things' (11–15).
You are a practical person. Careers which use these skills include catering, construction, manufacturing, engineering and transport.

Your highest score is in 'ideas' (16–20).
You are a creative person. These might be good areas for you to think about: design, fashion, performing arts, media, science.

1 25

THE PERFECT JOB
1
WHAT AM I GOING TO DO WHEN I LEAVE COLLEGE? ALL MY CLASSMATES SEEM TO HAVE PLANS.
LUCY IS THINKING ABOUT HER FUTURE.
2
WHAT ARE YOU GOING TO DO AFTER COLLEGE, JOSH?
I'M GOING TO WORK IN EXPORT SALES. I'VE ALREADY GOT A TRAINEESHIP LINED UP.
SOUNDS GREAT!
3
OH, NO. HERE'S BEN ...
I'M GOING TO WORK IN RETAIL SALES.
I'VE ALREADY GOT EXPERIENCE AS A SALES ASSISTANT, WITH MY PART-TIME JOB AT THE SUPERMARKET ...
AND MY EMPLOYERS ARE GOING TO TAKE ME ON AS A MANAGEMENT TRAINEE ...
OH, REALLY?
4
WHAT ARE YOU GOING TO DO, LUCY?
I'M NOT SURE ...
HOW ABOUT GOING INTO RETAIL THERAPY? AFTER ALL, YOU LOVE SHOPPING ...
RETAIL THERAPY? I HAVEN'T HEARD OF THAT JOB.
5
NO, BECAUSE I JUST MADE IT UP. RETAIL THERAPY – GOING SHOPPING TO ESCAPE FROM REALITY. HA HA!
OH, VERY FUNNY.
DON'T BE NASTY, BEN!
6
ON THE WAY HOME FROM COLLEGE ...
HI, MEL. HOW ARE YOU?
HI, LUCY. I'M GREAT, THANKS. COME INTO TOWN WITH ME.
BUT I HAVE TO DO MY HOMEWORK FOR COLLEGE ...
FORGET ABOUT THAT. LET'S GO SHOPPING!
OH ... ALRIGHT THEN ...
7
LUCY? YOU AREN'T GOING TO BELIEVE THIS, BUT I'VE JUST FOUND THE PERFECT JOB FOR YOU!
8
DO YOU LOVE TO SHOP?
THEN MAKE A CAREER OUT OF SHOPPING!
MYSTERY SHOPPER
WE ARE A LARGE MARKET RESEARCH COMPANY. WE NEED MYSTERY SHOPPERS IN THIS AREA. WE WANT TO EMPLOY PEOPLE OF ALL AGES FROM SCHOOL LEAVERS TO OLD AGE PENSIONERS. GO TO YOUR FAVOURITE STORES, ASK QUESTIONS ABOUT YOUR FAVOURITE PRODUCTS AND EVALUATE THE SERVICE YOU RECEIVE AS AN EVERYDAY CUSTOMER. IT'S A SATISFYING AND VARIED CAREER FOR SOMEONE WITH GOOD COMMUNICATION SKILLS AND A LOVE OF SHOPPING.
INTERESTED?
RING 1800 600600 AND SPEAK TO CATHY WARD.

2 Reading for detail

Match the speech bubbles to the characters from the story: Ben, Josh, Lucy and Mel.

EXAMPLE: 1 *Mel*

1 IT'S FUN GOING SHOPPING WITH LUCY.

2 I HOPE I GET A JOB SOON …

3 LUCY IS JUST A LOSER. NO WONDER SHE CAN'T GET A JOB!

4 BEN'S AN IDIOT. CAN'T HE SEE THAT LUCY'S REALLY WORRIED?

5 I REALLY SHOULD BE AT HOME, DOING MY HOMEWORK.

6 I'M GOING TO BE A TRAINEE MANAGER.

7 I'M GOING TO WORK WITH CUSTOMERS IN OTHER COUNTRIES.

8 THIS SEEMS LIKE THE IDEAL JOB FOR LUCY.

3 Working with words

a Find the words in the box which match the definitions. (All the words are on page 62.)

EXAMPLE: 1 *customer*

Tipp

career =
Karriere, Beruf, Laufbahn

career | college | customer | to employ | to evaluate | old age pensioner | part-time | product | sales assistant | school leaver | store | trainee | traineeship

1 a person who buys goods or a service
2 a person who has just finished school
3 a person who no longer works, because of his/her age
4 a person whose job is to sell goods in a shop
5 a position in which a company employs you and trains you to do a job
6 a person's professional life
7 another word for 'shop'
8 for only part of the normal working week
9 to decide how good or bad something is
10 to give someone a job

b There are three words/phrases too many. Write your own definitions for these three words/phrases.

4 Working with words: opposites

Find the opposites of these words in the text. Use a dictionary to check meanings if necessary.

EXAMPLE: 1 *full-time – part-time*

1 full-time	3 employee	5 serious	7 remember	9 hate
2 awful	4 trainer	6 nice	8 imperfect	10 give

Unit 7

5 Listening: mystery shopper

1 26

Lucy is telling her dad about the job as a mystery shopper.

a Listen to the conversation, then choose the summary which fits best.

1 The company wants to interview Lucy. Her dad thinks that mystery shopping is the ideal first job for Lucy. She isn't sure.
2 The company wants to interview Lucy. She is enthusiastic but her dad isn't sure that it's a good idea.
3 Lucy wants to phone the company but her dad thinks that she won't get the job.
4 The company has offered Lucy a job, but her dad thinks that she won't enjoy it.

b Listen to the conversation again. Make notes about the following points:

- Why is Lucy suitable for the job?
- What possible problems are there with the job?

6 Speaking: reasons for and against

Work with a partner. Discuss this question: Should Lucy apply for the job?
Look at your points from exercise 5. Can you find more reasons for or against?
Reach a decision and report back to the class, giving your reasons.

EXAMPLE:

We think that Lucy should/shouldn't apply for the job because ...

7 Building skills: mediation

Your friend finds the text opposite on a website. His English isn't very good, so he asks you what it's about.

Make notes in German to answer your friend's questions. Don't write full sentences.

EXAMPLE: 1 *Fragt nach zukunftsträchtigen Berufen im Bereich Herstellung*

1 Was will Sam Miller? Warum?
2 Was sagt der 'Job Guru' allgemein über Herstellung *(manufacturing)*?
3 Was macht eine CNC-Fachkraft *(CNC machinist)*?
4 Was macht ein/e CAD-Konstrukteur/in *(CAD technician)*?
5 Was macht ein/e Elektrotechniker/in *(electrical engineering technician)*?
6 Warum haben diese Berufe eine gute Zukunft?

Skill

Wie man eine Mediationsaufgabe bearbeitet

- Die Aufgabenstellung genau durchlesen:
  WAS? Müssen Sie den ganzen Inhalt vermitteln oder nur bestimmte Infos?
  WIE? Stichpunkte, ganze Sätze oder ein zusammenhängender Text?
- Eine Mediation ist keine Übersetzung. Man soll nicht den ganzen Text wortwörtlich übersetzen.
- Keine eigenen Ideen hinzufügen! Alles muss aus dem Text stammen.

http://www.

The Job guru

school & study | in & out | jobs | trends | comics

Dear Job Guru

I'm 15 years old and I'm going to leave school next year. I'm very practical and I'm interested in how things work. I also enjoy making things, so I think an apprenticeship in a technical field like manufacturing would be good for me. Which technical jobs will be most important in, say, 20 years' time? My friends say that manufacturing will be fully automated, so that there will be few manufacturing jobs. Is this true?

Yours Sam Miller

Dear Sam

I'm not going to claim that I can predict the future. In 20 years' time, many jobs will be ones we can't even dream of today! However, it seems certain that jobs in manufacturing are going to get more complex, as robots will carry out more and more of the simple tasks. There won't be much need for human 'button pushers'. Here are some jobs you might look at:

CNC machinist

Computer numerically controlled (CNC) tools can make very complicated shapes out of metal, plastic or wood. These might be used in motor vehicles, aircraft or even spacecraft. As a machinist, you would be responsible for setting up, programming and operating the machine.

CAD technician

A computer aided design (CAD) technician uses software to create 3D or 2D designs for buildings or machinery. You would normally work in a small team, with each person working on a different part of a project under a design engineer. CAD technicians work in a lot of different industries, including construction and car manufacturing.

Electrical engineering technician

An electrical engineering technician installs, maintains and repairs electrical equipment. You might work in a range of industries, including power generation, transport or construction. For example, you might install lighting, heating, air conditioning or lifts in a large building.

All of these jobs are ones with a good future. They all require skills that are relevant to a wide variety of industries, so they are unlikely to become out of date.

Good luck and have fun!

The Job Guru

(338 words)

8 Preparing for a job interview

Lucy decides to go to the job interview and prints interview tips from a website. Unfortunately she runs out of time and has to cross out some of the things on the list.

a Look at the list and write sentences about what Lucy is and isn't going to do.

EXAMPLES: 1 *She's going to buy new clothes for the interview.*
2 *She isn't going to …*

1	Buy new clothes for the interview.	6	Ask your parents to check your CV.
~~2~~	~~Get a haircut.~~	~~7~~	~~Find the interview location on Google Maps.~~
3	Look at the company website.	8	Watch the news on TV.
4	Use the internet to find out about the job.	~~9~~	~~Ask friends about their experiences with job interviews.~~
~~5~~	~~Do a practice interview with a friend.~~		

b You have been invited to a job interview. What are you going to do to prepare? Work with a partner. Each choose five things from the list above. Then compare your lists.

EXAMPLE:

A: *Are you going to (get a haircut)?*

B: *Yes, I am. / No, I'm not. How about you?*

Grammar

The *going to* future (Die Zukunft mit *going to*)

Aussage		Verneinung	
I'**m** You'**re** He'**s**/She'**s**/It'**s** We'**re**/They'**re**	**going to work.**	I'**m not** You **aren't*** He/She/It **isn't*** We/They **aren't***	**going to work.**

Frage		Kurzantworten	
Am I **Are** You **Is** he/she/it **Are** we/they	**going to work**?	Yes, I **am**. Yes, you **are**. Yes, he/she/it **is**. Yes, we/they **are**.	No, I'**m not**. No, you **aren't**.* No, he/she/it **isn't**.* No, we/they **aren't**.*

- Wir verwenden die Zukunft mit *going to,* um auszudrücken, was wir vorhaben oder planen.
  I'm going to get a job.
  Are you **going to phone** Cathy?
- Wir können mit dieser Form auch Voraussagen ausdrücken.
  You **aren't going to believe** this, but …

Zum Vergleich:
I'm going to phone Cathy. (Der Sprecher hat sich bereits entschlossen, Cathy anzurufen.)
I'll phone Cathy. (Der Sprecher entscheidet spontan, Cathy anzurufen.)

* Auch möglich: *you**'re not**, he**'s not**,* usw.

9 Doing a team-building task

Work in a group of about five to six students.

As part of a job interview you have to complete a team-building task. You have FIVE MINUTES to complete the task. If you go over the time limit, you won't get the job! First, choose a team leader.

Team leader	Turn to File 4 on page 136.
Team member A	Turn to File 1 on page 134.
Team member B	Turn to File 10 on page 137.
Team member C	Turn to File 3 on page 135.
Team member D	Turn to File 12 on page 138.
Team member E	Turn to File 7 on page 136.
(Extra team members: pick a letter A–E.)	

At the end of the task, the interview panel (your classmates) will ask about your roles. Explain what you have decided and why.

EXAMPLE:

Who's going to ... ?

(Anja)'s going to do that.

Why's that?

Because she's good at ...ing.

Useful phrases: *organizing a team*

Asking for a volunteer

Who wants to ... ?
Who's going to ... ?

Volunteering

I'll ...

Suggesting someone else

Why don't you ..., (Sven) ?
How about (Anja)?

Rejecting a suggestion

I don't think that's a good idea.

Summarizing roles

(Anja)'s going to ...

Backing up a decision

... because he's / she's / I'm (not) good at ...

TEST 2 Do you remember?

1 **You're on holiday in London. In the hostel *(Jugendherberge)* you meet a nice girl from New Zealand. She's looking for a good, cheap restaurant. Your guide book gives you the following information. Make three comparisons between the restaurants to help her to choose.**

Restaurants Notting Hill	Preis	Qualität
Siam Thai	£££	✧✧✧
Mumbai Curry	£	✧✧
Pronto Pizza	££	✧

Tipp: Sie brauchen dafür die Steigerungsformen der Adjektive *good* und *cheap*. Schauen Sie sich nochmals die Seite 39 an.

points 3

2 **In der Herberge gibt es eine rege Diskussion über den besten Film, den man je gesehen hat. Sie wollen daran Teil nehmen. Wie macht man das nett und höflich?**

a Alle reden durcheinander und Sie wollen sich zu Wort melden.
b Dave redet Quatsch: Sie wollen ihm höflich widersprechen.
c Sara schweigt: Sie möchten ihre Meinung hören.

Tipp: Nützliche Ausdrücke gibt's auf Seite 48.

points 3

3 **You're at a fair *(Jahrmarkt)* and your friends have persuaded you to see the fortune teller. Ask her three questions about the future.**

Tipp: Dafür brauchen Sie die *will*-Zukunft. Schauen Sie sich nochmals Seite 51 an.

points 3

4 **Ihre Mutter hat eine E-Mail von einer amerikanischen Bekannten, Mrs Barker, bekommen und will darauf antworten. Helfen Sie ihr mit folgenden Ausdrücken aus.**

a Eine höfliche Grußformel
b Dank für die erhaltene E-Mail
c Ein höflicher Schlusssatz, der zu weiterer Kommunikation ermuntert

Tipp: E-Mails Schreiben haben Sie in Unit 6 geübt.

points 3

5 **Sie machen nun ein Praktikum in England. Berichten Sie Ihrer Chefin, welche Aufgaben (unten) Sie schon erledigt haben und was Sie noch nicht gemacht haben.**

Reply to the German email from Mr Schmidt. ✓
Translate the company brochure into German. ×
Photocopy the applications for the new job. ✓

Tipp: Hier ist das *present perfect* gefragt. Schauen Sie sich nochmals Seite 59 an.

points 3

6 **You've been invited for a job interview. How are you going to prepare for it? Write three sentences.**

Tipp: Es geht um die Zukunft mit *going to*. Schauen Sie sich nochmals Seite 66 an.

points 3

How did you do?	
15–18 points	Excellent. Keep up the good work!
10–14 points	Good. Keep working hard so that you can get even more points in the next test (Unit 11).
less than 10 points	Take another look at the tasks you found difficult. Ask your teacher for help if you need it.

(Lösungen auf Seite 207.)

- giving advice
- describing how a person looks

Youth crime 8

WARM-UP

1 Which crime?

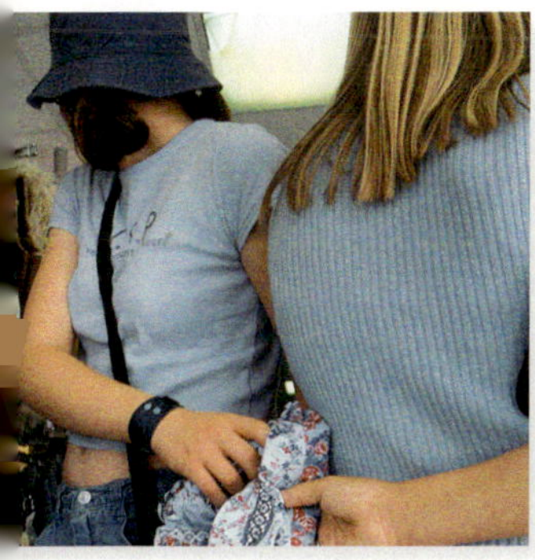

Complete the definitions of the crimes by matching the sentences parts.

1 Shoplifting is stealing ...
2 Possession of drugs is having ...
3 Illegal downloading is getting ...
4 Vandalism is destroying ...
5 Drunk driving is drinking ...
6 Telephone harassment is calling ...
7 Character assassination is making up ...
8 Assault is hitting ...

a someone.
b an illegal substance such as cannabis.
c lies about someone.
d something from a store.
e someone on the phone and not saying anything, or insulting them.
f a beer and then getting behind the wheel of a car.
g someone's property.
h a new film for free from the Internet.

2 Who says what?

Match the quotation to the person who said it.

1 'Help! I've been robbed!'
2 'I saw a crime take place.'
3 'I do things which are illegal.'
4 'It's my job to catch criminals.'
5 'I look after the criminals who live here.'
6 'I decide who is guilty and who is innocent.'
7 'People who have committed small crimes come to me and I help them stay honest.'

a the criminal
b the victim
c the witness/bystander
d the judge
e the police officer
f the probation officer
g the prison officer

3 Do you agree?

You are going to read three texts about bullying. Before you read, say whether you agree or disagree with the following statements.

1 Bullies target other people because they don't like them.
2 Bullies are self-confident.
3 Bullies are usually male.
4 Bullies are born that way.
5 In any group, bullies will be in the minority.

I don't agree with ...
I think (bullies) ...

4 Reading for gist

Stop Bullying Now UK **is an organization that gives advice about bullying. Read the texts quickly and say which one involves each of the following crimes.**

1 telephone harassment 2 character assassination 3 assault

2 02

Dear Stop Bullying Now UK,

I have a problem with a girl at school. Her name is Margot. Every time I say something in class, she makes comments about it to the person next to her. She tells everyone not to be friends with me. She got everyone in our maths class to sign a letter which said that no one liked me, then she wrote a really nasty 'biography' of my life and put it on the Internet. People actually believe the lies she tells about me. I hate my school now. I hate my life now. I don't see any way out of this except for suicide.

Please tell me what to do.

Liz, 16

A

Dear Stop Bullying Now UK,

There's a guy at my school (I'll call him John) who's having a really hard time, and I want to know how I can help him. John doesn't act macho like the other boys and so people think he could be gay. There are a lot of people who make fun of him. They call him terrible names that I don't want to repeat here, and some people think it's OK to hit him, too. I don't know if John is really gay or not, but no one should be treated this way.

I am not a very popular person at my school. I'm afraid that if I am nice to John, or if I tell the bullies to stop, they will tell everyone that I'm gay too, and then I will be in the same situation as John.

What should I do?

Abdul, 17

B

Dear Stop Bullying Now UK,

I got in trouble with the police because of an idiot named Kyle. All I did was call him a few times and send some text messages to his mobile telephone. He told the school director about it and she called the police. I couldn't believe it! I really hate this kid but I never hurt him! The police called my mum and she thinks they're stupid, too. Is it really true that what I did was illegal?

Sincerely yours,

Brett, 15

C

5 Reading for detail

Read the texts again and answer these questions.

1 Which letter writer ...
  a wants to kill himself/herself?
  b committed telephone harassment?
  c is afraid he/she will become a victim of bullying?

2 Copy and complete the table below. Who are the bullies, the victims and the bystanders in each situation?

	Letter A	*Letter B*	*Letter C*
Bully/Bullies	...	...	...
Victim	...	...	...
Bystander/s	...	...	*Brett's mum*

6 Speaking: giving advice

What should Abdul, Liz and Brett do? Use the phrases in the box.

Useful phrases: *giving advice*

In my opinion, he/she should ...
I think he/she should ...
The right thing to do would be to ...
Clearly, he/she should ...

Dealing with bullying	
... tell an adult.	... leave the victim alone.
... help the victim.	... say '...' to the bully.
... talk to ... in private.	... ignore the bullying.

7 Building skills: summarizing

With a partner or in a group, summarize each text in one or two sentences.

EXAMPLE:

The first text is written by someone who is very depressed because she is a victim of bullying. The bully is a girl at her school who told other people not to be friends with her and posted lies about her on the Internet.

Wie man einen Text zusammenfasst

Skill

- Geben Sie den Sinn soweit wie möglich in Ihren eigenen Worten wieder.
- Lassen Sie alle unwichtigen Details aus.
- Geben Sie keine eigene Meinung zum Text ab.
- Beginnen Sie so:

The first/second/third text is	*about* *written by*	*someone who ...*

8 Listening: a crime scene

2 03

How good a crime witness would you be? Listen to the CD. You will only hear the track once. You will be told to turn to a page at the back of the book very quickly. A few moments later, you will be told to turn back to this page.

a Now match the beginnings of the police officer's questions to their endings.

1	Will you be able to ...	a	you see the robber's faces?
2	Could ...	b	you remember the number plate of the vehicle?
3	Can ...	c	describe what happened?

b Give answers to the police officer's questions.

I can/could ... but I can't/couldn't ...

I will/won't be able to ...

9 Describing how a person looks

a Which person is being described?

1 He's got dark skin and he's bald.
2 He's got light skin and long hair.
3 He's wearing a black T-shirt and sunglasses.
4 He's wearing a black T-shirt and a cap.
5 He's got dark skin and long, curly hair.

b Partner A, turn to File 13 on page 138. Partner B, turn to File 8 on page 136. Draw the person that your partner describes.

10 Listening: what the bank robber looked like

2 04

a Listen to the girl who saw the bank robbery describe the bank robber that *she* saw to a police officer. Draw him on a piece of paper.

b Describe the bank robbers you saw, and their car. You may turn back to page 138 if you need to.

11 *Könnten* oder *konnten*?

Say whether *could* translates to *könnten* or *konnten*.

EXAMPLES: Could you give me your name and address, please? – *Könnten …*
Could you see how old he was – *Konnten …*

1 Could you please describe the robber?
2 I couldn't see his face because he was wearing a mask.
3 I could see the number plate on the car very clearly: VJ 6274.
4 Please don't ask me what kind of car it was because I couldn't tell you.

12 *Can, could* or *be able to*?

a Complete the sentences with one of the verbs and *can't* or *couldn't*.

find | live | play | see | tell | ~~watch~~

1 We *couldn't watch* the match because our TV was broken.
2 Why ... you ... me? Is it a secret?
3 He ... see the robber's face clearly.
4 You ... in this house. It's going to fall down any minute!
5 My brother takes lessons but he ... the piano very well yet.
6 I ... the address so I asked a lady on the street.

b Complete the sentences with *could*, *can*, or a form of *be able to*. Sometimes there is more than one correct answer.

1 *Can/Could* you tell us which way they went? They can't be far away.
2 My partner *can / is able to* draw people very well.
3 Tomorrow she ... get into her new flat.
4 When my grandfather was younger he ... run marathons.
5 ... you please give me some advice?
6 When ... we ... go swimming? In May or in June?

Grammar

can, could, be able to

Can/could werden nur in der Gegenwart und in der Vergangenheit verwendet. In allen anderen Zeitformen wird das Hilfsverb *be able to* verwendet.

	can/could	**be able to**
Gegenwart	She **can('t)** remember his face.	She **is(n't) able to** remember his face.
Vergangenheit	I **could(n't)** see the car clearly.	I **was(n't) able to** see the car clearly.
Perfekt	–	The police **have(n't) been able to** catch the robbers yet.
Zukunft	–	You'**ll be able to** help them. You **won't be able to** help them.

Crime doesn't pay! Pensioner caught shoplifting

24 January
When the water tap in his garden broke, pensioner Manfred K. (70) went to the DIY store and stole one. When the store's detective stopped him, Mr K. attacked him with pepper spray. '€170 for a water tap was too expensive for me,' said the thief. He stole for the first time in his life. The expensive punishment: €250 compensation to the store's detective, one year probation, €300 fine.

13 Reading for detail

Complete these sentences with information from the newspaper article.

1 ... was a 70-year-old pensioner.
2 He tried to ... a water tap from a ... .
3 Manfred attacked the ... .
4 The water tap normally cost ... .
5 Now, Manfred must ... €550 and see a probation officer. That's his ... .

14 Working with words

Match the verbs 1–4 to the phrases a–d.

1 pay	2 shoplift	a from a store	b someone with pepper spray
3 attack	4 stop	c a fine	d a thief from stealing

15 Translating: the greedy pensioner

a Match each sentence to a picture in the comic.

1 'You'll have to come with me, sir.'
2 'You mustn't steal again, Manfred!'
3 'I must have that water tap!'
4 'I don't have to do what you say!'

b Translate the sentences 1–4 into German. Use *müssen* three times and *dürfen* once.

16 *Has/have to* or *had to*?

a Complete the sentences with *have/has to* or *had to* and one of the verbs.

do | eat | drink | clean | work | pay | ~~go~~

1 People who commit terrible crimes *have to go* to prison.
2 He ... today, although the weather is so nice.
3 It was 39° so we ... a lot of water.
4 She ... her homework on the train this morning.
5 If you give the kids popcorn you will ... the floor afterwards.
6 They didn't ... any money for their pizza.
7 I don't ... because I'm not hungry.

b Make questions and answers with the words and *do/does*.

EXAMPLE:

Q Does he have to pay a fine?

A No, he doesn't have to pay anything.

1 Q: I/have to/call/the police
A: no/you/not have to/call/them
2 Q: she/have to/wear/glasses
A: no/she/not have to/wear/them
3 Q: what time/they/have to/leave
A: they/have to/leave/at six o'clock
4 Q: we/have to/walk very far
A: no/we/not have to/walk very far
5 Q: he/have to/wait very long
A: no/he/not have to/wait at all

c Rewrite the questions above in the past simple (with *did*).

EXAMPLE: Did he have to pay a fine?

Grammar

must, have to

Must wird nur in der Gegenwart verwendet. In allen anderen Zeitformen wird das Hilfsverb *have to* verwendet.

	must	have to
Gegenwart	You **must** pay the fine.	You **have to** pay the fine.
Vergangenheit	–	You **had to** call the police.
Perfekt	–	I **have had to** call the police three times this week.
Zukunft	–	You'll **have to** wait until the police arrive.

- *Must* entspricht „müssen" und drückt einen Befehl oder die Notwendigkeit aus, etwas zu tun:
  – I **must** finish my homework tonight.
- *Mustn't* drückt ebenfalls einen Befehl oder eine Notwendigkeit aus – etwas **nicht** zu tun.
  – I **mustn't** forget to post these letters on the way home.
- Achtung, *mustn't* hat eine völlig andere Bedeutung als *don't have to*:

You **mustn't** steal.	Sie **dürfen nicht** stehlen.
You **don't have to** steal.	Sie **müssen nicht** stehlen (weil es nicht nötig ist).

2
05

A trial in Fairy Tale Land – a play in four acts

FAIRY TALE LAND – Police are holding a wolf, Harry Wolf (45), at the police station in Fairy Tale Land. The police say Mr Wolf met a twelve-year-old girl in the wood and was able to find out from her that she was on her way to visit her grandmother, Mary-Ellen Woodenteeth (87). The girl also told Mr Wolf the location of Mrs Woodenteeth's house. Then, Mr Wolf went to the house and pretended to be Mrs Woodenteeth's granddaughter, and the elderly woman let him into the house. Mr Wolf then ate Mrs Woodenteeth. When the granddaughter arrived, he ate her, too. The two victims survived only because a woodsman, Randy Bigknife (29), was able to help them. Mr Bigknife cut open the belly of Mr Wolf while he was sleeping and pulled Mrs Woodenteeth and her granddaughter out. Then, Mr Bigknife filled Mr Wolf's belly with stones before he sewed it up, so that Mr Wolf could not run away. Mr Wolf, Mrs Woodenteeth and her granddaughter were all taken to hospital, and were let out the next day.

17 Speaking: a trial

You are going to role play Harry Wolf's trial. Your teacher will give you one of the following roles.

Mr Wolf, Mrs Woodenteeth, her granddaughter, Little Red Riding-Hood, Mr Bigknife, the police officer, the doctor, member(s) of the jury. Your teacher will play the judge.

Act I	The victims – MRS WOODENTEETH and LITTLE RED RIDING-HOOD – describe to the court what happened. The JURY ask them questions.
Act II	The witnesses – MR BIGKNIFE, the POLICE OFFICER and the DOCTOR – describe to the court what happened. The JURY ask them questions.
Act III	The accused – MR WOLF – tells his story. The JURY ask him questions.
Act IV	After some discussion and a vote, the JURY say MR WOLF is either 'guilty' or 'not guilty' of attempted murder. If he is guilty, the JUDGE decides what punishment to give him. If he is not guilty, music is played and he does a dance of joy (with stones in his belly).

a Before you start, say which people could use the following phrases?

1 He seemed very nice. I told him everything. Now I'm traumatized.
2 I found him in bed with an enormous belly. I could hear voices inside.
3 We got a telephone call to say that there was trouble at Mrs Woodenteeth's house.
4 I examined them. They looked like they had been eaten.
5 I thought he was my granddaughter. It was terrible.
6 You are all lying. I was at home watching television.

b Which phrases from the newspaper article could you use?

c Prepare what you are going to say during the trial and then perform it in class.

- explaining how a product works
- in a clothes shop
- talking about advertisements

Buying and selling 9

WARM-UP

1 Customers and salespeople

a Which of the phrases are shown in the pictures?

1 explain technical details
2 take a percentage off a price
3 sign a contract
4 send an invoice
5 pay cash for something
6 order a product or service
7 charge a price
8 deliver to a customer
9 take money from a customer
10 serve a customer
11 get a discount
12 pay with a credit card

b Use the wordlist at the back of the book to put the phrases above into the two categories on the right (one phrase fits both categories).

What a customer does
What a salesperson does

c Now, with a partner, use the above phrases to make statements and questions. Which group can make the most for each category?

EXAMPLE: *'We'll deliver the products to you tomorrow.'*

1 a salesperson to a customer
2 a salesperson to a colleague
3 a customer to a salesperson
4 a customer to a friend

2 Speaking: describing a selling process

Describe a selling process with some of the above phrases.

First, the customer ... Then, ...

3 Reading: a business idea

Read about Alex and Laura's business idea. What were the four reasons they started their business?

2 06

Alex and Laura got job training in school, but when they finished, they had trouble finding jobs. Instead of just sitting around and collecting unemployment money, they decided to start a business. Both of them liked seeing people having fun, so they decided to organize party events. Alex was a long-time player of LARPs (Live Action Role Playing Games), and wanted to organize them for other people. Laura had experience with children, so she knew how to organize a kids' party. Alex and Laura live in Germany, but they speak English, so they get lots of tourists and foreigners living in Germany as their customers.

4 Reading for detail

Read Alex and Laura's website and look at these customer comments. Who was at which party?

'We had so much fun dancing to that old music! And the photos we took of everyone in their costumes look great!' **1**

'The party was wonderful! I'm recommending your service to all the other parents I know.' **2**

'Your host was so funny, and the questions she asked were so clever. I didn't know any of the answers, but my guests loved the stuff they won.' **3**

'Thank you for a fantastic evening! Alex, you play the role of a dead body very well! You get an Oscar! Lol!' **4**

2 07

Kids' birthday party

Kids know how to have fun, and that's why we love kids' parties. We'll host your child's party at your home or, if you want, at one of our wonderful locations. We'll organize everything for you: the invitations, the decorations, the food and the games. And of course, we'll clean up after the fun is over. The birthday boy or girl can choose the decorations and the food. Our kids' party host has training and experience with children.

MURDER MYSTERY PARTY

Let your guests play detective! We'll send two hosts to your home to lead you through the game. We'll even let you murder one of them – well, not really, of course! It's great fun. Who will solve the mystery and be the next Sherlock Holmes or Miss Marple? Food, drink and clean-up services are also possible.

Roaring 20's flashback party

We'll arrive an hour before the party and decorate your home in the art-deco style of the 20's. We'll bring CDs of the best jazz music of the time. If you don't have a costume, we will dress you as a gangster or a Charleston lady.

Pop-culture trivia party

One of our party hosts comes to your home and leads you in a special trivia game that we created ourselves. Your guests will laugh and win great prizes. Food and drink services are also available.

– You or your guests don't speak German? No problem! Our hosts speak English! –

5 Writing: how much will it cost?

a In a group, choose an event from the website and decide how much Laura and Alex should charge for it. Add up all the services the event includes. There should be at least one optional service and one service which Laura and Alex charge 'per guest'. The groups that finish first should write their prices on the classroom board.

EXAMPLE:

	invitations	decorations	...	...	Total
Kids' birthday party:	€ X.XX per guest	€ XX.XX	...	...	€ ...

b Write sentences about your prices.

- The host's services will cost € ...
- If you invite only 10 guests, you'll pay € ...
- If you invite 50 guests, we'll charge € ...
- If ..., the event will cost € ...

6 Using *if* sentences type 1

Complete the customers' questions with the verbs.

EXAMPLE: If you *cook* for seven people, how much *will* you *charge?* (cook, charge)

1 If I ... my guests to win chocolate prizes, how much ... I ...? (want, pay)
2 What ... I ... if I ... the party in my home? (pay, have)
3 ... you ... my party if the children ... less than 5 years old? (organize, be)
4 How much ... a Murder Mystery party ... if I ... food or drink? (cost, not order)
5 What ... we ... if it ...? (do, rain)
6 If I ... more than 30 people, ... I ... a discount? (invite, get)
7 If I ... the costume you bring, ... I ... for it? (not like, pay)
8 If my daughter ... fun, ... we ... our money back? (not have, get)

7 Speaking: ordering a party service

Use the event prices on the board and role play conversations. One partner plays the role of either Laura or Alex. The other partner plays a customer who would like to order a party service. The customer should ask questions as in exercise 6.

Hello. I'm interested in ordering a party service.

Yes, of course. What would you like to know?

Grammar

if sentences type 1 (*if*-Sätze Typ 1)

Ein *if*-Satz sagt, was unter bestimmten Umständen geschehen wird. Der Satz hat zwei Teile:

If I **have** the party at home, ...	... **will** you **clean up**?
Der *if*-Teil nennt die Bedingung, ...	... der andere Teil nennt die Folge.
Der *if*-Teil steht in der einfachen Gegenwart, ...	... der Folgeteil in der *will*-Zukunft.

Steht der *if*-Teil zuerst, setzt man danach ein Komma. Steht der Folgeteil zuerst, setzt man kein Komma: You'**ll pay** more **if** you **order** food.

8 Listening: a party

2 08

a **Listen to Alex and Laura's description of one of these events. Which event are they describing?**

Barbecue party | Swimming pool party | Karaoke party | Vampire roleplay party | Holiday party (Christmas, Carnival, etc.) | Craft party

b **Listen again. Are the following statements true or false? Correct the false statements.**

1 Alex and Laura will sell the equipment to a buyer for €600.
2 They will explain how to use the equipment.
3 The speakers are loud enough for a big outdoor party.
4 The music is played from CDs.

9 Listening: how a product works

2 09

a **Listening for gist: Listen to Alex explaining to customers how to use a karaoke machine. His explanation has three parts. What is the order of the parts?**

- Tips for effective use
- Description of the equipment
- Operating the machine

b **Listening for detail: Listen again and answer these questions.**

1 What do you have to do before you can turn the machine on?
2 What two tips does Alex give about the microphone volume?
   - For each singer, you need to ...
   - If someone screams into the microphone, you need to ...
3 How could the speakers get damaged?

c **In which part does Alex use these words and phrases?**

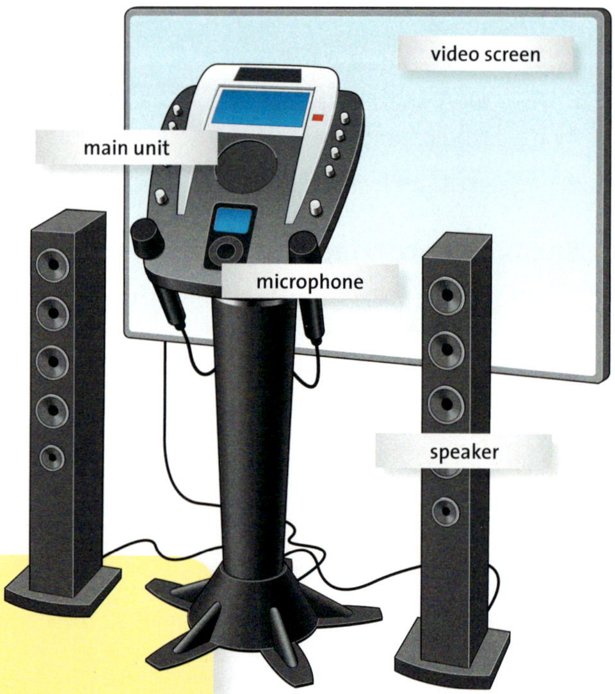

Useful phrases:
explaining how something works

1 There's / There are ...
2 It's got ...
3 First, you ...
4 Then, you ...
5 Plug the ... into the ...
6 ... like this ...
7 Make sure ...
8 If ...

10 *if* or *when?*

Complete the sentences with *if* or *when*.

1 I always buy an ice cream *when* I pass this shop.
2 *If* you pay cash for this, you get a 10% discount.
3 The clerk says 'thank you' ... she takes the customer's money.
4 I will buy more ... you give me a discount.
5 ... the salesperson can't answer your question, you'll find the answer on the Internet.
6 It's important to read everything carefully ... you sign a contract.
7 I usually eat something ... I get home from school.
8 ... you stick your head out of the window of a moving train, you will get hurt.
9 (To a person who may or may not have a laptop:) ... you use a laptop, keep it out of the hot sun.
10 (To a person who you know has a laptop:) ... you use your laptop, keep it out of the hot sun.

11 Building skills: doing a presentation

Explain how something that you use in your everyday life works. It can be anything you think is clever. You may need to research one or two facts about the thing. You do not have to bring it to class – you can draw a picture. Use the three-part format and the phrases that Alex used on **p. 80**.

Skill

Wie man einen Vortrag strukturiert

Introduction:
Hello! I'm going to tell you about ...
First, I'm going to describe the parts of the machine/tool.
Then, I'm going to tell you how to use it.
Finally, I'm going to give you some tips on how to use it effectively.

Moving on:
Now, I'm going to tell/describe/etc ...

Conclusion:
So, I hope you've enjoyed my presentation.
Thank you for your attention.
Does anyone have any questions?

Grammar

***if*/*when* sentences** (*if*/*When*-Sätze)

Man kann in beiden Teilen des Satzes die einfache Gegenwart verwenden, wenn man von allgemein gültigen Zusammenhängen spricht.

- *when* = „wenn" im Sinne von „dann, wenn" oder „immer wenn"
  When you sing, the volume indicator goes up and down.
- *if* = „wenn" im Sinne von „falls"
  If a singer screams like a rock star, the volume goes up too high.
  If you put the speakers in front of the singers, they can't hear anything.

12 A game: 'I'm packing a suitcase'

a Play 'I'm packing a suitcase' with pieces of clothing. Use colours and sizes (e.g. small, medium, large and extra-large).

EXAMPLE: **First player:** *I'm packing a suitcase and I'm packing brown sunglasses.*
Second player: *I'm packing a suitcase and I'm packing brown sunglasses and extra-large trousers.*

Today this person is wearing jeans and a red t-shirt.

Is it Patrick?

Yes, it is.

b Describe the clothes of someone in the class. The other people have to guess who it is.

13 A riddle

Solve this riddle. The answer is something you see on this page.

'When I am filled, I can point the way.
When I am empty, nothing moves me.
I have two skins: one on the outside and one inside.
What am I?'

Tipp

Wenn Sie Probleme mit der Aussprache des Wortes *clothes* haben, sprechen Sie es wie *close* (= schließen) aus.

14 Listening: in a clothes shop

2 / 10

a Listening for gist: Listen to three conversations and match each one to a picture.

b Listening for detail: Which of the useful phrases below do you hear?

Useful phrases: *in a clothes shop*

- a Any particular colour?
- b Hello. Can I help you?
- c Does it feel better?
- d How does it feel?
- e I have this green one, and this blue one.
- f I think it really suits you.
- g I'll see if we have it in another size.
- h Just a moment, please. I'll see what we have.
- i Right then. The cash desk is this way.
- j Thank you. Goodbye.
- k The changing rooms are this way.
- l The colour is just right for you.
- m This is the next size.
- n What size are you? Small, medium or large?
- o Would you like anything else?
- p Would you like to try it on?

15 Speaking: buying and selling clothes

a Jessica works in a clothing store in Germany where tourists often shop. Here is a typical dialogue she has with an English-speaking customer. Choose what she says from the useful phrases on page 82.

Jessica	English-speaking costumer
Jessica begrüßt die Kundin und fragt, ob sie helfen kann.	Yes, I'm looking for a summer dress.
Jessica fragt, welche Größe die Kundin hat.	Medium.
Jessica fragt, ob die Kundin eine bestimmte Farbe im Sinn hat.	Yes, blue or green.
Jessica sagt, dass sie nachschaut, was sie da haben. Jessica zeigt ein grünes und ein blaues Kleid.	The blue one is nice.
Jessica fragt, ob die Kundin das blaue Kleid anprobieren möchte.	Yes, please.
Jessica zeigt den Weg zu den Umkleidekabinen.	Thank you.
Die Kundin kommt von der Anprobe zurück. Jessica fragt, wie sie sich mit dem Kleid fühlt.	It's a bit small, somehow. It's too tight here under the arms.
Jessica sagt, dass sie nachschaut, ob das Kleid in einer Nummer größer da ist. Jessica bringt das Kleid in einer Nummer größer.	Thank you.
Die Kundin geht nochmal anprobieren und kommt wieder zurück. Jessica fragt, ob das Kleid besser sitzt.	Yes, it feels fine.
Jessica sagt, dass das Kleid der Kundin steht und dass die Farbe für sie genau richtig ist.	Yes, I'll take it.
Jessica fragt, ob die Kundin noch etwas anderes möchte.	No, thank you.
Jessica zeigt den Weg zur Kasse.	Thank you.
Jessica bedankt sich und verabschiedet sich.	

b Change roles and practise the dialogue again with a different item of clothing.

16 Speaking about advertisements

a Work with a partner.

What do you think these pictures could be advertising?

A *I think picture 1 is advertising ...*

B *I don't agree. I think it's an advert for ...*

b Now look at File 14 on page 138 for the answers.

c Tell your partner what the advertisements are saying about the products.

The advertisement says the product ...	is so good that ... will make ... is better than ...
With the product, ...	you will be able to ... you won't have to ...
Without the product, ...	you won't be able to ... you will have to ...

sunglasses
teeth
food
unappetizing/
tasteless
crowd/crowded
underground station

17 Project: creating an advertisement

Use one of the pictures below to create an advertisement for a product. Present your advertisement to the class.

Useful phrases: *advertisements*

- This picture advertises ...
- The slogan is ...
- The target group for this product is ...
- This advertisement would reach the most people ...

Target groups

men/women/teenagers/young adults/ older adults/professionals/wealthy people

Places

- on a poster/billboard on the subway/bus
- in a newspaper
- in a magazine
- during a television show like ...
- on a website like ...
- in a building like ...

- answering the telephone in an office
- telling visitors where to go in an office building

In and around the office 10

WARM-UP

1 Listening: what can you hear?

2 11 Listen and say which picture matches what you hear. There is one more picture than you need.

a

b

c

d

e

f

g

h

i

2 Office activities

Say what is happening in the pictures.

The man The woman The person The people Someone	in the kitchen at the desk in the conference room in picture b	is are	taking notes at a meeting. typing an email. working overtime. making photocopies. making coffee. answering the phone. taking a break. sorting the mail. greeting visitors.

3 A riddle

Find the thing on this page that goes around the world and yet stays in a corner.

Tipp

Mail bedeutet im Englischen meistens Post, nicht E-Mail, und ist unzählbar, daher: *three pieces of mail*, nicht ~~*three mails*~~.

4 Reading for gist

Read the text quickly and give each paragraph a heading. You have to make up one of them yourself.

• The corporation

• The man

• ...?

Walt Elias Disney

Walt Disney, Inc.

•

Walt Elias Disney moved to California in 1923 with a lot of creative ideas, but almost no money. He started creating some of the word's first animated films, but was not very successful. Then, in 1928, he invented the character Mickey Mouse, who became a sensation around the world. After that big breakthrough, Disney's life was one success after another. In 1937, he made *Snow White and the Seven Dwarfs*, the first ever full-length animated film. In 1955, he realized another kind of dream: a beautiful amusement park called Disneyland.

•

Walt Disney died in 1966 but his company Walt Disney Pictures has now made over 1,500 films. But Walt Disney Pictures also produces films under other names which you may have heard: Pixar Animation Studios, Touchstone Pictures and Miramax Films, just to name a few. At the global box office, Walt Disney films earned more than $1.2 billion in 2008.

•

But Disney's business is much more than movies. That is just one part of the gigantic Walt Disney Company. Other branches of the company include Parks and Resorts, Disney Cruise Lines, Disney Theatrical Entertainment, and Disney Publishing Worldwide – the world's largest publisher of children's books and magazines. Disney also owns the ABC television network, one of the 'Big Three' American TV networks, which shows news and other shows for adults. Even ESPN, the multinational sports entertainment company, has Disney as its parent company.

(236 words)

5 Reading for detail

Read the text again and answer the following questions.

1 What was Walt Disney's first big success?
2 Walt Disney made movies. What else did he do?
3 What is the connection between Disney and Pixar, Touchstone and Miramax?
4 Name five other parts of the Walt Disney Company.
5 What is a 'parent company'?

6 *Who or which?*

Match the sentence halves and complete them with *who* or *which*.

1 There are people all over the world ...
2 A cinema is a kind of theatre ...
3 Walt Disney was not the person ...
4 Walt Disney was a genius ...
5 Pixar is a studio ...
6 A parent company is a company ...

a created beautiful films and characters.
b owns another company.
c love Disney films.
d shows movies.
e invented animated films.
f produces computer-animated films.

7 Working with words: wordbuilding

a Copy the table and complete it with verbs from exercise 6 and the words in the box.

~~owner~~ | ownership | producer | production | creation | creator | invention | inventor

noun	*verb*	*person*
...	...	*(Besitzer) owner*
...	...	*(Erfinder) ...*
...	...	*(Produzent/Hersteller) ...*
...	...	*(Schöpfer) ...*

b Now translate the nouns in the column on the left of the table into German.

8 Using relative clauses

Choose one of the words, but don't say which. Use the expressions below to make sentences. Can the others in the class guess your word?

It's someone	who you see in a/an ... who works with a/an ... who has ...
It's something	which you use to ... which you see in ... which has ...

animator | keyboard | movie | pen | producer | receptionist | software developer | telephone | television

Grammar

Relative clauses (Relativsätze)

My brother is someone **who/that** loves Disney movies.
Disney has shops **which/that** sell DVDs, books, and other products.

Relativpronomen für Menschen: *who* oder (seltener) *that*.
Relativpronomen für Sachen: *which* oder *that*.

9 Speaking: at a reception desk

Aykan is taking a break, and you have to answer the phone.

Hello! Welcome to the offices of Disneyland Paris! I'm Aykan Kiliç, from Germany. I've been an intern here for about four months now. I work here at this reception desk where I answer the phone and greet visitors. Who are you here to see? Do you have an appointment?

Role play some dialogues between the caller (orange) and the receptionist (green).

Useful phrases: ***telephone phrases***

Receptionist:
Disney offices. *(your name)* speaking.
Just a moment. I'll put you through to him/her.
I'm sorry. He's/She's out of the office at the moment.
I'll give her the message when he/she gets back

Caller:
May I speak to ..., please?
This is *(your name)*.
When will he/she be back?
Can you give him/her a message, please?

1. **START** Say 'ring ring'.
2. Answer the phone in French: 'Bonjour, Disney.'
3. Ask if the person speaks English.
4. Answer positively.
5. Ask to speak to someone.
6. Ask for the caller's name.
7. Give your name.
8. Connect the caller.

(Alternatively, after "Give your name.":)

1. **START** Say 'ring ring'.
2. Answer the phone in English.
3. Ask to speak to someone.
4. Ask for the caller's name.
5. Give your name.
6. Say that the person is out of the office.
7. Ask when the person will be back.
8. Give a time.
9. Say you will call back.
10. **END** the phone call.

(Alternatively, after "Give a time.":)

1. Ask to leave a message.
2. Answer positively.
3. Leave a message.
4. Say you will give him/her the message.
5. **END** the phone call.

10 Working with words: office equipment

Which of following things can you find in the photo of Aykan's reception area on page 88?

chair | computer screen | drawer | envelopes | files | keyboard | mouse | pencils | pens | photocopier | plant | shelf

11 Departments in an office building

a Look at the symbols and find out where these departments/places are.

canteen | conference room | finance department | IT department | sales & marketing | car park

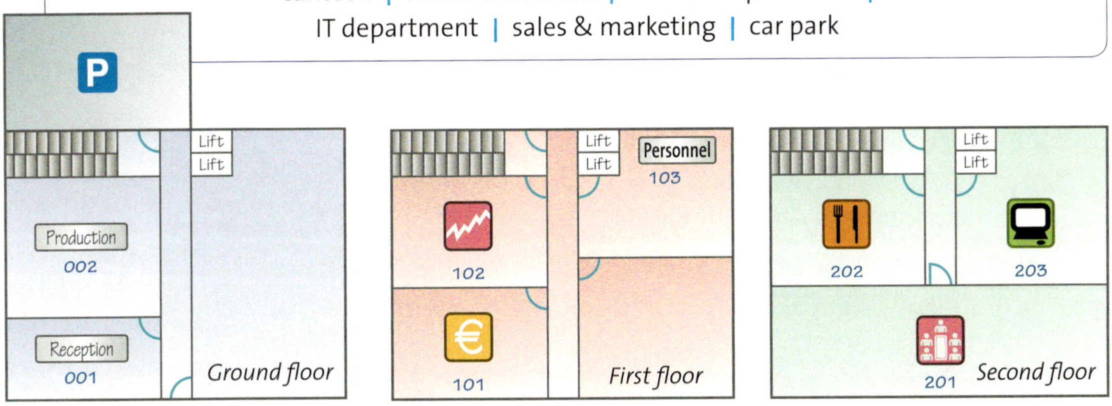

b Where do these visitors want to go?

1. *I'm here for a job interview.*
2. *Hi, we're from Paper King with some printer paper for your IT people.*
3. *There's a broken drinks machine somewhere in the building. I'm here to repair it.*
4. *Hi, I'm from Quick Print. I've got the new brochures you ordered.*
5. *I'm from LCL bank. I've got an appointment with Olivier Bertrand.*
6. *There's a big meeting somewhere and I'm catering the lunch.*
7. *Where can I park my car?*

12 Speaking: in an office building

Take the role of either the receptionist or the visitor and make dialogues like this:

Visitor:	I'm here for the job interview.
Receptionist:	You want the personnel department, then. That's room one-oh-three on the first floor. Just a moment. I'll phone to say that you're here.

13 Selling on the Internet

a What internet companies do you know? Make a list with a partner.

b Aykan has collected some Disney products which he wants to get rid of, but he doesn't know anyone who wants to take them. Where could he sell them?

2 13

The Story of Ebay

Pierre Omidyar was a software developer in California. One day in 1995, when he was 28 years old, he made a little website called AuctionWeb, where people could auction things off. The first thing he put on the site was a broken laser pointer. He thought this was funny and didn't think anyone would buy it. He was shocked when he saw that someone bought it for $14.83.

He sent the buyer an e-mail: 'Do you understand that the laser pointer you've bought is broken?' he wrote.

'Yes,' came the answer, 'I collect broken laser pointers!'

Pierre knew then that people could auction off anything on the internet and always find a buyer. He soon found talented people to join him in the company.

In 1997 they named the company Ebay after Pierre's consulting firm Echo Bay.

Two years later, the company opened offices near Berlin, Germany. There are now over 1,100 employees at this location. Most of them work in customer service. All of them need English in their jobs.

(175 words)

14 Reading for detail

Read the text and complete the sentences with numbers.

1 Pierre Omidyar has auctioned things off on the internet since ... .
2 Pierre Omidyar has auctioned things off on the internet for ... years.
3 The company has been called Ebay since ... .
4 The company has been called Ebay for ... years.
5 Ebay has had offices in Germany since ... .
6 Ebay has had offices in Germany for ... years.

15 *Since* or *for*?

Translate *seit* in the following sentences.

1 Seit 2003 hat die Firma ein neues Logo.
2 Ikea verkauft seit über 60 Jahren Möbel.
3 Seit 1976 verkauft H&M Kleidung außerhalb von Skandinavien.
4 ProSiebenSat.1 Media AG hat seit mehr als fünf Jahren einen deutschsprachigen Kanal in den USA.
5 Die Firma Ford Motor Co. ist berühmt, seitdem sie das „Model-T" macht.
6 Unsere Firma macht Gewinn, seitdem wir unseren neuen Chef haben.

16 Building skills: doing internet research

Choose a company and find out some interesting facts about it. Tell the class about it.

- What products or services does the company specialize in?
- Where does the company make and sell its products/services?
- What does the company do in Germany?
- What is the story of the company's founding?
- How many employees does the company have and where are they?
- How successful has the company been?
- What is your experience with the company and its products/services? Would you recommend them to a friend?

Skill

Wie man im Internet recherchiert

- Fast jede Firma hat ihre eigene Webseite, wo man Informationen finden kann.
- Wenn Sie eine Suchmaschine (z. B. Google) verwenden, schauen Sie sich aber nicht nur das erste Suchergebnis an.
- Bei Wikipedia können Sie zwischen Deutsch und Englisch hin und her klicken.
- Folgende Domains sind auf Englisch:
  – .edu (Universitäten usw. – vertrauenswürdige Informationen)
  – .com (USA) / .co.uk (GB) / .ca (Kanada) / .au (Australien)

Grammar

The present perfect with *since* and *for*
(Das Present Perfect mit *since* und *for*)

How long have they **been** employees?	*Wie lange sind sie schon Arbeitnehmer?*
He **has been** an employee **for** 10 years.	*Er ist seit 10 Jahren Arbeitnehmer.*
She **has been** an employee **since** 1995.	*Sie ist seit 1995 Arbeitnehmerin.*

- Wir verwenden nicht die Gegenwartsform, sondern das Present Perfect (= *have/has (not)* + **Partizip Perfekt** – s. Unit 6), wenn wir sagen oder fragen, wie lange etwas schon andauert.
- Deutsch „seit" = *since* oder *for*:
  – *since* + **Anfangszeitpunkt** (Frage: „seit wann?"): *since 10 o'clock / yesterday / last week / ...*
  – *for* + **Zeitspanne** (Frage: „wie lange schon?"): *for 10 minutes / two days / six weeks / ...*

17 A puzzle: who gets the green package?

You work for a package delivery service. You deliver packages every day to five companies in an industrial park. One of the packages, the green one, has lost its label today and you must figure out which company to deliver it to.

Each company manufactures a different product: body lotion, soup, nappies, hairpieces or plastic roses. Each company is owned by one of the five largest corporations in the world: Wal-Mart, Toyota Motor, BP, Royal Dutch Shell or Exxon Mobil. At each company, the mail is received by a different employee: the receptionist, the gardener, the boss's secretary, the security guard or the mail room attendant.

a Read the following information.

- The company which owns Birdhouse is Royal Dutch Shell.
- The company which gets the white package is called Pretty Pony.
- The products which Smell This makes are plastic roses.
- The company which is owned by BP is on the left of the company owned by Toyota Motor.
- The company which makes nappies is owned by BP.
- The employee who gets the red package is the mail room attendant.
- The company which is located in the centre makes soup.
- The company which gets the yellow package is next to the company where the boss's secretary receives the mail.
- The company which gets the blue package is next to the company where the receptionist receives the mail.
- The employee who receives the mail at the company which makes hairpieces is the gardener.
- The employee who receives the mail at Oh Baby is the security guard.
- The company which is owned by Exxon Mobil is next to Teen Cream.

b Copy the table and use it to help you solve the puzzle.

	Teen Cream	SMELL THIS	Birdhouse	Oh Baby	Pretty Pony
Parent company	*Wal Mart*	...	...	...	...
Product	*body lotion*	...	...	...	...
Employee	*receptionist*	...	...	...	...
Package colour	*yellow*	...	...	...	...

c Your teacher has the answer. After a few minutes, he or she can answer questions about the companies, but you must ask them in correct English.

Tipp

- Wenn Sie eine Lösung ausschließen können, schreiben Sie sie trotzdem in den Kasten, aber durchgestrichen, z. B. ~~nappies~~.
- Wenn Sie eine Lösung eindeutig zuordnen können, dann streichen Sie die übrigen Begriffe derselben Kategorie durch.

- talking about the environment
- describing a process

Our environment 11

WARM-UP

1 A questionnaire

Complete the questionnaire. When you have finished, compare your results with a partner. Who got the higher score? (See page 97 for the answer key.)

How green are you?

1 It's better to speak of 'our environment' than 'the environment' because …
a it belongs to us. b we're a part of it. c it's around us.

2 When you are the last person to leave a room at night, you turn off the light …
a always.
b if you expect to be away for more than five minutes.
c only if you're going to bed.

3 You're hungry, so you go to the supermarket for a snack. You buy …
a a bag of sweets.
b a bar of organic chocolate.
c some dried fruit and nuts which you put in a bag that you brought with you.

4 You used your moped to get to the supermarket. How often do you change the oil?
a Never. It's an electric moped.
b Never. It has a two-stroke engine.
c Every 6 months or 2000 km, like it says in the handbook.

5 You're thirsty, so you go back to the supermarket. You buy …
a a bottle of water in a glass bottle with a deposit.
b a can of Coke.
c a carton of chocolate-flavoured milk.

6 What does this symbol on a plastic container mean?
a This container is made from recycled plastic.
b This container can be recycled.
c It shows what type of plastic it is. It may or may not be recyclable where I live.

Green guerrillas

It's night in the city. The streets are quiet and many of the streetlights are broken. Areas of wasteland between housing estates are full of rubbish – old tyres and shopping trolleys.

In the darkness, something – someone – is moving. Figures in black are moving quickly through the streets. Their faces are hidden by ski masks. On their backs are rucksacks with heavy tools. In their hands are spades and pickaxes. ***The urban guerrillas*** are at work.

In the morning, the piles of rubbish and the old tyres have gone from the wasteland. Now there are garden beds with labels that say 'tomatoes', 'onions' and 'cabbages'. Two young apple trees have been planted. Local residents wake up to find leaflets in their letterboxes. The leaflets say 'Your area has been guerrilla gardened.' They explain what has been planted and give instructions about how to look after the plants.

This is guerrilla gardening, a peaceful form of direct action. Guerrilla gardeners find unused land and grow plants on it. They don't care who owns the land – if it isn't being used, it's fair game. Guerrilla gardener ***Andrew1206*** explains why. 'The city is an anonymous, unfriendly place. Why? Because people don't feel that it's theirs. The council, the police and the property developers tell them what to do. We want to take back control of the streets and the land between them. We want to show people that they have an environment that is worth caring for. Plants will grow anywhere. All they need is soil, light and water.'

To the local council, the guerrilla gardeners are just vandals. 'It isn't their land,' says councillor ***Bob Rogers.*** 'It's private land. They're just trespassers and vandals. They should keep to their own gardens.'

But many people in the area don't have a garden, because they live in tall blocks of flats. Local resident ***Anna Povey*** thinks that the guerrilla gardeners are doing a good job. 'It's much nicer to look at flowers and green plants, rather than dead grass and rubbish.'

Student ***Mal Allum*** shares a house with eight friends. They often pick vegetables from a local guerrilla garden. 'Why not? They're free and they taste great. We help to look after the garden. Lots of local people do.'

Not everybody values the guerrilla gardens – at first. Teenager ***Jack O'Brien*** vandalized the first guerrilla garden in the area. 'We pulled out the plants. It was just a laugh. Then we were sorry – what these guys are doing is quite cool, really. Nowadays we don't wreck the gardens, and we don't let other gangs wreck them either.'

(434 words)

2 Building skills: visualizing content

The diagram below shows the different attitudes towards guerrilla gardens which the people in the article express. Copy and complete the diagram with information from the text.

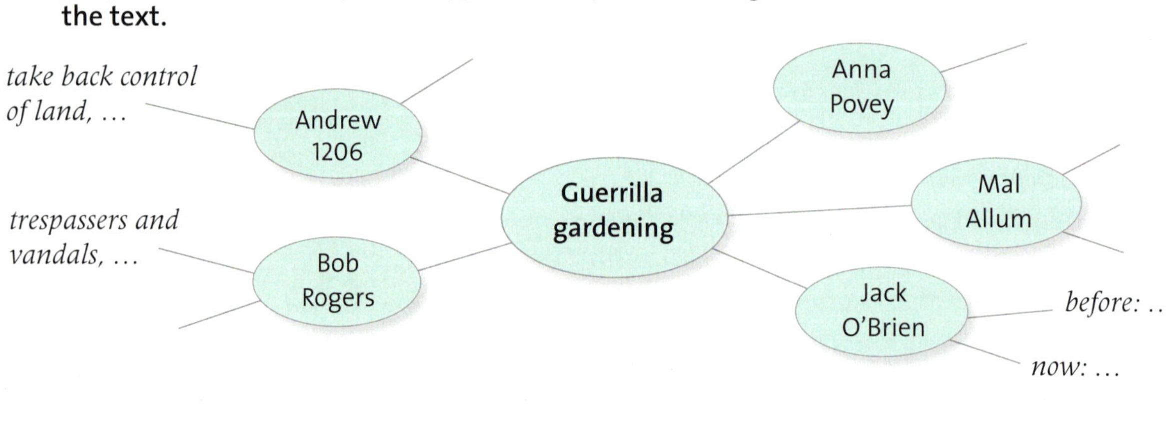

3 Building skills: organizing vocabulary

In the table below, things that are natural go in column A; those which are man-made go in column C. Those which are part natural and part man-made go in column B (e.g. garden beds are made by humans but contain soil and plants, which are natural).

a Copy and complete the table using the words in the box. They are all in the text.

A	B	C
natural		man-made
soil	*garden bed*	*streetlight*

apple tree | block of flats | cabbage | city | darkness | environment | flower | ~~garden bed~~ | letterbox | light | onion | plant | rubbish | ~~soil~~ | ~~streetlight~~ | tomato | vegetable | wasteland | water

b There may be more than one correct solution. Compare answers with a partner and discuss the reasons for any differences.

Skill

Texte und Vokabeln bildlich darstellen

Es gibt viele Möglichkeiten, Textinhalte und Vokabeln bildlich darzustellen, z. B. mit einer Mind Map (s. S. 94), mit einem Flussdiagramm oder mit einer Tabelle (s. oben).

Textverständnis

Bildliche Darstellung ist nützlich, um:

- komplizierte Textinhalte zu vereinfachen;
- unterschiedliche Standpunkte voneinander abzugrenzen bzw. Gemeinsamkeiten zu entdecken;
- Hauptinformationen eines Textes zusammenzufassen.

Einprägen von Vokabeln

Man lernt Vokabeln effektiver, wenn man sie in einen Zusammenhang bringt, etwa indem man sie bildlich anordnet. Man kann z. B. Vokabelgruppen, die zusammengehören, grafisch so anordnen, dass der Zusammenhang deutlich wird und man sie besser behält:

- Wortgruppen – thematisch verwandte Wörter, z. B. *environment, nature* (Mind Map, Mengendiagramm)
- Wortfamilien – Wörter, die denselben Stamm haben, z. B. *life, live, lively* (Tabelle)
- Antonyme – Wörter gegensätzlicher Bedeutung, z. B. *hot – cold* (Tabelle)

4 Speaking

Work in a small group. Discuss the following questions about the text on page 94.

- Could this happen in your town/city?
- Would you join them if they asked you?
- Is it important for us to grow our own food?
- What else could you do for the environment?

5 Mediation: Organic Community

Your friend is interested in environmental projects and finds this webpage. As his English isn't very good, he asks you to tell him what the page is about.

Make notes in German for your friend. You don't need to write complete sentences.

EXAMPLE: – *Praktische Projekte für Teilnehmer/innen jeder Altersgruppe und Herkunft*

ORGANIC COMMUNITY

Home | Projects

We aim to bring together people of all ages and backgrounds in practical projects that are creative and educational (e.g. cook-and-eat sessions, carpentry, grow your own food) in Hampshire and London. Experience of these projects gives young people a chance to help the environment and the communities in which they live.

Volunteer with us

Local Food Production

We develop fruit and vegetable gardens in schools and businesses. You can volunteer to assist us in land preparation and cultivation.

Living Buildings

We create green roofs and green walls on office buildings and council offices. A green roof includes a rooftop garden, a rainwater tank and a water recycling system.

Camps

We hold several camps each year for young people at Thorne Farm in Hampshire. We welcome volunteers to assist us at these weekend camps.

6 Writing: at your school

You want to have an outdoor leisure space at your school. It will be somewhere for students to relax and chat in nice, green surroundings. What things will you have in your leisure space? Draw a plan and write a description.

EXAMPLE: *We'll put a tree in the corner and a seat next to it. Then …*

There will be We'll put	a tree some plants a vegetable bed a pond a seat an area of grass	next to the door / gate / wall. in the northeast / northwest / southeast / southwest corner. on the north / south / east / west side. in the middle.

7 Listening: environment jobs

2 15 Read the job profiles, then listen to Callum, Zoe and Ethan talking about their jobs. Try to work out which job each of them does. One job is not done by any of them.

Gardener
Gardeners look after parks, gardens and green spaces. They usually plant flowers, bushes and trees, check the health of plants and spray fertilizer and pesticides. They also cut the grass, keep paths tidy and remove dead leaves and litter.

Arborist
Arborists look after trees in towns and cities and in the countryside. Some arborists work as tree surgeons: they climb up big trees to remove dead or damaged branches at heights of up to 36 metres. That's a dangerous and highly skilled job.

Forestry worker
Forestry workers develop, look after and protect forests. They plant, look after and cut down trees. They also put up fences and clear walking trails for the public to use. They sometimes also build roads through the forest. They may have to operate heavy machinery.

Countryside ranger
Countryside rangers look after areas of the countryside such as woods and national parks. They prevent damage, protect plants and wildlife, and make sure that land is safe for public use. They observe wildlife, keep records and write reports.

8 Tools of the trade

Identify the equipment in the pictures. Then decide which job from exercise 7 the item is used in. Some might be used in more than one job.

EXAMPLE: 1 *spade – gardener, forestry worker*

binoculars | chainsaw | gloves | GPS | hard hat | ladder | lawnmower | notebook / computer | spade | wheelbarrow

▶ Answer key, p. 93

1	a 0, b 2, c 1	If you chose **b**, you recognize that we can't get away from our environment, so we have to look after it.
2	a 2, b 1, c 0	If you chose **a**, you are careful about saving electricity.
3	a 0, b 1, c 2	Option **c** creates no waste, unlike the other two options.
4	a 2, b 0, c 1	Option **a** is the best. Option **b** is the worst because two-stroke motors cause most pollution.
5	a 2, b 1, c 0	Option **a** is the best because reusing containers uses less energy than recycling them. Option **c** is worst because drink cartons are often difficult to recycle.
6	a 0, b 0, c 2	Only option **c** is correct.

How did you do?

0–3 points	Poor. You don't care about our environment much.
4–7 points	Not bad. You think about our environment sometimes, but you could do much better.
8–10 points	Pretty good. You consider our environment before making choices.
11–12 points	Excellent. You care about our environment and you are well informed about green issues.

Unit 11

9 Listening: at a mail order company

2 16

The Green Thumb Mail Order Co. is an organic gardening supplier in Australia. Retail Manager Belinda Cundall is explaining to trainee Jamie Hayes how to process orders.

a **Read the sentences below and look up any words you don't know.**

b **Listen to the recording, then put the sentences in the correct order.**

EXAMPLE: *D, ...*

A The goods are checked against the packing list.
B The envelope is stuck to the outside of the box.
C The items on the list are selected from the warehouse.
D An Internet or telephone order is received.
E A packing list is printed out.
F The cardboard box is sealed.
G The post is collected at four o'clock.
H The box is taken to the mail room.
I The dispatch note and invoice are put in a transparent envelope.
J Live plants are packed carefully in special boxes.
K The goods are put in a cardboard box.

10 Writing: in the plant nursery

Now Jamie is going to work in the plant nursery, where the plants are grown. Tim Mills, the Nursery Manager, has written a list to explain what happens in the nursery.

Complete the list with the simple present passive of the verbs in brackets.

1 The pots *are filled* (fill) with soil.
2 A seed ... (put) in each pot
3 The pot ... (water).
4 The pots ... (label) with the name of the plant.
5 The pots ... (put) in a tray.
6 A barcode ... (stick) on the tray.
7 The tray ... (take) to the greenhouse.
8 The seed trays ... (look after) carefully for several weeks.
9 When the seeds have grown into plants, the barcode ... (scan).
10 The plants ... (enter) into the computer system as 'ready for sale'.

11 Speaking: describing a process

Choose a process that you know and describe it to your partner in the simple present passive.

Use phrases from the box to make the order clear. Your partner listens and takes notes.

First of all, ...
Then, ...
After that, ...
Finally, ...

12 Using the passive

What has been done to the wasteland in Grimetown? Use the phrases from the box in the present perfect passive.

EXAMPLE: *A sign has been put up.*

dig garden beds | make the shopping trolley into a wheelbarrow | paint the old car in bright colours | plant fruit trees | ~~put up a sign~~ | remove the rubbish | sow vegetable seeds | turn the oil drum into a compost bin | use the car tyres as plant pots

13 Writing a newspaper report

Write a report for the Grimetown Weekly News about the guerrilla garden above. Use the simple past passive. Start like this:

Another patch of wasteland in Grimetown was visited by the guerrilla gardeners last Thursday night. A sign was put up. It said 'Green is good.' A lot of rubbish was …

Grammar

The passive (Das Passiv)

	Aktiv	Passiv
Simple present	I **wash** the car.	The car **is washed** (by me).
Simple past	I **washed** the car.	The car **was washed** (by me).
Present perfect	I have **washed** the car.	The car **has been washed** (by me).

- In einem Aktivsatz sagen wir, wer etwas tut.
  In einem Passivsatz sagen wir, was mit einer Person oder Sache getan wird.
- Bildung des Passivs: Form von *to be* + Partizip Perfekt
  Gegenwart: *am/are/is* + Partizip Perfekt
  Vergangenheit: *was/were* + Partizip Perfekt
  Perfekt: *has/have been* + Partizip Perfekt
- Mit *by* können wir sagen, von wem etwas gemacht wird bzw. wurde. Meist verwenden wir jedoch das Passiv, wenn es nicht nötig (oder nicht möglich) ist zu sagen, wer etwas tut oder getan hat.

TEST 3 Do you remember?

1 **This is your friend Steffie. Your Irish online friend wants to know what she looks like. Write three sentences to describe her.**

Tipp: Personenbeschreibungen haben Sie in Unit 8 gemacht.

points 3

2 **Sie unternehmen einen Ausflug mit Ihrer Jugendgruppe. Ihr schottischer Austauschpartner Jack ist dabei. Erklären Sie ihm, was gemacht werden muss und was nicht.**

points 3

Ausflug 10.04. Bio-Bauernhof Sonnenwiese
- Abfahrt 07.30 Uhr vom Hauptbahnhof. Bitte pünktlich sein!
- Warme Kleidung mitbringen!
- Wir sind zu Mittag bei der Bauernfamilie eingeladen, Sie brauchen also kein Mittagessen mitzubringen.

Tipp: Hierfür benötigen Sie das Hilfsverb *have to* (müssen). Schauen Sie sich nochmals Seite 75 an, falls Sie Hilfe brauchen.

3 **Your favourite computer game is called 'Dschungelkönig'. Explain how to play the game.**

a Wenn der Affe *(monkey)* eine Banane frisst, verliert man einen Punkt. *points* 1
b Wenn der Tiger einen Affen frisst, gewinnt man zehn Punkte. *points* 1
c Wenn man keine Punkte mehr hat, ist das Spiel zu Ende. *points* 1

Tipp: Dafür brauchen Sie *if/when*-Sätze. Schauen Sie sich nochmals Seite 81 an.

4 **Sie rufen eine Firma an. Schreiben Sie Ihren Teil des Telefongesprächs:**

a Sie wollen Mr Francis sprechen.
b Man fragt nach Ihrem Namen: Antworten Sie.
c Man teilt Ihnen mit: Mr Francis ist nicht im Büro, aber er wird in zwei Stunden wieder da sein. Sie sagen, dass Sie zurückrufen werden.

Tipp: Falls Sie Hilfe brauchen, schauen Sie sich nochmals Seite 88 an.

points 3

5 **Name six objects you would find in an office.**

Tipp: Gegenstände in einem Büro haben Sie in Unit 10 gelernt.

points 3

6 **Explain what happens to the plants at the Green Thumb Mail Order Company. Use the verbs *put*, *stick* and *scan*.**

points 3

Tipp: Um Vorgänge zu beschreiben, verwenden wir oft das Passiv. Schauen Sie sich nochmals Seite 99 an, falls Sie Hilfe brauchen.

How did you do?	
15–18 points	Excellent. Keep up the good work!
10–14 points	Good. Keep working hard so that you can get even more points in the next test (Unit 15).
less than 10 points	Take another look at the tasks you found difficult. Ask your teacher for help if you need it.

(Lösungen auf Seite 207.)

- talking about interests, talents, likes and dislikes

The right job for me? 12

WARM-UP

1 The Game of Life

100 Americans took the survey below. For each question, think of the most typical answer. You get one Happiness Point for each survey-taker who gave your answer. If your answer is not in the results, you 'die' (you're out of the game). The winner is the person who 'dies' happiest.

EXAMPLE: *Name something a man calls his 'whole life'.*
Survey results: 51 Americans said 'job'; 33 Americans said 'family'; 6 Americans said 'sports'; 5 Americans said 'car'. (See File 9, page 137.)

In this example, if you guess 'job', you get **51 Happiness Points.** If you guess 'family', you get **33 Happiness Points**, etc. If you guess 'food' or 'computer', you **die**. (Answers that were given by only one survey-taker are not included in the results.)

Infancy (ages 0–1)

1 Which flavour *(Geschmacksrichtung)* of baby food tastes the best?

Childhood (ages 2–12)

2 What thing scares children the most?
3 Name something people are taught to hold correctly.

Adolescence (ages 13–17)

4 Name something young people do that makes their parents very nervous.
5 Name something people like doing at a party.

Early adulthood (ages 18–34)

6 Name a job women do where men often ask them out on dates.
7 When they've fallen in love, people neglect *(vernachlässigen)* things like school work. Name something else people neglect when they've just fallen in love.

Mid-adulthood (ages 35–64)

8 Name a job for which people have to work on Sundays.
9 Name an animal that adults imitate when they play with little kids.
10 Name something in the house that women use more than men.

Late adulthood (ages 64+)

11 Name an activity that makes your eyes tired.
12 Name a complaint people have about doctors.

2
17

From drop-out to professor: *a true story*

Talia Diaz was not a happy teenager. When she was 14, her parents divorced and she had to move with her mother from Puerto Rico to Texas, where she didn't know anyone. At high school, she didn't fit in with the other students and often had problems with the teachers. 'Everyone at school seemed to hate me, so I stopped going,' she remembers. Soon she became so miserable that she dropped out of school. She had no high school diploma and, therefore, no future – at least that's what some people thought.

But Talia wanted to have a profession with a future, so she decided to try again. She took the bus every day to a smaller school in another town. She studied hard and when she finally finished school, she was the second best in her class. She also discovered what she loved doing – mathematics. She managed to get into university and there she enjoyed learning more than ever.

Today, Talia is 23 and, believe it or not, she is studying for her PhD. She plans to become a math professor and share her passion for math with lots and lots of students. 'No one in high school expected me to get far in any profession. They wouldn't believe it if you told them that now I'm in an academic one!' says the future Dr Diaz.

(233 words)

2 Reading for detail

Read the text and correct these false statements.

1 Talia moved to Puerto Rico with her mother and father.
2 Talia liked her first high school in Texas and the people there.
3 Talia didn't like school so she got her diploma early.
4 Talia was the best in her class when she finished university.
5 Talia hates academics and never wants to be in a classroom again.
6 Talia is doing exactly what her high school teachers expected her to do.

3 Working with words

a Find the word in the text that means ...

1 to separate from one's husband or wife
2 to feel good in a social situation
3 to quit school
4 to find something for the first time
5 to give part of something to others
6 strong love

b Copy this table on a piece of paper, then complete it with words from the text.

EXAMPLES: Everyone at school seemed to hate me, so I stopped going.

Verb + *to*		Verb + *-ing*	
seem	*to hate*	*stop*	*going*
want	...	*love*	...
decide	...	...	...
...	...		
...	...		
...	...		

4 Ideal jobs

a These teenagers researched some jobs at on the Internet and found some they had never heard of before. Match each of them with their ideal job.

Andreas: I'*m interested* in working in teams with technicians and I'*m good at* organizing things.

Alina: I can *imagine* operating heavy machinery and I *hate* being indoors all the time.

Kevin: I *enjoy* working with people and I *love* working with my hands.

Sarah: I *like* working with precision tools and I *wouldn't mind* filling special orders.

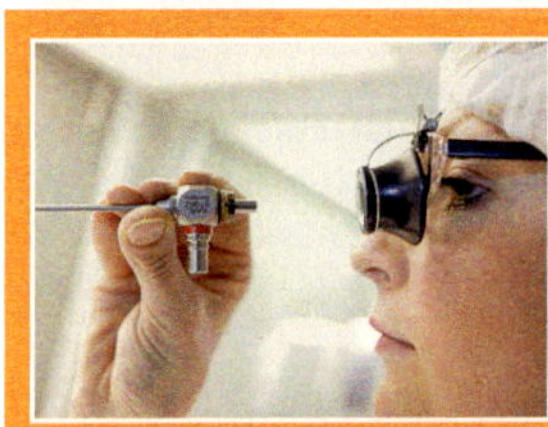

surgical instrument mechanic / *Chirurgiemechaniker/in*

orthopedic shoemaker *Orthopädische/r Schumacher/in*

forest machine operator / *Forstmaschinenführer/in*

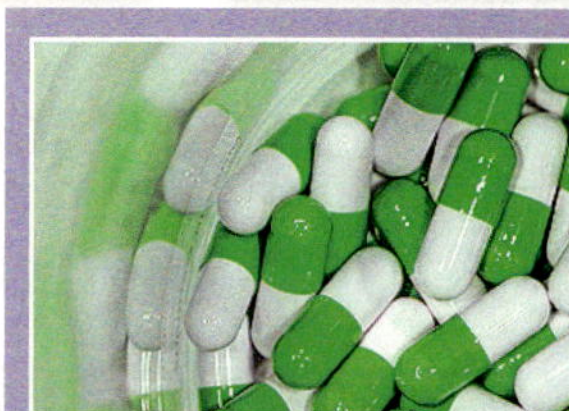

pharmaceutical business assistant / *Pharmazeutisch-kaufmännische/r Angestellte/r*

b Each phrase or verb in *italics* is followed by a verb. What form is the verb in? Add these verbs and phrases to your table from exercise 3b.

5 Interests, likes, dislikes and talents

Make sentences about someone you know (or change the verb forms and make them about yourself).

Sarah's good at working with people. She wants to become a nurse.

He's/She's interested in ...	He/She enjoys ...	He/She seems ...
He/She doesn't mind ...	He/She loves ...	He/She has decided ...
He's/She's good at ...	He/She hates ...	He/She plans ...
He/She likes ...	He/She wants ...	

Grammar

Verb + *-ing* form or infinitive with *to*
(Verb + *-ing*-Form oder *to*-Infinitiv)

Nach bestimmten Verben folgt die *-ing*-Form:
– z. B. Verben des Mögens und Nicht-Mögens: *enjoy, hate, like, love, (not) mind, prefer, ...:*
He **likes working** in a team.
– Nach einer Präposition (*at, in, of, on,* usw.):
You're **good at telling** stories.
Nach vielen anderen Verben folgt, wie im Deutschen, ein Infinitiv: *decide, hope, learn, offer, plan, seem, want, ...:*
– She **wants to work** with computers.

6 Save Dave! – a logic puzzle

It's Saturday night and your friends – Stacy, Tracy, Bobby, Bipsy and Dave – are having fun at five different clubs. You have to stay home and take care of your sick gerbil. You are taking its temperature when you get a text message on your mobile telephone:

Poor Dave! You have to save him! But where is he? You open your city's club guide and get the following information:

There are five clubs. They are next to each other on the same street. The clubs' names are: *Auntie's, The Sphinx, Midnight, Move it!, Lucky Lounge.*

► Each club has a different main attraction: go-go dancers, a panoramic view of the city, a magic show, a light-up dance floor, a giant fish tank.

► Each club plays a different kind of music: karaoke, reggae, punk, tango, techno.

2 18 Your other friends have left messages on your telephone. Listen and write down the clues. There is one piece of information for each friend. You find more clues in the local club guide. Use them to find Dave.

- ► *Auntie's* is on the left of the club that plays reggae music.
- ► The club that plays techno has a light-up dance floor.
- ► The bar with the panoramic view is next to the *Lucky Lounge.*
- ► *Move It!* plays tango music.
- ► The club that plays techno is on the right of the club that plays reggae, which is on the right of the club with the giant fish tank.
- ► The club with the go-go dancers is next to the club with the panoramic view.
- ► The club that has karaoke is at the end of the street, next to *Move It!*
- ► There is one more clue in the picture on the opposite page.

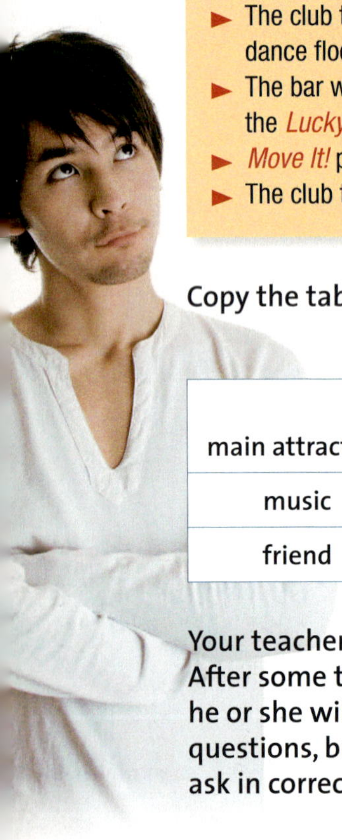

Copy the table and use it to help you solve the puzzle.

	Auntie's	The Sphinx	Midnight	Move it	lucky lounge
main attraction	...	...	...	...	...
music	...	...	...	...	...
friend	...	...	...	...	...

Your teacher has the answer. After some time has passed, he or she will answer questions, but only if you ask in correct English.

Tipp

- Wenn Sie eine Lösung ausschließen können, schreiben Sie sie trotzdem in den Kasten, aber durchgestrichen, z. B. ~~Lucky Lounge~~.
- Wenn Sie eine Lösung eindeutig zuordnen können, dann streichen Sie die übrigen Begriffe derselben Kategorie durch.

7 What was everyone doing?

Look at the picture and make sentences with the words in the box. Use the past continuous.

dance | laugh | kiss | play music | mIx a drink | make a video | ~~assist in a magic show~~ | take money from a guest

EXAMPLE: *When the power went out, Dave was assisting in a magic show.*

1	Dave	3	Mary and Marty	5	Wallace and Wllis	7	the bartender
2	Trudy	4	Ricky and Vicky	6	The DJ	8	the doorman

Grammar

The past continuous
(Die Verlaufsform der Vergangenheit)

Mit der Verlaufsform beschreiben wir eine längere Handlung, die in der Vergangenheit stattfand.

I/he/she/it	**was(n't)**	danc**ing**
you/we/they	**were(n't)**	danc**ing**

- Manchmal beschreibt die Verlaufsform eine Hintergrundhandlung, die zu einem bestimmten Zeitpunkt der Vergangenheit (z. B. *'when the power went out'*) vor sich ging:
  – We **were** danc**ing** when the power went out.
- Die Verlaufsform kann auch mehrere längere Handlungen beschreiben, die gleichzeitig passierten:
  – I **was** watch**ing** you while you **were** danc**ing**.

8 Using the past continuous

Philip is interested in making videos, but he's not very good at doing it!

Make sentences using *while* and the following phrases.

Philip made six videos. He filmed ...

EXAMPLE: *Scott while he was telling a joke.*

eat some breadcrumbs | play football | ~~tell a joke~~ | talk on the telephone | have fun at a club | chase a ball

Scott

some kids

some birds

his grandma

a dog

his friends

2 19

Six Tips For Making Better Videos

1 Shoot with the strongest light *behind* the camera.

Your viewers will be able to see the people and objects better. If the light is behind *them*, they will be too dark.

2 Learn when to pan and zoom.

One of the most common mistakes is moving the camera too much. Don't pan quickly from one subject to another. Not only does it look bad on the Internet, but it also slows down the online video stream. If you decide to pan, do it slowly. An even better technique is to take a shot of something and leave it there for 10–20 seconds, stop the recording and then take another shot.

3 Don't use the camera's zoom function.

This reduces the quality of your picture. If you need to get closer to your subject, 'zoom with your feet'.

4 Tell a story.

People will watch your videos to the end if they tell a story. For example, imagine you want to shoot an evening out at the disco. First, shoot yourself while you're getting ready at home. Then, take some good shots of the club to show what it looks like. Then, show your friends having fun. Finish with a shot of you riding home on the night bus. You've now told a story about the evening that will be interesting to watch.

5 Use the rule of thirds.

This is especially true if you're doing an interview or shooting a close-up of someone talking. Imagine your picture has four lines like a 'tic-tac-toe'* board. Then, imagine putting the eyes along the top line and the centre of their head on the left or the right line, even if it cuts a bit off the head.

This is more interesting than putting the person in the middle of the picture.

6 Remember: YouTube is a small screen.

When you are shooting videos to add to a video-sharing website, avoid wide scenes. You may want to begin with a wide shot of the setting to show the location, but after that, shoot close up.

* *'Drei gewinnt'*

(350 words)

9 Reading for detail

a As you can see from the pictures in exercise 8, Philip needs some advice on how to make better videos. Say which tips from the text would be useful for each of his videos.

EXAMPLE: *The video of Scott telling a joke – tip 1*

b With a partner, take it in turns to explain the tips in German.

10 Building skills: writing

Write some tips for something you know how to do. They can be humorous. Here are some suggestions.

- Tips for learning something
- Tips for talking to adults/parents
- Tips for making coffee/spaghetti/salad/etc.

Use as many of the useful phrases from the text as possible.

Useful phrases: *giving tips*

One of the most common mistakes is ...
A better technique is ...
For example, ...
First, ... Then, ...
This is especially true if ...
When you are ...*ing*, avoid ...
You may want to begin with ...

Skill

Wie man Texte richtig schreibt

- Nicht einfach drauflosschreiben! Machen Sie sich zuerst eine Übersicht über das, was Sie schreiben wollen. Sie können z. B. Überschriften machen und dazu alle Punkte auflisten, die Ihnen einfallen. Manchmal eignet sich eine Mind Map, um alles anschaulich um das Thema herum zu ordnen.
- Gliedern Sie Ihre Ideen in eine Einleitung (worum es in dem Text geht), einen Hauptteil und einen Schluss (kurze Zusammenfassung oder Fazit).
- Nachdem Sie Ihren Text geschrieben haben, prüfen Sie, ob die Länge stimmt und ob alles logisch und sprachlich korrekt ist. Es ist sogar völlig normal, einen ganz neuen Entwurf zu schreiben.
- Am wichtigsten ist es, dass Ihr Text klar und verständlich ist.

11 What's your sign?

a In English, Latin words are used for astrological signs. Match the Latin word to its English translation.

lion | bull | virgin | fish | scale | crab | archer | ram | twins | water carrier | mountain goat | scorpion

b Write the names of the signs on the board. Write the names of the people in the class under their signs.

EXAMPLE: *What's your sign? I'm a Capricorn.*

12 Speaking

I would say that most Libras are ...

I've heard that some Tauruses are ...

What characteristics do the different signs have?

analytical | communicative | courageous *(mutig)* | creative | determined *(entschlossen)* | emotional | generous *(großzügig)* | honest *(ehrlich)* | independent *(unabhängig)* | imaginative *(fantasievoll)* | loyal | optimistic | practical *(praktisch)* | rebellious *(rebellisch)* | sensitive *(sensible)* | unpredictable *(unberechenbar)*

13 Writing a horoscope

Make a group for every sign you have in your class. In your group, use one of the following texts to create a horoscope for a sign.

Horoscope for (sign) for the month of (month):

The month will begin (adverb) for you, dear (sign)! You have always been good at (verb + *-ing*) people, and this month you will do it to everyone! Your professional/school life is sure to bring lots of (adjective) (plural noun) and many reasons to feel (adjective). As Venus makes her way towards Earth, your love life will become (adjective). You will meet a/an (adjective) (profession), and romance will be in the air! But, be careful, dear (sign)! The stars say that you will be involved in a strange (type of machine) accident, where you could hurt your (body part).

Horoscope for (sign) for the month of (month):

This month, you will feel like (famous person) at (event), dear (sign)! The stars say you will enjoy (verb + *-ing*) at the beginning of the month, and your friends will be very (adjective) about this. The full moon on the 15th will make you feel (adjective), and you may not be able to control yourself. You should save money, because you will need to buy at least five (adjective) (plural noun). Watch out, someone you know may want your (noun). Give it freely and you will get twice as much back! If you decide to (verb) at the end of the month, do it (adverb)!

- talking about working abroad
- persuading somebody to do something

Working in Europe 13

WARM-UP

1 Euro-Quiz

How much do you know about the countries of the European Union? Complete the quiz to find out. Your teacher will tell you the answers when you have finished.

1 Which European country is this the flag of?
a Austria b France c Italy

2 Which country is this?
a Irland b Italy c Scotland

3 What is the capital of Poland?
a Prague b Budapest c Warsaw

4 The River Rhine flows through or along the border of four countries. Which of these is NOT one of them?
a Switzerland b Italy c Netherlands

5 What are the official languages of Belgium?
a Belgian and French b Dutch, French and German c French, Belgian and Dutch

6 In which European capital city is this building?
a Paris b London c Madrid

7 How many stars are there in the EU flag?
a 12 b 15 c 18

8 Which of these cities is not in Europe?
a Riga b Lisbon c Ankara d Athens

9 What is *das Mittelmeer* called in English?
a The Middle Sea b The Medium Ocean c The Mediterranean

10 Which of these languages is not an official language of the European Union?
a Turkish b English c German

11 Which of these countries joined the European Union first?
a Poland b Austria c Germany

12 Which of these countries joined the European Union last?
a Latvia b Czech Republic c Romania

Searching for love and adventure in the UK

Some come for love, some for adventure and some to further their career. Yet foreign nurses in the UK all have one thing in common: the National Health Service needs them desperately. Nurses who speak good English find it easy to get work here.

2
20

Love was what brought **Alja** to Britain. She met Paul, a builder, while he was working in Latvia. He persuaded her to give up her nursing job at a hospital in Riga and move to Edinburgh. That was three years ago.

Alja completed an adaptation course at Edinburgh Royal Infirmary. The adaptation course made sure that her skills were up-to-date, and showed her the British way of doing things.

'In Latvia we were short of equipment and resources. If you broke an instrument, it would be difficult to get a replacement. Here everything is up-to-date and everything is available.'

Sometimes, though, Alja is lonely and misses the day-to-day contact with her family. 'I used to see my sister every day, so it's hard being such a long way from her. If I could get more time off work, I would take the children to Riga to see her in the summer. Maybe next year …'

Grigor is ambitious. He arrived here two years ago with a degree in nursing from Bulgaria and a diploma from Russia, where he worked for three years.

He is a senior staff nurse on the Accident and Emergency ward at the Edinburgh Royal Infirmary. He enjoys his work, but the pay could be better. 'Nurses are never paid enough. That's true all over the world, even though we work hard.'

Grigor has a close bunch of friends in Edinburgh, but he doesn't want to stay in Britain for ever. He wants to go back home to Bulgaria one day: 'I'm not exactly homesick, but it's true that "There's no place like home," as the British say. If I wanted to settle down, I'd choose a Bulgarian girl, not a British girl. But for now my career is the important thing.'

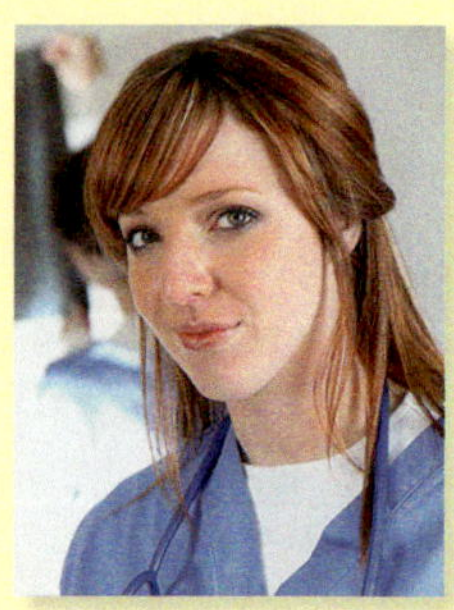

Marisol comes from Spain – a country which has plenty of nurses. 23-year-old Marisol wanted a broad range of experience – and that was hard to find at home. 'I was a community nurse in Barcelona, it was a dead-end job.'

However, it's the social life that keeps her here, as much as her work on a surgical ward at the Royal Infirmary. Edinburgh is a multicultural community: 'Scotland is not only for the Scottish! There are people from many countries here. Being a foreigner here is good fun – not a problem.'

She certainly wasn't attracted to Britain by the money. 'If I wanted to make good money, I would go to Saudi Arabia. The pay here is worse than back home.'

(466 words)

2 Reading for gist

Read the text quickly, then match the speech bubbles to the people in the text.

EXAMPLE: 1 *Grigor*

1 I want to be successful in my profession.

2 There aren't enough good job opportunities back home.

3 I wish I could see my family more often.

4 I fell in love with someone from another country.

5 I definitely plan to return home – but not yet.

6 It's nice to work in a well-equipped hospital.

7 It's a lot of fun living and working here.

8 I'd prefer to marry someone from the same background as me.

3 Reading for detail

Read the text again and complete these sentences in your own words.

1 When Alja met Paul, she was *a nurse at a hospital in Riga.*
2 In comparison with Latvian hospitals, the Royal Infirmary has ...
3 Next year, Alja hopes ...
4 Grigor wants to ...
5 He isn't very satisfied with ...
6 Although he likes Scottish people, Grigor would prefer ...
7 Marisol wasn't happy with ...
8 She really enjoys being ...
9 Money wasn't the main reason ...

4 Working with words

Complete the translations with expressions from the text.

1 *Freundschaft interessiert ihn nicht, er will nur* ***beruflich weiterkommen****.* (Introduction)
He isn't interested in friendship, he just wants to *further his career*.

2 *Ohne meine Familie* ***wäre*** *ich* ***einsam****.* (Alja)
I would ... without my family.

3 *In diesem Job ist es schwierig,* ***Urlaub zu bekommen****.* (Alja)
It's difficult to ... in this job.

4 *Meine Freunde* ***würden mir fehlen****, wenn ich von Madrid wegginge.* (Alja)
I would ... my friends if I left Madrid.

5 *Ich würde mich eher in Deutschland als in der Schweiz* ***niederlassen****.* (Grigor)
I would rather ... in Germany than in Switzerland.

6 *Krystyn hat* ***einen festen Freundeskreis*** *in Berlin.* (Grigor)
Krystyn has ... in Berlin.

7 *Ich bin viel herumgereist,* aber ***daheim ist es am schönsten****.* (Grigor)
I've travelled a lot, but ... .

8 ***Privat unternehme*** *ich sehr viel: Ich bin immer auf Partys.* (Marisol)
My ... is very busy: I'm going to lots of parties.

5 Speaking: working abroad

Work in a small group. Discuss: If you decided to work in another European country, which country would you choose, and why?

I would work in ... because ...
I wouldn't want to work in ... because ...
Personally, I find ... more interesting than ... because ...
What do you think of ... as a place to work?

6 Using *if* sentences type 2

a You're trying to persuade your friend to go on a working holiday in southern Europe. All he/she sees are problems, so he/she doesn't want to go. Try to convince your friend.

buy a phrasebook | get a lift with my dad's friend | ~~get casual jobs~~ | go to an internet café | go to McDonalds | phone home | sleep on the beach | spend the day in a shopping mall | try busking | use our medical insurance |

EXAMPLE: 1 *If we ran out of money, we'd get casual jobs.*

1 What would we do if we ran out of money?
2 Where would we stay if the hostel was full?
3 What would we do if we couldn't get jobs?
4 How would we travel if we couldn't afford train tickets?
5 What would we do if we couldn't speak the language?
6 What would we do if one of us got sick?
7 What would we eat if we didn't like the local food?
8 What would we do if we got homesick?
9 How would we talk to our parents if our mobile phones were stolen?
10 How would we stay warm if the weather was bad?

b Now role play the situation with a partner. You can make up your own problems and solutions if you like. When you have practised, record your conversation and play it back to the class.

Grammar

_if_ sentences type 2 (*if*-Sätze Typ 2)

In *if*-Sätzen des Typs 2 wird die Situation als theoretisch möglich, aber kaum wahrscheinlich betrachtet.

If I **left** Germany, I**'d** (= would) **miss** my family.
Wenn ich Deutschland verlassen würde, würde mir meine Familie fehlen.
Would you **be** homesick if you **lived** abroad?
Würdest du Heimweh haben, wenn du im Ausland lebtest?

- *If*-Teil = *if* + simple past, Folgeteil = *would* + **Infinitiv**
- Der *if*-Teil kann hinter dem Folgeteil stehen. In diesem Fall steht kein Komma dazwischen.

! Im *if*-Teil steht kein *would*. (*If I ~~would leave~~ Germany, ...*)

7 Listening: am I allowed to use my 'handy'?

Lukas Schmidt from Nürnberg has just started a job as a hospital porter in Manchester, England. He wants to ask a colleague, Emma Watts, about the hospital rules, but he's finding it difficult to explain what he means.

a Complete the dialogue with useful phrases from the box below.

Lukas: Emma?
Emma: Yes?
Lukas: *(quietly)* Am I allowed to use my handy in the hospital?
Emma: ...[1]
Lukas: *(louder)* Am I allowed to use my handy?
Emma: Your hanky? Your handkerchief? Of course you are. Have you got a cold?
Lukas: No, no. ...[2] My *handy*.
Emma: Sorry, Lukas. ...[3] I don't know what a 'handy' is.
Lukas: Oh, ...[4] It's a phone that you carry around in your pocket. Look, here it is ... *(He gets out his mobile phone.)* ... [5]
Emma: Ah! ...[6] your *mobile phone*?
Lukas: Mobile phone?
Emma: ...[7]
Lukas: Oh, right. Mobile phone, not 'handy'. ...[8]
Emma: That's OK. ...[9]
Lukas: Hmm, my English is really bad, I think ...
Emma: No, Lukas, it's great. Really. But to answer your question: no, you aren't allowed to use your phone – not on the ward. So you'd better turn it off now, before the nurse comes ...

Useful phrases: *dealing with communication difficulties*

Dealing with misunderstandings
- a I must have used the wrong word.
- b Sorry, I don't know what you mean.
- c You've misunderstood me.

Checking and confirming meaning
- d What's this called in English?
- e You mean ... ?
- f Yes, that's right.

Apologizing and replying
- g Sorry about the misunderstanding.
- h That's OK. Everybody makes mistakes.

When you didn't hear
- i Sorry, I didn't quite catch that.
- j You're speaking a bit fast for me.

2 21 **b** Now listen to the conversation to check your answers.

8 Building skills: paraphrasing

Work with a partner.

Student A: Look at this page. Student B: Turn to File 6 on page 136.

Student A: You don't know the English for these words. How could you explain them to an English speaker? Explain them to your partner using the useful phrases. Can he/she guess the correct word?

Useful phrases: ***paraphrasing***

It's a thing that you use to ...
It's a kind of ... (that ...)
It's a person who ...
It's a place where ...
It's when you ...

1 Krankenschwester/-pfleger
2 Heimweh haben
3 Bezahlung
4 Krankenhaus
5 Sprachführer

9 Building skills: dealing with communication difficulties

You've just arrived at the airport in London to start your working holiday. You realize that you've lost something important. You go to the lost property office.

Work with a partner. One of you is the traveller and one of you is the lost property office attendant. Role play the dialogue.

A: Traveller	B: Lost property office attendant
Begrüßen Sie den Beamten/die Beamtin.	Grüßen Sie zurück und fragen, womit Sie helfen können.
Sagen Sie, dass Sie Ihren Reisepass verloren haben. Da Sie nicht wissen, wie es auf Englisch heißt, versuchen Sie es mit 'travel pass'.	Reagieren Sie mit höflichem Unverständnis.
Umschreiben Sie: ein kleines Buch mit Foto, man kann damit ins Ausland reisen.	Jetzt verstehen Sie; sagen Sie, dass es *passport* heißt. Fragen Sie nach dem Namen des Passinhabers.
Sie verstehen den Beamten/die Beamtin akustisch nicht.	Wiederholen Sie die Frage.
Sagen Sie Ihren Namen.	Schauen Sie nach. Sie finden den Pass und überreichen Sie ihn/ihr.
Bedanken Sie sich überschwänglich und verabschieden Sie sich.	Verabschieden Sie sich ebenfalls.

Skill

Wie man Verständigungsschwierigkeiten überwindet

Wie Sie Missverständnisse vermeiden:
- Bemühen Sie sich um eine gute Aussprache.
- Hören Sie genau zu: Wie sagen es die Muttersprachler?
- Lernen Sie aus Ihren Fehlern, sodass Sie nicht die gleichen Fehler wiederholen.

Wenn Sie nicht verstehen, was jemand gesagt hat, können Sie:
- um Wiederholung bitten: *Sorry, could you repeat that?*
- um eine Erklärung bitten: *I don't quite understand. What do you mean by that?*

Wenn jemand Sie nicht versteht, sollten Sie versuchen, den Grund aufzuklären:
- Hat man Sie rein akustisch nicht verstanden? (Den Satz deutlich wiederholen.)
- War Ihre Aussprache/Betonung falsch? (Das scheinbar problematische Wort in einzelne Silben getrennt nochmals wiederholen.)
- Haben Sie das falsche Wort gebraucht? (Es mit einem anderen Wort versuchen.)

Wenn Ihnen das richtige Wort nicht einfällt:
- Umschreiben Sie es (siehe **Useful Phrases:** *dealing with communication difficulties,* S. 113).
- Verwenden Sie nichtverbale Mittel wie Gestik (z. B. auf den Gegenstand zeigen).

Ganz wichtig: Humor bewahren und höflich bleiben!

10 Working with words: false friends

False friends *(falsche Freunde)* can cause confusion when you speak English. Here are some English words that look similar to German ones – but mean something different.

Copy and complete the table with the real German meanings. Use a dictionary if you need to.

Englisch	heißt nicht ...	sondern ...
actual	*aktuell*	...
chef	*Chef/in*	...
handy	*Handy*	...
warehouse	*Warenhaus*	...
gift	*Gift*	...
become	*bekommen*	...
spend	*spenden*	...
sensible	*sensibel*	...
meaning	*Meinung*	...

11 Reading: health care jobs

These Germans are all members of a European networking site for health care workers.

a Match each ID card to the correct 'About me' profile.

b List the duties which are mentioned for each job.

EXAMPLE: 1 *health services officer: check patients' documents, …*

2 22

1

About me
I'm a health services officer in a large general hospital in Hessen. When patients arrive, I check that they have all the necessary documents. Patients are often nervous: wouldn't you be if you were going in for an operation? So I have to be calm and friendly as I help them to fill in the forms. It's not unusual to have English-speaking patients, so I often have to use English at work. Then I have to put all the details on computer and phone the medical insurance company if there are any questions about the patient's insurance.

2

About me
What I like about my job as a medical assistant in a doctor's surgery is that it's so varied. In reception I answer the phone and book appointments for patients, I greet the patients when they arrive and swipe their chip cards to bring up their details on screen. It's a small practice and I'm often called in to assist the doctor with examinations and minor operations, to take blood samples and things like that. In the quiet times, there's always plenty of administrative work to do – letters and emails need to be written to patients, medical supply companies and specialists, invoices need to be paid. There's never a dull moment.

3

About me
I recently qualified as a dental assistant. I assist the dentist in the treatment room. When it's a patient's turn I fetch him or her from the waiting room, fill up the water glass and hand the patient's file to the dentist. Some of the patients are nervous, of course, so I try to make them relax. During the examination or treatment I pass instruments to the dentist and help with the treatment. I hope to get my X-ray certificate so that I can take responsibility for X-rays of the patients' teeth. After treatment I disinfect the surfaces and sterilize the instruments. I'm learning to do denture repairs and laboratory work.

12 Job skills and qualities

Which of these skills and qualities would each of the jobs require? Some may be required by two or all three jobs. Give reasons.

EXAMPLE: *All three jobs require a friendly patient manner because they all involve working with patients.*

a a friendly patient manner
b good hand-to-eye coordination
c the ability to multi-task
d data entry skills
e foreign language skills
f first aid skills
g administrative skills
h thoroughness and attention to detail
i good safety awareness

- making an emergency call
- understanding other cultures

It's an emergency! 14

WARM-UP

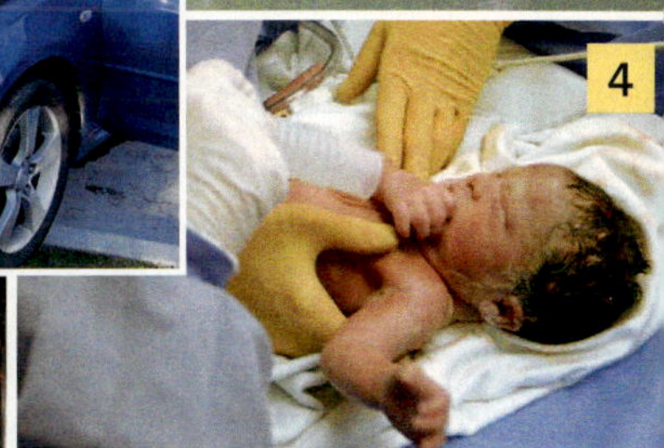

1 Emergencies

a Match the photos to the emergencies.

fire | flood | car accident | giving birth | robbery | power failure

b What would you do in these situations?

I would	try	to help the person/people who ... to stop the ...
	call	the police. an ambulance. the fire brigade
	stay lose my	cool.

2 A first-aid kit

What would you need each of these things for?

You need ... to protect yourself against germs.

pull something out of the skin
clean a wound
cover a wound
tape a bandage
wrap an injured joint
hold something in place
cut a bandage
reduce swelling
reduce pain

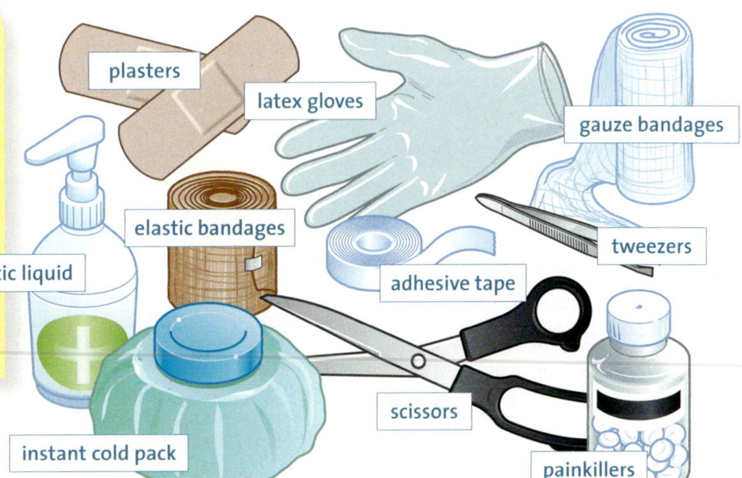

2 23

Woman gives birth on Ferris wheel

A baby was born on a Ferris wheel yesterday after the wheel stopped suddenly and kept the mother and 172 other passengers trapped hundreds of feet above the ground for over six hours. A fire had broken out in the control room, which caused a power failure.

The ten passengers closest to the ground were lowered to the ground with ropes. The mother and her family were at the top of the wheel and therefore too far from the ground to be rescued. A doctor was able to communicate with them via intercom.

The rescue team were planning how to get the other passengers to the ground when the wheel's power was restored.

Maria Lee, the mother, had spent the day with her family at the amusement park and had planned to spend only the usual 40 minutes on the Ferris wheel.

(148 words)

3 Reading for detail

What happened on the Ferris wheel? Make sentences.

1	A fire ...	a	were lowered	I	... at the top of the wheel.
2	Passengers ...	b	broke out	II	... to the ground with ropes.
3	A woman	c	gave birth	III	... in the control room.

4 Using the past perfect

Decide which event happened first. Then make a sentence with *after*.

EXAMPLE: A mother gave birth on a Ferris wheel.
A mother spent the day at the amusement park.
***After** a mother **had spent** the day at the amusement park, she gave birth on a Ferris wheel.*

1 A ferris wheel stopped.
A fire broke out in the control room.

2 Mrs Lee got on the Ferris wheel.
Mrs Lee gave birth to a baby.

3 The mother finally went to hospital.
The mother was trapped for over six hours.

4 10 passengers were able to go home.
Rescue workers lowered 10 passengers to the ground with ropes.

5 Power was restored to the wheel.
The wheel started again.

Grammar

The past perfect (Die Vorvergangenheit)

Mit der Vorvergangenheit beschreiben wir, was bereits **vor** einem Zeitpunkt in der Vergangenheit geschehen war.

fire broke out → fire brigade came → NOW

After the fire **had broken out**, the fire brigade came.

- Vorvergangenheit: *had (not)* + **Partizip Perfekt**
- Die Formen sind für alle Personen gleich.

5 Listening: at the Ferris wheel

2 24

Listen and match the speakers to the people who were at the Ferris wheel. There is one extra person.

a emergency call centre dispatcher

b fire fighter

c mother

d civil defence rescuer

e police officer

f paramedic

g electrician

6 Using *if* sentences type 3

After the fire a newspaper reporter wrote about what might have happened.

Complete the report by making *if* sentences type 3.

EXAMPLE: The Ferris wheel didn't stop. Mrs Lee was on the ride for only a short time.
If the Ferris wheel ***hadn't stopped****, Mrs Lee* ***would have been*** *on the ride for only a short time.*

1 The fire brigade arrived too late. The fire was much worse.
2 The Ferris wheel operator forgot to use the fire extinguisher. The wheel didn't stop.
3 The dispatcher didn't call the civil defence rescue squad. The police officer called them.
4 Mrs Lee was closer to the ground. She was rescued before the baby came.
5 There were complications with the birth. There was a tragedy.

Grammar

if sentences type 3

In *if*-Sätzen Typ 3 überlegt man: „Was wäre gewesen, wenn ...?“.
Tatsächlich war aber alles ganz anders.

If there **hadn't been** a fire, the wheel **wouldn't have stopped**.
(But there was a fire, so the wheel stopped.)

- *if*-Teil: Vorvergangenheit (= *had (not)* + **Partizip Perfekt**):
  If the mother **had known** the wheel would stop, ...
- Folgeteil: *would (not) have* + **Partizip Perfekt:**
  ... she **wouldn't have gone** on it.

Making an emergency call

1 Say what happened, e.g. a car accident.
2 Say which emergency service you need: ambulance, fire brigade, or police.
3 Give as much information as possible about the location of the emergency. The necessary information will depend on whether you are in an urban or rural area, and include:

a	exact address or location
b	street name and number
c	city/town
d	nearest cross road or street
e	landmarks and distance from landmark
f	your name
g	phone number from where the call is being made
h	number and condition of the people who have been hurt, including level of consciousness, breathing and circulation

7 Listening: an emergency call

2 25

a Before you listen, read the tips in the text above.

b Listen to the emergency call. Which information from the above list does the caller give? Which information is not given?

c Listen again. Which questions does the dispatcher ask?

- What's your emergency?
- Where are you?
- Are you hurt?
- How many people have been hurt?
- Is he conscious?
- Is he breathing?
- Does he have a pulse?
- What's your name?
- Are you calling from a mobile telephone?
- Can you give me your number, please?

8 Writing a dialogue

With a partner, write a dialogue between an emergency call centre dispatcher and someone who is at the location of an emergency. Make your dialogue as realistic as possible. Present your dialogue to the rest of the class.

9 Ridiculous emergency hotline calls

35 % of all emergency hotline calls are not true emergencies. All of the following calls were made to emergency hotlines in the USA, but only three of them are real emergencies.

Complete the sentences with verbs in the past perfect. You have to use one of the verbs twice.

bite | drink | (not) have | hit | leave | ~~lock~~ | (not) make | see | snow

EXAMPLE: A woman called because she *had locked* her keys in her car.

1 A man called to report that he ... an elephant walking down the street. He was not hallucinating; it was true.
2 A woman called because a fast food restaurant ... her burger the way she wanted it.
3 A woman called because she ... a cookbook and she wanted advice on how to roast her turkey.
4 A man called because he ... a deer with his car. He thought it was dead. He put it in the back seat of his car and while he was driving home, it woke up and bit him in the neck.
5 A child called from the back of his mother's car because she was driving too fast and she ... a lot of alcohol.
6 A man called because he wanted a police officer to come and scrape the ice off his car window. It ... heavily during the night.
7 A woman called because her pet chimpanzee ... her friend. The woman was badly injured.
8 A woman called because she ... a man beat someone with a baseball bat – in a movie.
9 After a policeman ... her house, a woman called the emergency hotline and said she needed him to come back. When asked what the emergency was, the woman said she thought the policeman was attractive and wanted to ask him out on a date. The dispatcher sent him back – to arrest her for misusing the hotline.

10 Listening: what did they say?

2 26

Write what each caller said using the past perfect. Use *'d* for *had*.

EXAMPLE: CALLER: 'I left my keys on the driving seat.'
*The caller said she'**d left** her keys on the driving seat.*

11 What Rudy did and what he might have done

*The day Rudy got his driving licence **should** have been the best day of his life. Unfortunately, he made a bad choice which decided the rest of his life.*

a Tell what Rudy did (events 1–10) in the simple past.

EXAMPLE: 1 *Rudy **took** his driving test.*

b Now look at what might have happened, and make *if* sentences type 3.

EXAMPLE: 1 *If he **had failed** his driving test, he **would have ridden** his bicycle everywhere and he **would have become** very fit.*

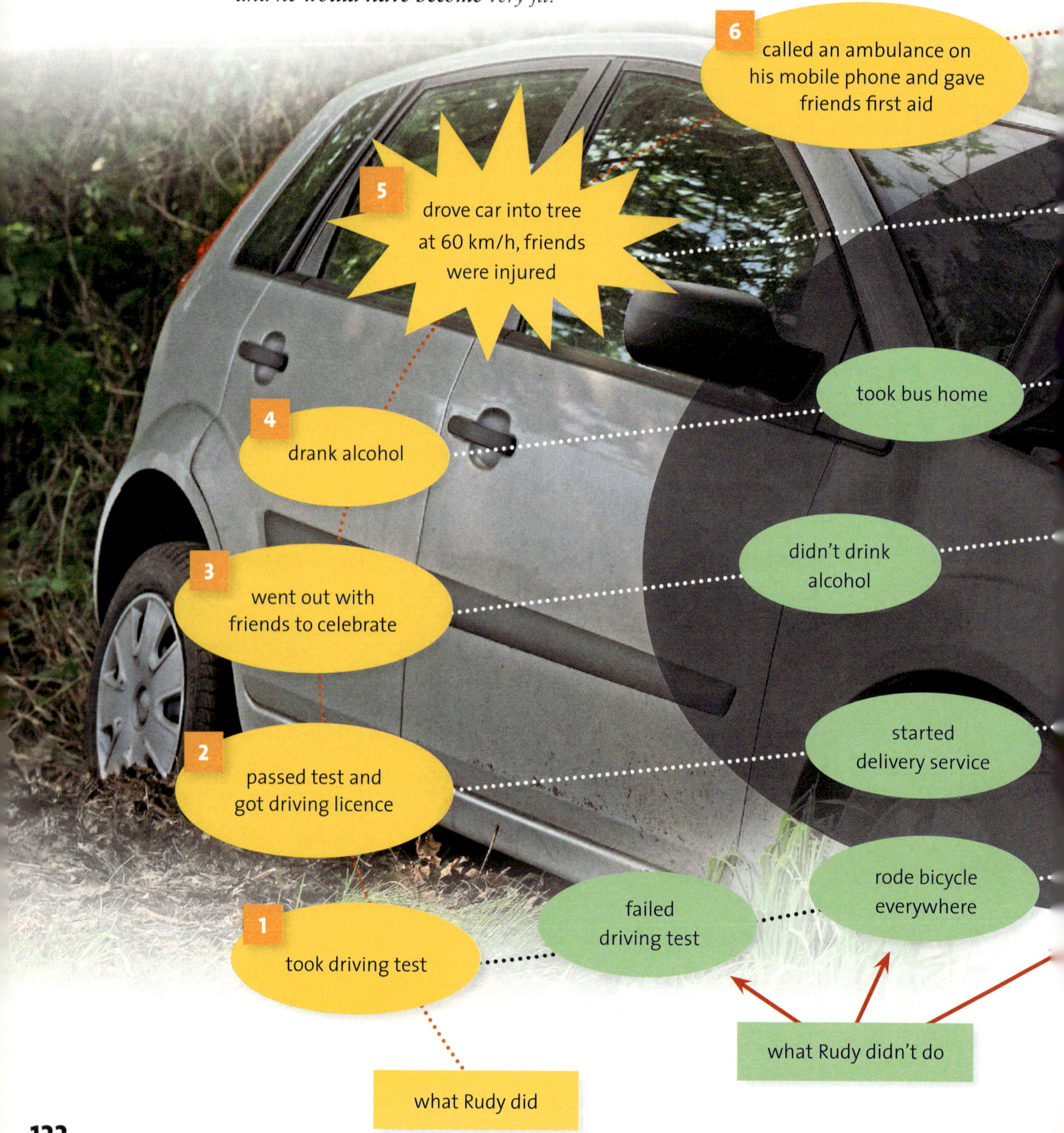

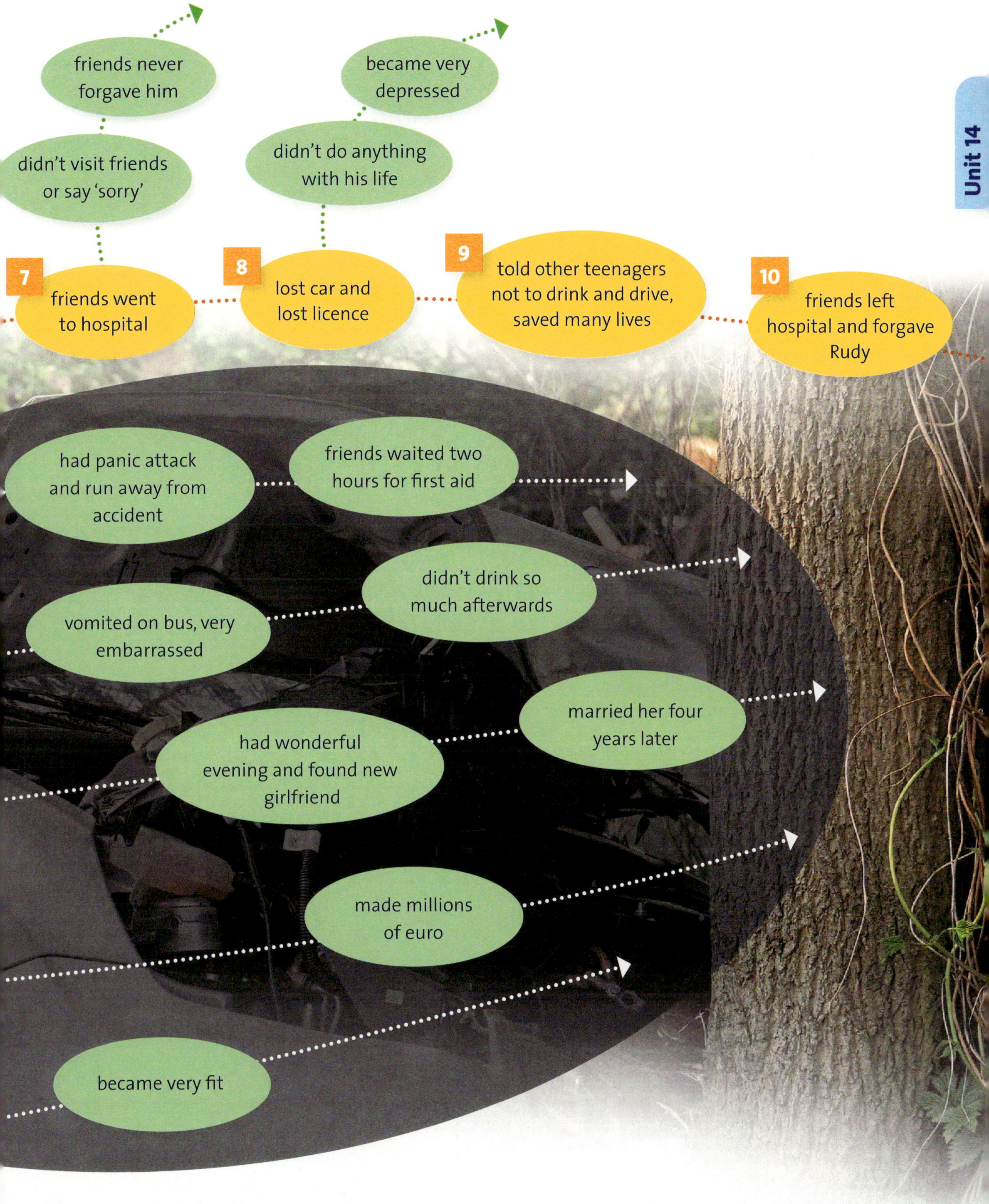

12 Writing about an emergency

Describe an emergency that you or someone you know has experienced. Then, say what would have prevented the emergency or what would have made it worse.

13 Listening: typical stereotypes

a What cultural stereotypes can you think of?

2 27 **b** Listen to what one of these young women has to say about stereotypes. Who is talking: Kally, Olga or Jing?

14 A comic

a Read the comic. Where do these sentences belong?

Help her! | We don't eat from sunrise to sunset. | Get your stinky salami out of my face! | Here, try some. | We're all the same, really. | That's strange!

b Check your answer with a partner. What is the lesson of the story?

- taking part in a discussion
- taking notes from a voicemail message

Globalization 15

WARM-UP

1 Consumer items

Where do you think these items were made?

EXAMPLE: *I think the camera was made in Japan.*

China	India	Italy	Japan	Switzerland	Vietnam

camera | jeans | mp3 player | trainers | T-Shirt | watch

2 Speaking: where were your things made?

a Look at the labels in items around you, e.g. your shoes, your partner's T-shirt, things in your school bag. Tell the class where the things were made.

EXAMPLES:

My mp3 player was made in Korea.

Markus' T-shirt was made in Indonesia.

b Discuss in class: Why weren't these things made in Germany?

What does globalization mean to you?

2
28

We hear a lot about 'globalization' these days, but what does this buzzword actually mean to the person in the street? We interviewed some people in London's Hyde Park to find out. Here are some of their replies.

Hollie, 18, student from London

Globalization? Well, I think of the Internet first of all. It has completely changed how we communicate with each other.

Nowadays we can contact people on the other side of the world instantly – all with the click of a mouse. I've got relatives in Australia and I can keep in touch with them by email and instant messaging and Skype. That's all part of globalization.

If you want information about anything, you can get it on the Internet. That's amazing when you think about it, isn't it? It means that we can share ideas and information with people anywhere.

Alain, 34, tourist from Quebec

For me, when I hear the word 'globalization' I think of big, multinational companies – you know, like McDonalds and Microsoft and Shell and Toyota. They are rich and powerful and their managers get millions of dollars each year. Meanwhile, there are workers in the Third World who earn less than ten dollars a day. I think that globalization has helped to create that unfair world.

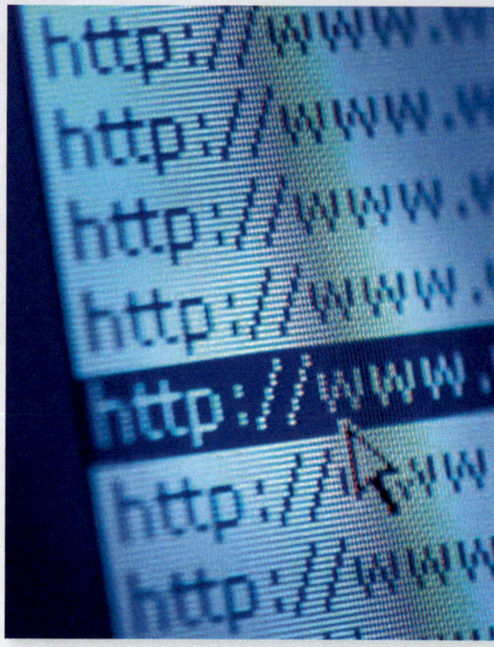

How? Because in a globalized world, big companies have too much power. They can do what they like and governments can't control them.

Anna, 29, originally from Dublin, now working in London

Globalization means that goods and services can be bought and sold freely around the world. Everyone is better off because of globalization – the producers and the consumers. Consumers get cheaper and more varied goods, and the producers get more potential customers.

Maybe you drive a car from Japan, watch a TV from China and wear a suit which was made in Indonesia. With your breakfast you drink coffee from Brazil or tea from India. For dinner you eat beef from Holland and potatoes from Israel and drink a glass of Australian wine. That's globalization!

OK, I admit that some workers in the Third World get paid very little for their hard work. But if global markets for their goods didn't exist, they probably wouldn't have a job at all. Which would you rather have – ten dollars a day or nothing?

(390 words)

3 Reading for detail

Read the text, then answer the questions.

1 What does Hollie think of when she hears the word 'globalization'?
2 How does she contact her family in Australia?
3 Why is it easy for people to share ideas and information nowadays?
4 What is unfair about globalization, in Alain's view?
5 Why can't governments control multinational companies, according to Alain?
6 Why does everyone benefit from globalization, according to Anna?
7 What examples of globalization does she give?
8 What might happen without globalization, according to Anna?

4 Making a mind map

Make a mind map about globalization using information from the text. You can start like this:

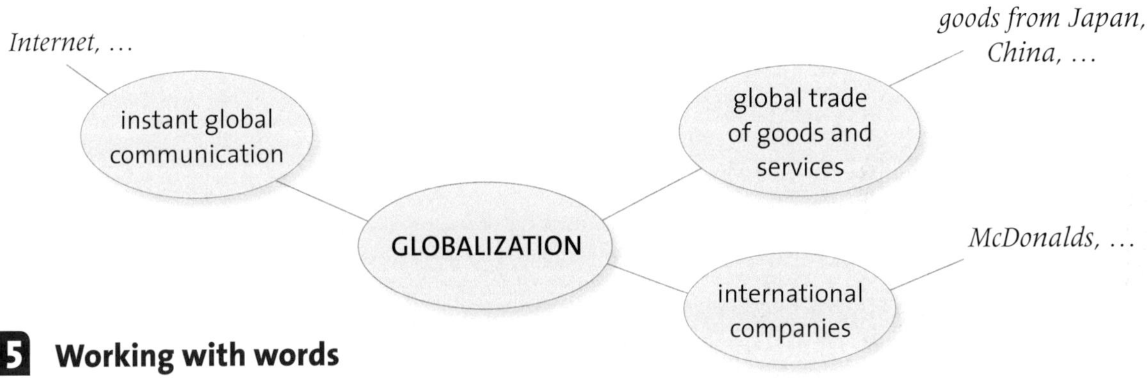

5 Working with words

a Match the words to the definitions.

1	buzzword	a	person who buys goods and/or services
2	amazing	b	group of people who control a country by making laws, etc.
3	multinational	c	objects which are bought and sold
4	government	d	an expression that is currently fashionable
5	consumer	e	things that people do for each other, especially for money
6	goods	f	not limited to just one country
7	services	g	place where goods are bought and sold; people prepared to buy a product
8	market	h	very surprising

b Complete the sentences with the words from above. There are two words you don't need.

1 'Teamwork' is our manager's latest ... – she's always talking about how important it is.
2 They're not exactly a ... company: they're based in Vienna with one small office in Prague.
3 Are ... concerned about fairness, or do they just want the best goods at the lowest price?
4 What ... does a marketing agency offer to its customers?
5 I don't think you'll find a ... for your products in Germany – Germans won't buy them.
6 The speed of change in computing over the last few decades has been ... . Who would have predicted it?

Chocolate *that leaves a bad taste*

2 29

It looks yummy, that chocolate bar, doesn't it?

But before you take a bite, think about how it was produced.

A 12-year-old boy, Siaka, picked some of the cocoa which was used to make that chocolate bar. Siaka was born in Mali, but two years ago he went to Côte d'Ivoire to look for work. A local farmer 'bought' Siaka for $28 from an employment agent. Since then Siaka has been working for the farmer, picking cocoa, rice and cotton.

The farmer promised him $1 a day for his work. But so far he hasn't paid him anything. All Siaka gets is food and a bed in a hut with no windows. For that, he has to work all day in the fields.

Because chocolate prices are low, farmers have to use cheap workers. The cheapest workers are child slaves like Siaka.

200,000 children work on cocoa farms in Côte d'Ivoire, the world's biggest exporter of cocoa. Côte d'Ivoire farms produce nearly half the world's cocoa. Most of the cheap chocolate you see on supermarket shelves comes from there.

'People who are drinking cocoa and eating chocolate are drinking and eating the blood of children.' *Salia Kante, Director, Save the Children Fund in Mali*

www.info.fairtrade.net

Not hungry anymore?

FAIRTRADE

If you prefer your chocolate slavery-free, choose a brand with the Fairtrade logo. Fairtrade makes sure that farmers get a fair price for their produce. They aren't allowed to use slave labour or child labour and they have to pay their workers a fair wage.

Fairer all round – Fairtrade chocolate

(263 words)

6 Mediation: fair trade

You are giving a talk to a youth group on the subject 'Fairer Handel – faire Welt'. Summarize the relevant information from the text in German. Do not translate the text word for word.

7 Writing an email to a chocolate company

a Which questions would you ask a chocolate company?

EXAMPLES: *Where does your chocolate come from? Why don't you use Fairtrade chocolate?*

b Now write an email to the company. Start like this:

Dear Sir or Madam
I like your chocolate and often buy it, but recently I read a leaflet about child slavery on cocoa plantations, …

8 Different opinions

Are these people in favour of or against the Fairtrade movement?

1 Fairtrade tells local producers how to run their businesses. That makes them less competitive in the global market.

2 Sure, buying Fairtrade goods makes us rich Westerners feel good about ourselves. But it also helps the poor.

3 Fairtrade makes very little difference to a worker's income – only a few cents a day.

4 Supermarkets make a lot of money out of Fairtrade products. They sell them for a high price, but only a tiny profit goes to the farmers.

5 Fairtrade helps producers to earn a good profit. They put that money back into their communities.

6 If you only earn two dollars a day, another 20 cents is a big difference.

9 Building skills: taking part in a discussion

Work in two groups.

Group A: You want to boycott all non-Fairtrade chocolate products and organize a protest action outside your local supermarket.

Group B: You aren't persuaded by the Fairtrade scheme. You don't want to damage local businesses and cause trouble.

Useful phrases: *taking part in a discussion*

Giving an opinion
(Personally,) I think/feel/believe that ...
It seems to me that ...
If you ask me, ...

Giving reasons
You see, ...
The reason is that ...

Agreeing with an opinion
Yes, I agree.
That's right/true.

Asking for agreement
Don't you agree?
..., don't you think?

Disagreeing with an opinion
I don't agree.
In fact, I think that ...

Skill

Wie man an einer Diskussion teilnimmt

- Lernen Sie die Formulierungen oben in dem Kasten *Useful phrases*.
- Legen Sie sich ein paar Fragen und Antworten zum Thema zurecht.
- Bleiben Sie immer ruhig und denken Sie nach, bevor Sie sprechen.
- Gehen Sie auf Ihre Gesprächspartner ein und halten Sie Blickkontakt.
- Beteiligen Sie sich und hören Sie nicht bloß still zu.

10 How do goods get from A to B?

How do goods get from one side of the world to the other? It's a complicated process. Most goods are still sent by sea. Below are just some of the jobs involved.

Match the job descriptions to the photos.

A This person is a member of a ship's crew. He/She carries out duties on the deck, in the engine room or in the galley (ship's kitchen).

B This person loads and unloads cargo from ships. These days, most of the cargo is in containers. He/She operates heavy machinery including cranes and large forklift trucks.

C This person plans the most efficient ways of transporting goods by road, rail, air and sea.

D This person transports goods between suppliers and customers. He/She works from depots, distribution centres and warehouses.

E This person works in airports or ports to inspect imports, collect customs duty and prevent illegal trade.

11 Listening: an urgent voicemail message

2 30

You work for a freight forwarding company.

a Listen to the message once. Which of these sentences best summarizes the content?

1 A container of Fairtrade Easter bunnies has not arrived in South Africa.
2 A container of Fairtrade Easter bunnies has been damaged in an accident on its way to South Africa.
3 The caller wants to send a container of Fairtrade Easter bunnies from South Africa to Germany.

b Listen to the message again and make notes in German for your boss, the logistics manager, Tanja Lindt-Haase. Copy and complete this form.

12 Using tenses

a Complete the text with the simple present, the present continuous and the present perfect of the verbs in brackets.

Siaka *has worked* [1] (work) on Coulibaly's farm since the age of ten. He ... [2] (not see) his family for two years. Every day he ... [3] (start) work at six o'clock and ... [4] (work) in the fields for ten hours. Today Siaka and his friend Brahima ... [5] (work) in the coffee plantation. The sun ... [6] (shine) and it's very hot, but the boys ... [7] (carry) heavy sacks of coffee beans.
Coulibaly ... [8] (not pay) the boys for their work yet. 'I ... [9] (not have) any money myself,' he says. 'At the moment the exporters ... [10] (not pay) so little for coffee and cocoa, it's hard to make a living.'

b Complete the text with the simple past, the past continuous and the past perfect of the verbs in brackets.

Alain Dubois from Quebec *visited* [1] (visit) London last year. Alain ... [2] (walk) in Hyde Park when a reporter ... [3] (come) up to him. She ... [4] (want) to ask him some questions. She ... [5] (ask) his opinion about globalization.
Alain ... [6] (talk) about the problem of rich multinational companies like McDonalds and Microsoft. He ... [7] (say) that globalization ... [8] (be) very bad. However, Alain ... [9] (forget) to mention something: before the interview he ... [10] (eat) lunch in McDonalds and he ... [11] (enjoy) it very much!
After the interview, Alain ... [12] (go) to an internet café. He ... [13] (write) an email to his girlfriend back home in Quebec. He ... [14] (tell) her about the conversation he ... [15] (have) with the reporter. Alain ... [16] software from Microsoft to write the email. While he ... [17] (write), Alain ... [18] (think): 'Maybe globalization has some advantages after all!'

Overview of present and past tenses

Grammar

(Überblick der Gegenwarts- und Vergangenheitsformen)

Simple present (einfache Gegenwart)
We always **buy** Fairtrade chocolate.
- Etwas geschieht immer, regelmäßig oder nie.

Present continuous (Verlaufsform der Gegenwart)
Siaka **is working** in the rice fields today.
- Etwas geschieht gerade, d.h. es ist noch nicht zu Ende; es ist vorübergehend.

Simple past (einfache Vergangenheit)
The container **left** Hamburg yesterday afternoon.
- Etwas geschah zu einem bestimmten Zeitpunkt in der Vergangenheit.

Past continuous (Verlaufsform der Vergangenheit)
Alain **was walking** in the park when the reporter spoke to him.
- Etwas ging vor sich, d.h. es war noch nicht zu Ende, als etwas anderes geschah.

Present perfect
Thanks to globalization, rich countries **have become** even richer.
- Etwas ist irgendwann in der Vergangenheit in dem Zeitraum bis zum jetzigen Augenblick passiert.

Siaka **has been** a child slave for three years now.
- Etwas dauert über die gesamte Zeit bis zum jetzigen Augenblick an.

Past perfect
After Siaka **had worked** on the plantation for three years, he was able to return home.
- Etwas war bereits beendet, bevor etwas anderes geschah.

TEST 4 Do you remember?

1 **You're writing your personal profile for a jobs website. Write three sentences to describe your career interests.**

Tipp: Sie können dafür Ausdrücke wie *I'm interested in … I enjoy … I've decided …* verwenden. Sehen Sie sich Seite 103 an, falls Sie Hilfe brauchen.

points 3

2 **Sie waren auf einer Party, bei der es eine Rauferei gab. Schildern Sie Ihrem englischen Freund Jules, was gerade vor sich ging, als der Streit ausgebrochen ist. Denken Sie sich drei Dinge aus.**

Tipp: Sie brauchen dafür die Verlaufsform der Vergangenheit. Schauen Sie sich nochmals Seite 105 an.

points 3

3 **Bei einem Vorstellungsgespräch will man Ihren Unternehmungsgeist und Ihre Eigeninitiative prüfen. Denken Sie sich Antworten auf die Fragen des Interviewers aus:**

a 'What would you do if you missed your bus to work?'

b 'What would you do if your computer broke down?'

c 'What would you do if you got locked in the office overnight?'

Tipp: Es handelt sich hier um *if*-Sätze Typ 2 *(Was wäre, wenn … ?)* Falls Sie Hilfe brauchen, schauen Sie sich nochmals Seite 112 an.

points 3

4 **Sie plaudern in einer Disko mit einem freundlichen irischen Jungen, aber Sie haben Mühe, sich zu verständigen. Was sagen Sie?**

a Sie haben etwas akustisch nicht verstanden.

b Sie haben wohl das falsche Wort gebraucht.

c Er redet zu schnell.

Tipp: Nützliche Sätze für Verständnisschwierigkeiten gab es in Unit 13.

points 3

5 **Ein Raubüberfall hat gerade stattgefunden und jemand ist dabei verletzt worden. Machen Sie einen Notruf und erklären Sie, was passiert ist und welche Notdienste gebraucht werden.**

Tipp: Notfallsituationen haben Sie in Unit 14 gemacht.

points 3

6 **Your English friend Jules has been given an essay topic: 'How globalization affects me'. Unfortunately he has no idea what to write. Give him three tips.**

Tipp: Ebenfalls ratlos? Lesen Sie nochmals Seite 126.

points 3

How did you do?	
15–18 points	Excellent. You've worked hard and learned a lot!
11–14 points	You've made good progress. Well done!
less than 10 points	Take another look at the tasks you found difficult. Ask your teacher for help if you need it.

(Lösungen auf Seite 207.)

Anhang

FILES 1–14

File 1 Unit 7, Exercise 9

Team member A
You are an experienced camper and you are good at making fires. You can't swim and you are allergic to fish.

File 2 Unit 2, Exercise 9

Referee's directions for 'An International Love Story'

1	a.	*Gut, dass Grammatik fürs Ausgehen keine Voraussetzung ist. Trotzdem:* Wait here until your next turn.
	b.	Your parents are pretty cool. Go to square 2.
2	a.	*Ihr beide also.* Great! Go to square 3 (not square 3A).
	b.	*Keiner von euch?* Oh no! Go to square 3A (not square 3).
3	a.	'Smart' means *klug* in English. Very good! Wait until your next turn.
	b.	'Annoying' means *nervig* in English. Very bad thing to say! Go back to square 2 and wait there.
3A	a.	*Nur eine Woche? Musstest du deinen Führerschein danach abgeben?* Wait until your next turn.
	b.	Now you can drive your dates around. What fun! Go to square 3B.
3B	a.	*Oft also.* Wait until your next turn.
	b.	*Manchmal also.* Wait until your next turn
	c.	*Nie also.* Wait until your next turn.
	d.	*Immer also.* Wonderful! Go to square 3C.
3C	a.	*Du warst höflich zu dem Lehrer.* Very nice. Go to square 4.
	b.	*Du warst unhöflich zu dem Lehrer!* Terrible! Go back to square 3B and wait there until your next turn.
4	a.	'Brand' means *Marke* in English. You said the right thing. Wait here until your next turn.
	b.	'Brand' means *Marke* in English. For the German word *Brand*, we say 'fire'. Go back one square and wait there until your next turn.
5	a.	You said, *'Bezahlst du?'* Very un-cool. Go back to square 4 and wait there until your next turn.
	b.	You said, *'Wie wäre es mit einem Film?'* That's a fine idea for a first date. Wait here until your next turn.
6		(Wait here until your next turn.)
7	a.	You said, *'Das macht mir nichts aus.'* Very strange thing to say! Go back to square 6.
	b.	You said, *'Was für eine Überraschung!'* Very good. Wait here until your next turn.
8	a.	'Menu' means *Speisekarte* in English. You both went to the hospital. For the German word *Menü*, we say 'a meal with more than one course' *(Gang)*. Go back to square 7.
	b.	That's fine. Wait here until your next turn.
9		(Wait here until your next turn.)
10	a.	'Pot' means *Teekanne* in English. Very good! Wait here until your next turn.
	b.	*In einer Blechdose also?* Very strange! *Teekanne* is 'pot' in English. Go back to square 9 and wait there until your next turn.

11	a.	Very good! 'Curious' means *neugierig* in English. Go to square 12.
	b.	*Der Kunde findet dich auch sehr seltsam.* 'Curious' means *neugierig*, and is a better thing to say. Wait here until your next turn.
12	a.	*Schon verlobt?* Oh no! Go to square 13A.
	b.	*Der Kunde ist geschieden.* That's no problem. Go to square 13 and wait there until your next turn.
13	a.	'Handy' just means *nützlich* in English. Wait here until your next turn.
	b.	Very good. That's the American word. Go to square 14 and wait there until your next turn.
	c.	Very good. That's the British word. Go to square 14 and wait there until your next turn.
13A		(Wait here until your next turn.)
13B	a.	*Du lehnst die Einladung also ab. Ziemlich feige von dir.* Wait here until your next turn.
	b.	*Du nimmst die Einladung also an. Sehr mutig.* Go to square 13C.
13C	a.	*Du bleibst in der Kirche? Na gut, dann bleibst du eben auch auf diesem Feld sitzen, bis du wieder dran bist.*
	b.	Yes! Go for it! Go to square 14.
14		(Wait here until your next turn.)
15	a.	*Du wünschst dir, deine große Liebe mit einer Glatze wiederzusehen?* Very strange! Go back to square 14.
	b.	'See you soon!' is *Bis bald!* in English. Very good. Wait here until your next turn.
16	a.	*Du bist auf einen tollen Römer / eine tolle Römerin gestoßen.* Good for you! Go to square 17.
	b.	*Der Römer / Die Römerin wäre natürlich viel besser gewesen.* The German word *Roman* is 'novel' in English. Go to square 17A.
17		(Wait here until your next turn.)
17A	a.	*Ein Künstler.* Very romantic! Go to square 17B.
	b.	You thought 'photograph' means *Fotograf* in German. It means *Foto*. A *Fotograf* is a 'photographer' in English. Have fun with your photo and wait here until your next turn.
17B	a.	'Great' means *großartig*. Very nice thing to say. Go to square 17C.
	b.	'Gross' means *ekelhaft* in English. Oops! Go back to square 17A and wait there until your next turn.
	c.	'Tall' means *groß*. Wait here until your next turn.
17C	a.	You don't reply 'please' if someone says 'thank you'! Wait here until your next turn.
	b.	Very nice! Go to square 18 and wait there until your next turn.
18	a.	In English, 'pepperoni' is a kind of salami. Oops! Go back one square.
	b.	'Pepper' is *Paprika* in German. Very good! Go to square 19! 'Pepper' is also the English word for the spice *Pfeffer*.
	c.	Shrimps? They're not vegetarian. What were you thinking? Wait here until your next turn.

File 3 Unit 7, Exercise 9

Team member C
You are good at fixing electrical and electronic things such as computers. You remember that there are some chocolate bars in the cabin of the boat. It may be difficult for other team members to find them.

File 4 Unit 7, Exercise 9

Team leader
Read out the situation to your team.
We were on a boat in the Pacific Ocean. Unfortunately the boat sank. Now we are on a desert island without any food and drink. We are cold and hungry. We need to ...

- *make a fire to keep us warm*
- *get our water bottles from the sunken boat*
- *catch fish to eat;*
- *build a shelter*
- *fix the radio so that we can get help.*

Organize your team so that everyone has a task that he/she is good at.
When you have finished, report back to the class. Answer their questions with the help of your team mates.

File 5 Unit 4, Exercise 2

a **Partner B:** ask your partner where the following buildings are.
1 underground station 2 shopping centre 3 police station 4 post office

b Now unscramble the sentences and answer your partner's questions
1 The bus station is ... the block / between / and / of flats / the library
2 The hospital is ... the / opposite / cinema
3 The car park is ... the shopping centre / on / in / front of / Holloway Road
4 The pharmacy is ... to / next / hospital / the

c Now complete your list with the buildings H–O.

File 6 Unit 13, Exercise 8

Student B
You don't know the English for these words. How could you explain them to an English speaker? Explain them to your partner using the 'Useful phrases'. Can he/she guess the correct word?

1 Station
2 Ausländer/in
3 Unfall
4 ehrgeizig
5 Fahrkarte

Useful phrases: *paraphrasing*

It's a thing that you use to ...
It's a kind of ... (that ...)
It's a person who ...
It's a place where ...
It's when you ...

File 7 Unit 7, Exercise 9

Team member E
You are a very good swimmer but unfortunately you have broken your leg. You are a trainee electrician.

File 8 Unit 8, Exercise 9b

Partner B: The woman I saw was very short and corpulent. She was wearing a grass skirt (from Hawaii) and a bikini top. She had two small eyes in the middle of her face. She had lots and lots of long, curly hair. There were mice in her hair.

Files

File 9 Unit 12, Exercise 1

Answers for 'The Game of Life'

These are the most common answers that were given to the questions. Any answer that was only given once is not included. Give yourself one 'Happiness Point' for each answer given that you guess correctly.

1
31 banana
19 apple
11 peach *(Pfirsich)*
8 carrots
5 pears *(Birne)*
5 sweet potato *(Süßkartoffel)*
4 pea *(Erbse)*
3 apricot
2 plum *(Pflaume)*

2
53 the dark
17 monsters/nightmares *(Alpträume)*
6 loud noises *(laute Geräusche)*
6 thunder *(Donner)*
4 strangers *(fremde Leute)*

3
41 pencil/pen
28 silverware *(Besteck)*
9 golf club *(Golfschläger)*
7 baby
5 chopsticks

4
30 drive a car
22 climb things
5 chat on the computer
4 date
4 play in street
4 stay out late

5
27 dance
23 talk
19 eat
14 drink
11 play games
3 meet people

6
43 secretary / office work
30 waitress
15 model
6 nurse
4 flight attendant

7
31 friends
23 job
19 eating right
10 family
6 housework

8
51 clergyperson *(Geistliche/r)*
8 waitress/waiter
7 nurse
5 police officer
4 gas station attendant *(Tankwart/in)*
3 physician *(Arzt/Ärztin)*
2 bus driver
2 fire fighter

9
46 horse
30 dog
10 bear
3 lion
3 monkey/ape

10
35 stove / oven *(Herd / Ofen)*
9 vacuum cleaner *(Staubsauger)*
7 telephone
6 washing machine
5 makeup
5 mirror

11
76 reading
7 driving a car
5 sewing *(nähen)*
3 computer work
3 swimming
2 watching TV

12
54 too expensive
20 late
7 don't listen
7 too busy / in a hurry *(zu beschäftigt / in Eile)*
4 don't explain enough *(nicht genug erklären)*

File 10 Unit 7, Exercise 9

Team member B

You are an experienced camper and you are good at making fires. You can't swim and you are allergic to fish.

File 11 Unit 8, Exercise 8

File 13 Unit 8, Exercise 9b

Partner A: I saw a very tall man running away. He was very thin. He was at least two metres tall, and his trousers were too short. He had a very small head with very large eyes and a long, thin nose. He was bald. He had tattoos all over his arms.

File 12 Unit 7, Exercise 9

Team member D
You worked on a building site last summer holiday and you like making things from wood. You can't swim very well.

File 14 Unit 9, Exercise 16

Suggested answers

1 toothpaste

2 ketchup

3 bicycle

Grammatikübersicht

Personal pronouns and possessive adjectives (S. 8, 12)

subject pronouns	object pronouns	reflexive pronouns	possessive adjectives
I	me	myself	my
you	you	yourself	your
he/she/it	him/her/it	himself/herself/itself	his/her/its
we	us	ourselves	our
you	you	yourselves	your
they	them	themselves	their

The verb *to be* (S. 8, 24)

	simple present	simple past
I	am	was
you	are	were
he/she/it	is	was
we	are	were
you	are	were
they	are	were

The simple present (S. 20)

Aussage		Verneinung		Fragen			Kurzantworten					
I You We They	work.	I You We They	**don't** work.	**Do**	I you we they	work?	Yes,	I you we they	**do**.	No,	I you we they	**don't**.
He She It	work**s**.	He She It	**doesn't** work.	**Does**	he she it	work?	Yes,	he she it	**does**.	No,	he she it	**doesn't**.

- Bei *he, she, it* muss das ‚s' mit: *he/she/it work**s**, play**s**, live**s***.
- Besonderheiten der -*s*-Endung:
  - auf Verbendung -*ch*, -*sh*, -*s*, -*x* folgt **-*es***: *watch* → *watch**es***, *wash* → *wash**es***, *kiss* → *kiss**es***, *fax* → *fax**es***
  - Konsonant + -*y* wird Konsonant + **-*ies***: *try* → ***tries***, *fly* → ***flies***
  - Sonderformen: *do* → ***does***, *go* → ***goes***, *have* → ***has***
- Verneinung mit dem Hilfsverb *do*: *I **don't** work, he **doesn't** work.*
- Fragen mit dem Hilfsverb *do*: ***Do** you work? **Does** she work?*
- Kurzantworten mit dem Hilfsverb *do*: *Yes, … **do/does**. No, … **don't/doesn't**.*
- Die einfache Gegenwart beschreibt etwas, das immer, regelmäßig oder nie geschieht.
- Signalwörter: *always* (immer), *usually* (normalerweise), *often* (oft), *sometimes* (manchmal), *never* (nie), *on Mondays* (montags), *every (day, week, Tuesday, etc.)* usw.

The present continuous (S. 35)

Aussage		Verneinung		Frage	
I'm		I'm **not**		**Am** I	
You'**re**		You'**re not** / You **aren't**		**Are** you	
He'**s**		He'**s not** / He **isn't**		**Is** he	
She'**s**		She'**s not** / She **isn't**		**Is** she	
It'**s**	work**ing**.	It'**s not** / It **isn't**	work**ing**.	**Is** it	work**ing**?
We'**re**		We'**re not** / We **aren't**		**Are** we	
They'**re**		You'**re not** / You **aren't**		**Are** you	
You'**re**		They'**re not** / They **aren't**		**Are** they	

- Mit der Verlaufsform der Gegenwart sagen wir, dass etwas gerade jetzt geschieht und noch nicht abgeschlossen ist: **I'm standing** outside the cinema.
- Die einfache Gegenwart beschreibt etwas, das immer, regelmäßig oder nie geschieht: I **go** to the shops **every Saturday / on Saturdays**.

The simple past (S. 27)

Aussage	Verneinung	Frage	Kurzantworten
a) regelmäßige Verben			
She listen**ed**.	She **didn't** listen.	**Did** she listen?	Yes, she **did.** / No, she **didn't**.
We work**ed**.	We **didn't** work.	**Did** we work?	Yes, we **did**. / No, we **didn't**.
b) unregelmäßige Verben			
I flew.	I **didn't** fly.	**Did** I fly?	Yes, I **did.** / No, **I didn't.**
They **came**.	They **didn't** come.	**Did** they come?	Yes, they **did.** / No, they **didn't.**

- Die Vergangenheitsform der Verben ist für alle Personen *(I, you, he/she/it, we, you, they)* gleich.
- Regelmäßige Verben: Endung *-(e)d*
- Unregelmäßige Verben: eigene Formen (s. Liste S. 206)
- Verneinung mit *didn't*. (Nach *didn't* steht die Grund-, nicht die Vergangenheitsform des Verbs!)
- Fragen und Kurzantworten mit *did*. (Auch nach *did* steht die Grundform des Verbs!)
- Die Vergangenheitsform verwenden wir, wenn wir sagen, was zu einem bestimmten Zeitpunkt oder in einem bestimmten Zeitraum der Vergangenheit abgeschlossen wurde.
- Signalwörter: *yesterday, last week/month, last Tuesday, (two years) ago.*

The past continuous (S. 105)

Mit der Verlaufsform beschreiben wir eine längere Handlung, die in der Vergangenheit stattfand.

I/he/she/it	**was(n't)**	danc**ing**
you/we/they	**were(n't)**	danc**ing**

- Manchmal beschreibt die Verlaufsform eine Hintergrundhandlung, die zu einem bestimmten Zeitpunkt der Vergangenheit (z. B. *'when the power went out'*) vor sich ging:
  – We **were** danc**ing** when the power went out.
- Die Verlaufsform kann auch mehrere längere Handlungen beschreiben, die gleichzeitig passierten:
  – I **was** watch**ing** you while you **were** danc**ing.**

The present perfect (S. 59)

Aussage			**Verneinung**		
I/You/We/They	**have**	start**ed**.	I/You/We/They	**haven't** (have not)	finish**ed**.
He/She/It	**has**	**gone**.	He/She/It	**hasn't** (has not)	**gone**.
Frage			**Kurzantworten**		
Have	I/you/we/they	start**ed**?	Yes, / No,	I/you/we/they	**have**. / **haven't**.
Has	he/she/it	**gone**?	Yes, / No,	he/she/it	**has**. / **hasn't**.

- Present Perfect: *have/has (not)* + **Partizip Perfekt** (3. Form des Verbs)
- Partizip Perfekt: regelmäßige Verben: Endung *-(e)d*; unregelmäßige Verben: eigene Formen (s. Liste S. 206)
- Wir verwenden das Present Perfect, wenn wir sagen wollen, dass etwas irgendwann in der Zeit bis jetzt geschehen ist.
- Signalwörter: *just, ever, never, already, so far, yet, before.*

The present perfect with *since* and *for* (S. 91)

How long have they **been** employees?	*Wie lange sind sie schon Arbeitnehmer?*
He **has been** an employee **for** 10 years.	*Er ist seit 10 Jahren Arbeitnehmer.*
She **has been** an employee **since** 1995.	*Sie ist seit 1995 Arbeitnehmerin.*

- Wir verwenden nicht die Gegenwartsform, sondern das Present Perfect (= *have/has (not)* + **Partizip Perfekt** – s. Unit 6), wenn wir sagen oder fragen, wie lange etwas schon andauert.
- Deutsch „seit" = *since* oder *for*:
  – *since* + **Anfangszeitpunkt** (Frage: „seit wann?"): *since 10 o'clock / yesterday / last week / ...*
  – *for* + **Zeitspanne** (Frage: „wie lange schon?"): *for 10 minutes / two days / six weeks / ...*

The past perfect (S. 118)

Mit der Vorvergangenheit beschreiben wir, was bereits **vor** einem Zeitpunkt in der Vergangenheit geschehen war.

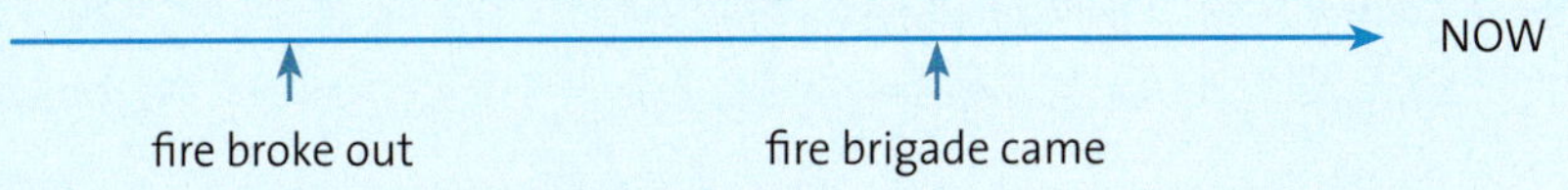

After the fire **had broken out**, the fire brigade came.

- Vorvergangenheit: *had (not)* + **Partizip Perfekt**
- Die Formen sind für alle Personen gleich.

Grammar

The *will* future (S. 51)

Aussage	Verneinung
I/... **will be here** tomorrow.	I/... **won't be** here in the year 2050.
Frage	**Kurzantwort**
Will I/... get the job?	Yes, I/...**will**. / No, I/... **won't**.

- Die Zukunft mit *will*: *will* + Grundform des Verbs – für alle Personen gleich
- Verneinung: *won't (= will not)* + Grundform des Verbs – für alle Personen gleich
- Mit *will/won't* sagen wir, was in der Zukunft sein oder nicht sein wird.
  - In 2050 there **will be** free power.
  - There **won't be** as many young people.
  - **Will** the world **be** a more dangerous place? – Yes, it **will**. / No, it **won't**.
- Wir verwenden *will/won't* auch bei spontanen Entscheidungen, Versprechen und Angeboten.
  - What does this mean? – I'**ll explain** it to you.

The *going to* future (S. 66)

Aussage		Verneinung	
I'**m** You'**re** He'**s**/She'**s**/It'**s** We'**re**/They'**re**	**going to work.**	I'**m not** You **aren't*** He/She/It **isn't*** We/They **aren't***	**going to work.**
Frage		**Kurzantworten**	
Am I **Are** You **Is** he/she/it **Are** we/they	**going to work**?	Yes, I **am**. Yes, you **are**. Yes, he/she/it **is**. Yes, we/they **are**.	No, I'**m not**. No, you **aren't**.* No, he/she/it **isn't**.* No, we/they **aren't**.*

- Wir verwenden die Zukunft mit *going to*, um auszudrücken, was wir vorhaben oder planen.
  I'm going to get a job.
  Are you **going to phone** Cathy?
- Wir können mit dieser Form auch Voraussagen ausdrücken.
  You **aren't going to believe** this, but ...

Zum Vergleich:
I'm going to phone Cathy. (Der Sprecher hat sich bereits entschlossen, Cathy anzurufen.)
I'll phone Cathy. (Der Sprecher entscheidet spontan, Cathy anzurufen.)

* Auch möglich: *you**'re not**, he**'s not**, usw.*

if/*when* sentences (S. 81)

Man kann in beiden Teilen des Satzes die einfache Gegenwart verwenden, wenn man von allgemein gültigen Zusammenhängen spricht.

- *when* = „wenn" im Sinne von „dann, wenn" oder „immer wenn"
  When you sing, the volume indicator goes up and down.

- *if* = „wenn" im Sinne von „falls"
  If a singer screams like a rock star, the volume goes up too high.
  If you put the speakers in front of the singers, they can't hear anything.

if sentences type 1 (S. 79)

Ein *if*-Satz sagt, was unter bestimmten Umständen geschehen wird. Der Satz hat zwei Teile:

If I **have** the party at home, ...	... **will** you **clean up**?
Der *if*-Teil nennt die Bedingung, ...	... der andere Teil nennt die Folge.
Der *if*-Teil steht in der einfachen Gegenwart, ...	... der Folgeteil in der *will*-Zukunft.

Steht der *if*-Teil zuerst, setzt man danach ein Komma. Steht der Folgeteil zuerst, setzt man kein Komma: You'**ll pay** more **if** you **order** food.

if sentences type 2 (S. 112)

In *if*-Sätzen des Typs 2 wird die Situation als theoretisch möglich, aber kaum wahrscheinlich betrachtet.

If I **left** Germany, **I'd** (= would) **miss** my family.
Wenn ich Deutschland verlassen würde, würde mir meine Familie fehlen.
Would you **be** homesick if you **lived** abroad?
Würdest du Heimweh haben, wenn du im Ausland lebtest?

- *If*-Teil = *if* + simple past, Folgeteil = *would* + **Infinitiv**
- Der *if*-Teil kann hinter dem Folgeteil stehen. In diesem Fall steht kein Komma dazwischen.

! Im *if*-Teil steht kein *would*. *(If I ~~would leave~~ Germany, ...)*

if sentences type 3 (S. 119)

In *if*-Sätzen Typ 3 überlegt man: „Was wäre gewesen, wenn ...?".
Tatsächlich war aber alles ganz anders.

If there **hadn't been** a fire, the wheel **wouldn't have stopped**.
(But there was a fire, so the wheel stopped.)

- *if*-Teil: Vorvergangenheit (= *had (not)* + **Partizip Perfekt**):
  If the mother **had known** the wheel would stop, ...
- Folgeteil: *would (not) have* + **Partizip Perfekt:**
  ... she **wouldn't have gone** on it.

The passive (S. 99)

	Aktiv	Passiv
Simple present	I **wash** the car.	The car **is washed** (by me).
Simple past	I **washed** the car.	The car **was washed** (by me).
Present perfect	I have **washed** the car.	The car **has been washed** (by me).

- In einem Aktivsatz sagen wir, wer etwas tut.
  In einem Passivsatz sagen wir, was mit einer Person oder Sache getan wird.
- Bildung des Passivs: Form von *to be* + Partizip Perfekt
  Gegenwart: *am/are/is* + Partizip Perfekt
  Vergangenheit: *was/were* + Partizip Perfekt
  Perfekt: *has/have been* + Partizip Perfekt
- Mit *by* können wir sagen, von wem etwas gemacht wird bzw. wurde. Meist verwenden wir jedoch das Passiv, wenn es nicht nötig (oder nicht möglich) ist zu sagen, wer etwas tut oder getan hat.

can, could, be able to (S. 73)

Can/could werden nur in der Gegenwart und in der Vergangenheit verwendet. In allen anderen Zeitformen wird das Hilfsverb *be able to* verwendet.

	can/could	be able to
Gegenwart	She **can(t)** remember his face.	She **is(n't) able to** remember his face.
Vergangenheit	I **could(n't)** see the car clearly.	I **was(n't) able to** see the car clearly.
Perfekt	–	The police **have(n't) been able to** catch the robbers yet.
Zukunft	–	You**'ll be able to** help them. You **won't be able to** help them.

must, have to (S. 75)

Must wird nur in der Gegenwart verwendet. In allen anderen Zeitformen wird das Hilfsverb *have to* verwendet.

	must	have to
Gegenwart	You **must** pay the fine.	You **have to** pay the fine.
Vergangenheit	–	You **had to** call the police.
Perfekt	–	I **have had to** call the police three times this week.
Zukunft	–	You**'ll have to** wait until the police arrive.

- *Must* entspricht „müssen" und drückt einen Befehl oder die Notwendigkeit aus, etwas zu tun:
  – I **must** finish my homework tonight.
- *Mustn't* drückt ebenfalls einen Befehl oder eine Notwendigkeit aus – etwas **nicht** zu tun.
  – I **mustn't** forget to post these letters on the way home.
- Achtung, *mustn't* hat eine völlig andere Bedeutung als *don't have to*:

You **mustn't** steal.	Sie **dürfen nicht** stehlen.
You **don't have to** steal.	Sie **müssen nicht** stehlen (weil es nicht nötig ist).

Comparative and superlative adjectives (S. 39)

eine Silbe	*-er, -est*	fast, **faster**, **fastest**
eine Silbe, die auf Vokal + Konsonant endet	*letzter Buchstabe wird gedoppelt -er, -est*	fit, **fitter**, **fittest**
endet mit y	*-ier, -iest*	happy, **happier**, **happiest**
zwei oder mehr Silben	*more, most*	interesting, more **interesting**, most **interesting**
unregelmäßig		good, better, best bad, worse, worst

Making comparisons:
A bus is bigger **than** a car.
I think Bangkok is **as** interesting **as** Moscow.
The bus is **not as** expensive **as** a taxi.

Adverbs (S. 43)

Ein Adverb beschreibt ein Verb. Es sagt uns, wie etwas getan wird.

Bildung des Adverbs		
regelmäßig: + *-ly*	Fred is a **careful** cook.	He cooks **carefully**.
Es gibt aber wichtige Ausnahmen.		
y-Endung: + *ily* *ic*-Endung: + *ally*	Martha is a **happy** cook. Sue is a **fantastic** cook.	She cooks **happily**. She cooks **fantastically**.
ohne Änderung unregelmäßig	Esther is a **fast** cook. Jing is a **good** cook.	She cooks **fast**. She cooks **well**.

much, many, a lot of (S. 11)

Welches Wort man benutzt, hängt davon ab, ob das Substantiv zählbar oder nicht zählbar ist. Bei nicht zählbaren Substantiven in einem Aussagesatz verwendet man normalerweise nicht *much*, sondern *a lot of*.

	zählbares Substantiv, z. B. *object*	**nicht zählbares Substantiv, z. B. *money***
Aussagesatz	There are **many** objects. There are **a lot of** objects.	~~This costs **much** money.~~ This costs **a lot of** money.
Verneinung	There aren't **many** objects. There aren't **a lot of** objects.	This doesn't cost **much** money. This doesn't cost **a lot of** money.

Relative clauses (S. 87)

My brother is someone **who/that** loves Disney movies.
Disney has shops **which/that** sell DVDs, books, and other products.

Relativpronomen für Menschen: *who* oder (seltener) *that*.
Relativpronomen für Sachen: *which* oder *that*.

Grundwortschatz

Diese Liste enthält ca. 700 Grundwörter, die in **Keep Going** als bekannt vorausgesetzt werden. Nicht aufgeführt, jedoch vorausgesetzt, sind internationale Wörter (Taxi, Fax, TV usw.) und einige sehr elementare Wörter wie Pronomen, Zahlen und Tage.

A

about ungefähr, fast; herum
above über, oben
across hinüber, herüber, (quer) durch
actor Schauspieler
actually eigentlich, tatsächlich
address Adresse
advertising Werbung, Werbebranche
after nach
afternoon Nachmittag
afterwards nachher, danach
again wieder
against gegen
age Zeitalter, Alter
ago vor
air Luft
aircraft, airplane Flugzeug
airport Flughafen
alcohol Alkohol
all alle(s)
almost fast, beinahe
alone allein(e)
along entlang
already schon, bereits
also auch, außerdem
although obwohl
altogether insgesamt
always immer
animal Tier
another noch eine
answer; to answer Antwort, Lösung; (be)antworten
any irgendwelche, jede/r/s
anyone jemand, jede/r
anything etwas, alles
anywhere irgendwo(hin)
apple Apfel
arm Arm
to arrange arrangieren
arrival Ankunft
to arrive ankommen, eintreffen
as wie, als, da, weil
to ask fragen, bitten
aunt Tante
away weg, entfernt

B

baby Säugling, Baby
bad schlecht, schlimm
bag Tüte, (Reise-)Tasche
ball Ball
banana Banane
bathroom Bad(ezimmer)
to be sein
beach Strand
beautiful schön
because weil
to become werden
bed Bett
bedroom Schlafzimmer
before vor(her)
to begin beginnen
beginning Anfang
behind hinter, hinten
to believe glauben
below unter, unten
best beste/r/s
better besser
between zwischen
bicycle Fahrrad
big groß
bike (Fahr-)Rad
bird Vogel
birthday Geburtstag
bit, a ~ ein bisschen, ein wenig
to bite beißen
black schwarz
blood Blut
blue blau
boat Boot, Schiff
body Körper
book; to book Buch; buchen, bestellen
boring langweilig
born geboren
both beide
bottle Flasche
bottom unterer Teil
boy Junge
boyfriend Freund
box Kasten, Kiste, Schachtel
bread Brot
breakfast Frühstück
bridge Brücke
brother Bruder
brown braun
bus (Linien-)Bus
bus stop Bushaltestelle
business Geschäft, Firma, Sache
busy (viel)beschäftigt, arbeitsreich, hektisch
but aber, sondern, außer
butter Butter
to buy kaufen

C

(phone) call; to call (Telefon-)Anruf; anrufen, rufen
camera Fotoapparat, Kamera
can können, dürfen
car Auto
car park Parkplatz
careful vorsichtig, sorgfältig
cat Katze
chair Stuhl
chance Chance, Gelegenheit
change; to change (Ver-)Änderung; (aus) wechseln, (sich) ändern
cheap billig, günstig
cheese Käse
chicken Huhn, Hähnchen
child (children) Kind(er)
chips Pommes frites
chocolate Schokolade
choice Wahl, Auswahl
to choose (aus)wählen
Christmas Weihnachten
church Kirche
cinema Kino
city (Groß-)Stadt
class Klasse
clean; to clean sauber, rein; säubern, reinigen
clear klar, deutlich
clock Uhr
to close schließen
close nahe, eng
clothes Kleidung, Kleider
coffee Kaffee
cold kalt
to collect sammeln; abholen
colour Farbe
to come kommen
complete; to complete vollständig; vervollständigen, ausfüllen
to continue fortfahren, weitermachen
to cook kochen, braten, backen
correct; to correct richtig, genau; korrigieren, berichtigen
to cost kosten
could konnte/n, könnte/n
country Land, Staat
cousin Cousin/e
cow Kuh
crazy verrückt
to cut schneiden, ab-, zuschneiden

D

to dance tanzen
dangerous gefährlich
dark Dunkelheit; dunkel
daughter Tochter
day Tag
dead tot
dear liebe/r
to decide (sich) entscheiden, beschließen
to describe beschreiben
desk Schreibtisch, Pult
diary Tagebuch; Terminkalender
different anders, verschieden
difficult schwer, schwierig
dinner (Abend-)Essen
direct direkt, gerade
dirty schmutzig
to discover entdecken
dislike; to dislike Abneigung; nicht mögen
to do tun, machen
doctor Arzt, Ärztin
dog Hund
door Tür
down herunter, hinunter, unten
to draw zeichnen
dream; to dream Traum; träumen
dress; to dress Kleid; (sich) anziehen

drink; to drink Getränk; trinken
to drive fahren
driver Fahrer/in
during während

E

each jede/r/s
early früh
earth Erde
easy leicht, einfach
to eat essen
egg Ei
elephant Elefant
end; to end Ende, Schluss; (be)enden
ending Schluss, Ende
energy Energie
enough ausreichend, genug
etc. usw.
even sogar (noch)
evening Abend
ever je(mals)
every jede/r/s
everybody jede/r
everyday Alltags
everyone jede/r/s, alle
everything alles
everywhere überall
exact(ly) exakt, genau
example Beispiel
exciting aufregend, spannend
excuse me Entschuldigung
exercise Übung
exercise book (Schul-)Heft
expensive teuer
to explain erklären
eye Auge

F

face Gesicht
fact Tatsache
false falsch, unwahr
family Familie
famous berühmt
far weit (entfernt)
farm Bauernhof
fashion Mode
fast schnell
fat dick
father Vater
to feel (sich) fühlen
to fight (be)kämpfen
to fill füllen
to find finden, suchen
fine gut, schön, fein
finger Finger
finish; to finish Ende; (be)enden
fire Feuer
first erste/r/s, zuerst
fish Fisch(e)
flat Wohnung
flower Blume
food Essen, Nahrung
foot (feet) Fuß (Füße)
football Fußball
footballer Fußballspieler/in
for für, denn
forbidden verboten
to forget vergessen
fork Gabel
free kostenlos, frei
free time Freizeit
fresh frisch
friend Freund/in
friendly freund(schaft)lich
from von
front, in ~ of vor
fruit Obst, Frucht
fun Spaß, Vergnügen
funny lustig, komisch
future Zukunft, zukünftig

G

game Spiel
garden Garten
general allgemein
Germany Deutschland
to get holen, bekommen
girl Mädchen
girlfriend Freundin
to give geben, schenken
glass Glas
global weltweit, Welt-, umfassend
globalized globalisiert
to go gehen, fahren
God Gott
gold, golden Gold, golden
good (better, best) gut
good morning guten Morgen
goodbye auf Wiedersehen
granddaughter Enkelin
grandfather Großvater
grandmother Großmutter
grandparents Großeltern
grass Gras
great groß(artig)
green grün
grey grau
guest Gast

H

hair Haar(e)
hand Hand
to happen geschehen, passieren
happy glücklich, froh
hard schwer
hat Hut
hate; to hate Hass; hassen, überhaupt nicht mögen
to have haben
head Kopf
to hear hören
heavy schwer
helicopter Hubschrauber
to help helfen
helpful hilfreich, nützlich
her ihr
here hier
herself sie (sich) selbst
him ihn, ihm
himself er (sich) selbst
his sein/e
to hit schlagen
to hold halten, festhalten
holiday Ferien, Urlaub, Feiertag
home, at ~ zu Hause
homework Hausaufgabe(n)
to hope hoffen
horse Pferd
hospital Krankenhaus
hot heiß, warm
hour Stunde
house Haus
how wie
however jedoch
hungry hungrig

I

ice Eis
ice cream (Speise-)Eis
idea Idee, Gedanke
if wenn, falls, ob
ill krank
important wichtig
interest Interesse
interested, to be ~ in sich interessieren für
interesting interessant
international international
to interview interviewen
into in ... hinein
to introduce vorstellen

J

jeans Jeans
joke Witz, Scherz
just einfach, nur, genau

K

to keep (be)halten
to kill töten, umbringen
kilogram Kilo(gramm)
king König
kitchen Küche
knife Messer
to know kennen, wissen

L

lady Dame
land; to land Land; landen
language Sprache
large groß, umfangreich
last (month) letzte(n Monat)
late spät
to laugh lachen
to learn lernen, erfahren
learner Lerner/in
to leave verlassen
leg Bein
less (than) weniger (als)
lesson (Unterrichts-) Stunde
to let lassen
letter Buchstabe, Brief
library Bibliothek
to lie liegen; lügen
life Leben
like mögen, gern haben
likely wahrscheinlich
list Liste
to listen zuhören, anhören
little; a little klein; ein wenig, etwas
live; to live live; leben, wohnen
long lang
to look sehen; aussehen
to look at ansehen
to look for suchen
to lose verlieren
lot, a ~ of viel, viele
to love sb/sth jdn lieben, etw sehr gern mögen
lovely schön, hübsch, reizend
luck Glück
lunch Mittagessen

M

machine Maschine, Gerät
magazine Zeitschrift
magic Magie, Zauberei, Zauberkunst
main Haupt-
to make machen, tun
man Mann, (der) Mensch
many viele
map Karte, Plan

math(ematic)s Mathe(matik)
may dürfen, können, mögen
me mir, mich
meal Essen, Mahlzeit
meaning Bedeutung
meat Fleisch
media Medien
medium mittlere; Medium, Mittel
to meet treffen, begegnen
metal Metall
metre (BE)/meter (AE) Meter
middle Mitte
might könnte(n) (vielleicht)
milk Milch
minute Minute
mistake Fehler, Irrtum
mixture Mischung
moment Moment
money Geld
month Monat
moon Mond
more mehr
morning Morgen
most(ly) beinahe, fast
mother Mutter
mountain Berg
mouse, mice Maus, Mäuse
to move (sich) bewegen; umziehen
multinational multinational
murder Mord
music Musik
must müssen
myself (ich) selbst

N

name Name
nature Natur
near nahe
nearly beinahe, fast
to need brauchen, benötigen
neighbour Nachbar/in
never nie(mals)
new neu
news Nachricht(en)
next to neben
nice schön, nett
night Nacht
nobody niemand
normal normal
nothing nichts
now nun, jetzt
number Nummer, Zahl

O

o'clock Uhr
of course natürlich, selbstverständlich
office Büro, Amt
often oft, häufig
old alt
once einmal, einst, sobald
only nur, einzig
onto auf
open; to open offen; öffnen
opposite gegenüber
or oder
other andere/r/s
our unser/e
out of (her)aus
outside draußen
over there dort (drüben)
own; to own eigene/r/s; besitzen

P

page Seite
paint; to paint Farbe; malen
pair Paar
paper Papier, Zeitung
parents Eltern
part Teil
passport (Reise-)Pass
to pay (be)zahlen
pen Stift
pepper Pfeffer, Paprika
per pro, per
perfect vollkommen, perfekt
perhaps vielleicht, eventuell
person Mensch, Person
pet Haustier
phone; to phone Telefon; anrufen
phone number Telefonnummer
picture Bild
piece of Stück, Teil von
place Stelle, Platz, Ort
plan; to plan Plan; planen
plane Flugzeug
plant Pflanze
to play spielen
player Spieler/in
plenty of viel, reichlich
point Punkt
police; police officer Polizei; Polizist/in
police station Polizeiwache
polite höflich
poor arm, schlecht, mangelhaft
possible möglich
postcard Postkarte
post office Postamt
potato Kartoffel
pound Pfund
to practise üben
to prefer vorziehen, lieber mögen
present Geschenk
pretty hübsch
price (Kauf-)Preis
private privat
probably wahrscheinlich
problem Problem
project Projekt
to put setzen, stellen, legen

Q

quarter Viertel
queen Königin
question Frage
quick schnell, rasch
quiet ruhig, still
quite ziemlich, ganz

R

radio Funkgerät
railway station Bahnhof
rain; to rain Regen; regnen
to read lesen
real echt, wirklich
really wirklich, eigentlich
red rot
religion Religion
to remember (sich) erinnern (an)
rest of Rest des
rice Reis
rich reich
to ride fahren
right rechts, rechte/r/s, richtig; Recht
road (Land-)Straße
role Rolle
room Zimmer, Raum
rule Regel
to run laufen

S

sad traurig
safe sicher
salad Salat
salt Salz
same gleiche/r/s, der-, die-, dasselbe
sandwich Sandwich
to save (money) (Geld) sparen
to say sagen
school, schoolwork Schule, Schularbeit
science Naturwissenschaft
sea (die) See
second zweite/r/s; Sekunde
to see sehen
see you later bis später
to seem scheinen
to sell verkaufen
to send schicken
sentence Satz
shall sollen, werden
shape Form, Gestalt
to share sich teilen
shop Laden, Geschäft
shop assistant Verkäufer/in
short kurz, klein, knapp
to shout schreien
to show zeigen
sick krank
silly dumm, blöd
since da, weil, seit
to sing singen
sister Schwester
to sit sitzen
skirt Rock
to sleep schlafen
slow langsam
small klein
to smile lächeln
snow; to snow Schnee; schneien
so so, deshalb
soft weich, sanft
some einige, etwas
somebody jemand
someone jemand
something etwas
sometimes manchmal
somewhere irgendwo(hin)
son Sohn
song Lied
soon bald
sorry traurig; Verzeihung
sort Art, Typ, Sorte
soup Suppe
space Weltraum
to speak (to) sprechen (mit)
special besondere/r/s, speziell
to spend (Geld) ausgeben; (Zeit) verbringen
spoon Löffel
sport Sport
to stand stehen
start; to start Beginn; anfangen, starten
to stay bleiben
still still, trotzdem, (immer) noch
to stop anhalten
store Laden, Geschäft
story Geschichte
straightaway sofort
street Straße
strong stark, kräftig

student Student/in, Lernende/r
to study studieren, lernen
stupid blöd, bescheuert
suddenly plötzlich
sun Sonne
supermarket Supermarkt
surprise Überraschung
sweet süß
to swim schwimmen
swimming pool Schwimmbad, -becken

T

table Tisch, Tabelle
to take nehmen, dauern
to talk sprechen
tall groß
tea Tee
to teach unterrichten
teacher Lehrer/in
team Mannschaft
telephone; to telephone Telefon; telefonieren
television Fernsehen, Fernseher
to tell sagen, erzählen
thanks; thank you Dank; danke
that das, dass
theatre Theater
their ihr/e
them ihnen, sie
then dann
these diese
they sie
thin dünn
thing Sache, Ding
to think denken
thirsty durstig
this dies, diese/r/s
those jene
through durch (... hindurch)
to throw werfen
ticket Karte, Fahrschein
till bis
time Zeit, Mal
tired müde
today heute
together zusammen
toilet Toilette
tomato Tomate
tomorrow morgen
tonight heute Abend/Nacht
too zu; auch
tooth (teeth) Zahn (Zähne)
top oberer Teil
tourist Tourist/in
towards auf ... zu
town Stadt
to travel reisen, fahren
tree Baum
trousers Hose
true richtig, wahr
to try versuchen
T-shirt T-Shirt
typical typisch

U

uncle Onkel
to understand verstehen
university Universität
until bis
us uns
to use benutzen, gebrauchen, verwenden
useful nützlich
usual(ly) gewöhnlich, normal(erweise)

V

vegetable Gemüse
very sehr
village Dorf
to visit besuchen
visitor Besucher/in, Gast

W

to wait warten
waiter Kellner
waitress Kellnerin
walk; to walk Spaziergang; gehen
to want wollen
warm warm
washing Wäsche
to watch (an)sehen
water Wasser
way Weg; Art, Weise
to wear tragen, anhaben
weather Wetter
week Woche
weekend Wochenende
welcome; to welcome willkommen; willkommen heißen
what was, welche/r/s
when wenn, als, wann
where wo(hin)
whether ob
which welche/r/s
while während
white weiß
who wer, der/die/das, welche(r/s)
whole ganze/r/s
whose wessen, dessen
why warum
will werde(n), wollen
to win gewinnen
wind Wind
winner Gewinner/in
wish; to wish Wunsch; wünschen
with mit, bei
within innerhalb (von), in
without ohne
wolf Wolf
woman Frau
wonderful wunderbar, -voll
wood Holz; Wald
word Wort
to work arbeiten
workplace Arbeitsplatz
world Welt
would würde/n
to write schreiben
wrong falsch

Y

year Jahr
yesterday gestern
young jung
your dein/e, Ihr/e, euer/e
yourself du/Sie selbst, (Sie) sich

Chronologisches Wörterverzeichnis

Dieses Wörterverzeichnis enthält alle Wörter aus **Keep Going**, die nicht in der Liste des Grundwortschatzes enthalten sind, d. h. die nicht als bekannt vorausgesetzt werden.

T = das Wort befindet sich im *Transcript* (Hörübung). **F** = das Wort befindet sich in den *Files*.
≈ = Wort mit gleicher Bedeutung; ≠ = Wort mit gegensätzlicher Bedeutung; ⚠ = *Achtung!*

iː	ɪ	e	æ	ɑː	ɒ	ɔː	ʊ	uː	ʌ	ɜː	ə
see	sit	ten	bad	arm	got	saw	put	too	cut	bird	about
tʃ	dʒ	ʃ	ʒ	θ	ð	ŋ	s	z	v	w	
chips	jet	ship	garage	thing	the	ring	ice	as	very	wet	

Let's go!

S. 6	**empire** ['empaɪə]	Many countries were part of Britain's empire.	*Reich*
	character ['kærəktə]	James Bond is a character, not a real person.	*Charakter, (Film-, Roman-) Figur, Person*
	nightmare ['naɪtmeə]	I have horrible nightmares when I go to sleep.	*Albtraum*
	favourite ['feɪvərɪt]	Chips are my favourite food.	*Lieblings-*
	tool [tuːl]	A hammer is a useful tool.	*Werkzeug*
	rock [rɒk]	There are big rocks in the mountains.	*Stein, Fels*
	robot ['rəʊbɒt]	R2-D2 is the little robot from *Star Wars*.	*Roboter*
	intelligent [ɪn'telɪdʒənt]	⚠ *Aussprache!*	*intelligent*
	electricity [ɪˌlek'trɪsəti]	Electricity is a sort of energy.	*Elektrizität*
	light [laɪt]	There isn't enough light in here. I can't see.	*Licht, Lampe, Leuchte*
	dragon ['drægən]	A dragon is a sort of monster.	*Drachen*
	forest ['fɒrɪst]	There are millions of trees in the forest.	*Wald*
	breath [breθ]	You can see people's breath on a cold day.	*Atem*
	breath of fire [ˌbreθ əv 'faɪə]		die Fähigkeit, Feuer zu speien
	to build [bɪld]	They are building a house.	*bauen, aufbauen, errichten*
	guy [gaɪ]	Hi guys! How's life?	*Typ, Kumpel*
	lake [leɪk]	In English the *Bodensee* is called Lake Constance.	*See*
	magic wand [ˌmædʒɪk 'wɒnd]	Harry Potter points his magic wand at Voldemort.	*Zauberstab*
	darkness ['dɑːknəs]	≠ light	*Dunkelheit, Finsternis*
	underwater [ˌʌndə'wɔːtə]	I can swim 25 metres underwater, then I need more air.	*unter Wasser*
	elf [elf]	It was a story about magic, dragons and elves.	*Kobold, Elfe*
	extremely [ɪk'striːmli]	≈ very	*äußerst*
	clever ['klevə]	≠ stupid	*klug, schlau, clever*
	medicine ['medsn]	If you get ill again, take this medicine.	*Arznei, Medizin*
S. 7	**to copy** ['kɒpi]	Can I copy your work, please?	*abschreiben, kopieren*
	information [ˌɪnfə'meɪʃn]	I need more information to answer the question.	*Angaben, Informationen*
	strength [streŋθ]	Bodybuilding improves your strength.	*Stärke, Kraft*
	factor ['fæktə]	⚠ *Aussprache!*	*Faktor*
	intelligence [ɪn'telɪdʒəns]	The IQ test finds out a person's intelligence.	*Intelligenz*
	to translate [træns'leɪt]	Can you translate this into German, please?	*übersetzen*
S. 8	**to breathe** [briːð]	There's no air in here. I can't breathe!	*atmen*

tʃ	dʒ	ʃ	ʒ	θ	ð	ŋ	s	z	v	w
chips	jet	ship	garage	thing	the	ring	ice	as	very	wet

	to breathe fire [ˌbriːð 'faɪə]	Dragons breathe fire.	*Feuer speien*
	popular (with sb) ['pɒpjələ]	He's popular at school. Everyone likes him.	*beliebt (bei jdm)*
	not ... yet [nɒt 'jet]	I haven't done it yet. I'll do it tomorrow.	*noch nicht*
	someday ['sʌmdeɪ]	I'll see her again someday, I don't know when.	*irgendwann*
	to mean [miːn]	I don't understand: what does this word mean?	*bedeuten, heißen*
	complicated ['kɒmplɪkeɪtɪd]	The story is too complicated to explain now.	*kompliziert*
	criminal ['krɪmɪnl]	The police are looking for the criminal.	*Verbrecher/in, Kriminelle/r*
	adventure [əd'ventʃə]	The trip will be very exciting, a great adventure.	*Abenteuer*
	talented ['tæləntɪd]	He's talented: he plays music very well.	*talentiert*
S. 9	**to program** ['prəʊgræm]	The IT expert is programming the computer.	*programmieren*
	programmer ['prəʊgræmə]	She works as a computer programmer.	*Programmierer/in*
	detail ['diːteɪl]	This report is good, but a few details are wrong.	*Detail, Einzelheit*
	statement ['steɪtmənt]	Is this a statement or a question?	*Aussage, Behauptung*
	advertisement [əd'vɜːtɪsmənt]	I found the job in a newspaper advertisement.	*Anzeige, Inserat*
	company ['kʌmpəni]	Microsoft is a large company.	*Gesellschaft, Firma*
	creative [kri'eɪtɪv]	We need some creative ideas to solve this problem.	*kreativ*
	product ['prɒdʌkt]	The company makes several different products.	*Produkt*
	training ['treɪnɪŋ]	You need training to do this job.	*Ausbildung*
	professional [prə'feʃənl]	He's a professional musician, not an amateur.	*Berufs-, professionell, berufsmäßig*
S. 10	**(the) following** [ðə 'fɒləʊɪŋ]	To make a pizza, you need the following: ...	*(der/die/das) folgende*
	category ['kætəgəri]	Which category does a tomato belong in: vegetable or fruit?	*Kategorie, Klasse*
	hidden ['hɪdn]	It must be hidden: I can't find it.	*verborgen, versteckt*
	object ['ɒbdʒɪkt]	In English we call all objects 'it'.	*Gegenstand, Objekt*
	gap [gæp]	There's a gap here. Something is missing.	*Lücke*
	bracket ['brækɪt]	Put it in brackets like this: ( )	*Klammer*
	to design [dɪ'zaɪn]	She designs and makes her own clothes.	*entwerfen, gestalten, konstruieren, bauen*
	especially [ɪ'speʃəli]	It's for everyone, not especially for teenagers.	*besonders, eigens, extra*
	adult ['ædʌlt]	This game is only for adults, not for children.	*erwachsen, Erwachsene/r*
	to click [klɪk]	Click this link to go to the webpage.	*klicken, anklicken*
	to allow [ə'laʊ]	I can't allow you to come in here, it's private.	*erlauben, gestatten*
	to be allowed to do sth [bi ə'laʊd tə duː]	It's my dad's: we aren't allowed to use it.	*etw tun dürfen*
	(for) free [fə 'friː]	You can play for free. It doesn't cost anything.	*kostenlos, gratis*
	herd [hɜːd]	There are 30 elephants in this herd.	*Herde*
	display [dɪ'spleɪ]	The phone's display shows the caller's number.	*Anzeige, Display*
	corner ['kɔːnə]	This table is round, so there aren't any corners.	*Ecke*
S. 11	**skill** [skɪl]	You don't need a lot of skill to win, just luck.	*Fähigkeit, Fertigkeit*
	phrase [freɪz]	Could you explain the phrase '...', please?	*Formulierung, Satzteil*
	background ['bækgraʊnd]	That's Mark in the background in this photo.	*Hintergrund*
	foreground ['fɔːgraʊnd]	Mel is in the foreground, so you can see her clearly.	*Vordergrund*

i:	ɪ	e	æ	ɑ:	ɒ	ɔ:	ʊ	u:	ʌ	3:	ə
see	sit	ten	bad	arm	got	saw	put	too	cut	bird	about

	beach umbrella ['bi:tʃ ʌmbrelə]	A beach umbrella keeps you cool in the hot sun.	*Sonnenschirm*
	sandal ['sændl]	Sandals are comfortable in hot weather.	*Sandale*
	gift [gɪft]	I don't want any money for it: it's a gift.	*Geschenk*
	strawberry ['strɔ:bəri]	Strawberries are my favourite fruit.	*Erdbeere*
	finally ['faɪnəli]	'I've done it at last.' – 'Finally!'	*zuletzt, endlich*
	once [wʌns]	'Have you been to France?' – 'Yes, but only once.'	*einmal*
S. 12	**to race** [reɪs]	These cars race at the Nürburgring.	*um die Wette fahren*
	sure [ʃʊə]	It might be true, but I can't be sure.	*sicher(lich), (na) klar*
	blind [blaɪnd]	The blind man uses a white stick.	*blind*
	to sound [saʊnd]	That sounds wrong. Are you sure it's right?	*klingen*
	at least [ət 'li:st]	We need at least €100, maybe more.	*zumindest, wenigstens*
	race [reɪs]	The Dakar Rally is a famous race in Africa.	*(Wett-)Rennen*
	to hit sb off the road [ˌhɪt ɒf ðə 'rəʊd]	I was cycling along, then a car hit me off the road.	*jdn von der Straße drängen*
	to beat (sb) [bi:t]	Germany beat England 2:0.	*(jdn) schlagen*
	to hurt oneself [hɜ:t]	Did you hurt yourself when you fell off your bike?	*sich wehtun*
	to fall over [ˌfɔ:l 'əʊvə]	He didn't just fall over: somebody pushed him.	*hinfallen*
	addicted [ə'dɪktɪd]	I can't stop playing this game: I'm addicted.	*süchtig*
	to surprise sb [sə'praɪz]	The answer surprised him: he didn't expect it.	*jdn überraschen*
	to call [kɔ:l]	Hey, don't call me an idiot!	*nennen*
	leader ['li:də]	Jed's the leader, he always decides what to do.	*Führer/in*

Unit 1

S. 13	**running** ['rʌnɪŋ]	Running is quicker than walking.	*Laufen*
	skiing ['ski:ɪŋ]	We go skiing in the Alps.	*Skifahren*
	to ride [raɪd]	Beth rides her pony every morning.	*reiten*
	gymnastics [dʒɪm'næstɪks]	You need to be flexible to do gymnastics.	*Turnen*
	karate [kə'rɑ:ti]	Karate and judo both come from Japan.	*Karate*
	healthy ['helθi]	Fruit is a healthy food, but chocolate isn't.	*gesund*
S. 14	**gist** [dʒɪst]	I don't understand all the details, but I get the gist.	*das Wesentliche*
	to skim [skɪm]	Just skim the text, don't read it all yet.	*(Text) überfliegen*
	heading ['hedɪŋ]	Headings tell you what the text is about.	*Überschrift*
	homeless ['həʊmləs]	Many homeless people sleep in the park at night.	*obdachlos*
	reality [ri'æləti]	Dreams and reality aren't often the same.	*Wirklichkeit*
	brilliant ['brɪliənt]	I'm not a brilliant artist, but I'm quite good.	*genial, glänzend*
	bright [braɪt]	≈ clever	*intelligent, aufgeweckt*
	to be mad about sth [bi 'mæd əbaʊt]	He's mad about sport, he can't get enough of it.	*nach etw verrückt sein*
	difference ['dɪfrəns]	I'm Canadian, not American. There's a difference!	*Unterschied*
	smart [smɑ:t]	I only wear smart clothes for work, not at home.	*schick, elegant*
	cardboard ['kɑ:dbɔ:d]	The apples are in a cardboard box.	*Pappe*

	member ['membə]	You aren't a member of the golf club, so you can't play.	*Mitglied*
	to last [lɑːst]	The film lasts 90 minutes.	*dauern*
	to follow ['fɒləʊ]	You have to follow the rules.	*folgen*
	soccer ['sɒkə]	*BE:* football	*Fußball*
	court [kɔːt]	We have a tennis court in our garden.	*Spielfeld*
	break [breɪk]	That's enough work. It's time for a break.	*Pause*
	in total [ɪn 'təʊtl]	£10, £5 and £5.50 ... how much is that in total?	*insgesamt*
	referee [ˌrefə'riː]	The referee starts the game.	*Schiedsrichter/in*
	to throw [θrəʊ]	You can't throw the ball: you have to kick it.	*werfen*
	male [meɪl]	It's an all-male team: no girls allowed.	*männlich*
	female ['fiːmeɪl]	It's an all-female team: girls only.	*weiblich*
	mixed [mɪkst]	It's a mixed team: both boys and girls can join.	*gemischt*
	to come true [ˌkʌm 'truː]	Dreams sometimes come true.	*wahr werden*
	medal ['medl]	The best player wins a gold medal.	*Medaille*
	fame [feɪm]	Fame is when everyone knows who you are.	*Ruhm*
	competition [ˌkɒmpə'tɪʃn]	Only one team can win the competition.	*Wettbewerb*
	home [həʊm]	He needs a home – somewhere to live.	*Zuhause, Wohnung, Haus*
	to give sth up [ˌgɪv 'ʌp]	You should give up chocolate, it's bad for you.	*etw aufgeben, mit etw aufhoren*
	drug [drʌg]	Cannabis is an illegal drug.	*Droge*
	alcohol ['ælkəhɒl]	Whisky and vodka contain lots of alcohol.	*Alkohol*
	to improve [ɪm'pruːv]	The weather is improving. It gets better every day.	*verbessern, (sich) bessern*
	relationship [rɪ'leɪʃnʃɪp]	He has a good relationship with his parents.	*Verhältnis, Beziehung*
	several ['sevrəl]	There are several cars in the car park – about 20.	*mehrere*
	coach [kəʊtʃ]	The coach tells the players what to do.	*Trainer/in*
	instructor [ɪn'strʌktə]	I'm a sports instructor. I teach football and hockey.	*Lehrer/in, Trainer/in*
S. 15	**carefully** ['keəfəli]	Listen carefully: you mustn't miss anything.	*sorgfältig*
	goalkeeper ['gəʊlkiːpə]	A goalkeeper stays in the goal area all the time.	*Torwart/in*
	defender [dɪ'fendə]	A defender tries to stop the other team from scoring goals.	*Verteidiger/in*
	captain ['kæptɪn]	The captain is the leader of the team.	*Kapitän/in*
	striker ['straɪkə]	A striker tries to score a goal.	*Stürmer/in*
	choice [tʃɔɪs]	There isn't a choice, we must do it.	*Wahl, Auswahl*
	opinion [ə'pɪniən]	In my opinion, you're wrong.	*Meinung*
	to read out [ˌriːd 'aʊt]	Please can you read out the question for all of us?	*(laut) vorlesen*
	independent [ˌɪndɪ'pendənt]	I'm independent: I don't like to work in a team.	*unabhängig*
	runner ['rʌnə]	He's a good runner: 100 metres in 10 seconds.	*Läufer/in*
	to laugh [lɑːf]	Don't laugh, it isn't funny.	*lachen*
	to joke [dʒəʊk]	'You're joking!' – 'No, I'm serious.'	*scherzen*
	gentle ['dʒentl]	Ben's very gentle, he wouldn't hurt anybody.	*sanft*
	giant ['dʒaɪənt]	He's very big, a real giant.	*Riese*
	calm [kɑːm]	Stay calm, don't shout.	*ruhig*
	tall [tɔːl]	She's 1.6 metres tall.	*groß (Körpergröße)*

i:	ɪ	e	æ	ɑ:	ɒ	ɔ:	ʊ	u:	ʌ	ɜ:	ə
see	sit	ten	bad	arm	got	saw	put	too	cut	bird	about

	overweight [ˌəʊvəˈweɪt]	I weigh 90 kilos. I'm a bit overweight.	*übergewichtig*
	aggressive [əˈgresɪv]	That child is aggressive. He often hits the others.	*aggressiv*
	cooperative [kəʊˈɒpərətɪv]	A cooperative person works well with others.	*kooperativ*
S. 16	**research** [rɪˈsɜːtʃ]	After 20 years' research, he got a Nobel Prize for science.	*Forschung, Recherche*
	to report [rɪˈpɔːt]	Report to the class what you find out.	*berichten*
	current [ˈkʌrənt]	The current team is different to last year's.	*aktuell*
	trophy [ˈtrəʊfi]	The winning team's name is on the trophy.	*Trophäe, Pokal*
	to hold [həʊld]	Can we hold a concert at school?	*halten, abhalten, veranstalten*
	to take part in sth [teɪk ˈpɑːt ɪn]	Please take part in the next meeting.	*an etw teilnehmen*
	to take place [teɪk ˈpleɪs]	Where do the meetings take place?	*stattfinden*
	to support [səˈpɔːt]	It's important to support poor people.	*unterstützen*
	businesswoman [ˈbɪznəswʊmən]	I'm a businesswoman: I have my own business.	*Geschäftsfrau*
	to get in touch with sb [get ɪn ˈtʌtʃ wɪð]	You can get in touch with me by phone or email.	*sich mit jdm in Verbindung setzen*
	trainee [treɪˈniː]	The trainees work here for three years.	*Auszubildende/r*
	leisure [ˈleʒə]	⚠ *Aussprache!*	*Freizeit*
	to draw sth up [ˌdrɔː ˈʌp]	I'll draw up a list of questions.	*etw aufstellen, entwerfen, aufsetzen*
	timetable [ˈtaɪmteɪbl]	Which lesson is next in your timetable?	*Stundenplan*
	to take turns [teɪk ˈtɜːnz]	Let's take turns: you can go first, then me.	*sich abwechseln*
	routine [ruːˈtiːn]	He always follows the same routine.	*Routine*
	daily routine [ˌdeɪli ruːˈtiːn]	Exercise is part of my daily routine.	*Tagesablauf*
	college [ˈkɒlɪdʒ]	Are you going to college when you finish school?	*Berufsschule*
S. 17	**staff** [stɑːf]	'How many staff work at the centre?' – 'About 50.'	*Personal, Belegschaft, Angestellte*
	to maintain [meɪnˈteɪn]	I maintain the machines so that they work well.	*warten, unterhalten*
	equipment [ɪˈkwɪpmənt]	Do you know how to use the equipment?	*Geräte*
	gym [dʒɪm]	Arnold is very fit. He goes to the gym every day.	*Fitness-Studio*
	to make sure [ˌmeɪk ˈʃʊə]	Make sure that the computer is working properly.	*sicherstellen, gewährleisten*
	safe [seɪf]	≠ dangerous	*sicher*
	to break down [ˌbreɪk ˈdaʊn]	This machine breaks down all the time.	*kaputtgehen*
	to fix sth [fɪks]	Can you fix the problem with my car?	*etw reparieren, flicken*
	odd jobs [ˌɒd ˈdʒɒbz]	I don't have anything special to do, just odd jobs.	*die anfallenden Arbeiten*
	sign [saɪn]	The sign says 'No smoking'.	*Schild*
	to put up [ˌpʊt ˈʌp]	Let's put up photos on the wall.	*aufstellen*
	to be responsible for sth [bi rɪˈspɒnsəbl fə]	Who is responsible for food at the party?	*für etw zuständig sein*
	safety [ˈseɪfti]	Safety is important: nobody must get hurt.	*Sicherheit*
	user [ˈjuːzə]	Users of the pool must follow the rules.	*Nutzer/in, Benutzer/in*
	certificate [səˈtɪfɪkət]	If you pass the test, you get a certificate.	*Zeugnis, Zertifikat, Diplom*

tʃ	dʒ	ʃ	ʒ	θ	ð	ŋ	s	z	v	w
chips	jet	ship	garage	thing	the	ring	ice	as	very	wet

first aid [ˌfɜːst ˈeɪd]	This man is sick. Does anyone here know first aid?	*Erste Hilfe*
lifesaving [ˈlaɪfseɪvɪŋ]	The lifesaving equipment is next to the pool.	*Lebensrettung*
to sit around [ˌsɪt əˈraʊnd]	I don't do much, I just sit around.	*herumsitzen*
class [klɑːs]	Sue takes a French class on Thursday evenings.	*Kurs*
to check [tʃek]	Can I check your ID, please?	*überprüfen*
membership [ˈmembəʃɪp]	How much does one year's membership cost?	*Mitgliedschaft*
to send sth out [ˌsend ˈaʊt]	Spam emailers send out millions of emails.	*etw verschicken*
to keep sb informed [kiːp ɪnˈfɔːmd]	Keep me informed about any changes.	*jdn auf dem laufenden halten*
to assist sb with sth [əˈsɪst]	I assist Mrs Patrick with her work.	*jdm bei etw helfen*
to run sth [rʌn]	Mrs Patrick runs the centre. We do what she says.	*etw betreiben, leiten, führen*
to hire sb [ˈhaɪə]	We need to hire three new people.	*jdn einstellen*
to supervise [ˈsuːpəvaɪz]	You must supervise young children in the pool.	*beaufsichtigen, kontrollieren*
to vacuum [ˈvækjuəm]	I vacuum the rooms to keep them clean.	*staubsaugen*
carpet [ˈkɑːpɪt]	The carpet feels nice and warm under my feet.	*Teppich*
to mop [mɒp]	I'm mopping the floor. That's why it's wet.	*(auf)wischen*
to polish [ˈpɒlɪʃ]	I polish all the metal so that it shines.	*polieren*
floor [flɔː]	Don't sit on the floor. Get a chair.	*Fußboden*
to empty [ˈempti]	Empty the bottle before you throw it away.	*leeren*
bin [bɪn]	Don't leave that paper on the floor. Put it in the bin.	*Mülleimer*
expression [ɪkˈspreʃn]	'Excuse me' is a polite expression.	*Ausdruck*
to match [mætʃ]	Match the names to the photos.	*zuordnen*
meaning [ˈmiːnɪŋ]	I don't understand the meaning of this word.	*Bedeutung*
possibility [ˌpɒsəˈbɪləti]	There are two possibilities: right or wrong.	*Möglichkeit*
task [tɑːsk]	I can't do this task. It's too difficult.	*Aufgabe*
S. 18 **trade** [treɪd]	Jack wants to learn a trade.	*Handel, Gewerbe, Branche*
to identify [aɪˈdentɪfaɪ]	Can you identify this? I don't know what it is.	*herausfinden, erkennen, identifizieren*
mystery [ˈmɪstri]	Nobody knows: it's a mystery.	*Rätsel, Geheimnis*
to belong to sb [bɪˈlɒŋ tə]	'Does this belong to you?' – 'Yes, it's mine.'	*jdm gehören*
briefcase [ˈbriːfkeɪs]	I keep paper, a pen and my laptop in my briefcase.	*Aktentasche*
cash register [ˈkæʃ redʒɪstə]	Please go to the cash register to pay for that.	*Registrierkasse*
drill [drɪl]	I need a drill to make a hole in the metal.	*Bohrer*
printer [ˈprɪntə]	Put some more paper in the printer.	*Drucker*
toolbox [ˈtuːlbɒks]	I have a lot of tools in my toolbox.	*Werkzeugkasten*
vacuum cleaner [ˈvækjuəm kliːnə]	You need a vacuum cleaner to keep the carpet clean.	*Staubsauger*
appointment [əˈpɔɪntmənt]	I have an appointment with Mrs Smith at 1 p.m.	*Termin*
to discuss [dɪˈskʌs]	Can I discuss this problem with you, please?	*besprechen, erörtern, diskutieren*
exercise machine [ˈeksəsaɪz məʃiːn]	This exercise machine will help you to get fit.	*Trainings-/Fitnessgerät*
... speaking [ˈspiːkɪŋ]	Cathy Jones speaking. How can I help you?	*am Apparat*
I'm afraid ... [aɪm əˈfreɪd]	I'm afraid I can't help. Sorry!	*Leider ...*

i:	ɪ	e	æ	ɑ:	ɒ	ɔ:	ʊ	u:	ʌ	ɜ:	ə
see	sit	ten	bad	arm	got	saw	put	too	cut	bird	about

	though [ðəʊ]	Barry Smith can help you, though.	*aber, allerdings*
T	**You're welcome.** [jɔ: 'welkəm]	'Thanks.' – 'You're welcome.'	*Bitte sehr. Gern geschehen.*
S. 19	**manager** ['mænɪdʒə]	The managers run the company.	*Geschäftsführer/in, Leiter/in*
	conversation [ˌkɒnvə'seɪʃn]	Don't listen to our conversation. It's private.	*Gespräch, Unterhaltung*
	instructions [ɪn'strʌkʃnz]	Read the instructions before you use the machine.	*Anleitung*
	to suit [su:t]	Thursday doesn't suit me. How about Friday?	*passen*
S. 20	**to enjoy sth** [ɪn'dʒɔɪ]	'Do you enjoy swimming?' – 'No, I don't like it.'	*etw genießen, gern haben*
	to get up [ˌget 'ʌp]	What time do you get up in the morning?	*aufstehen*
	attention [ə'tenʃn]	Please can I have your attention, everyone?	*Aufmerksamkeit*
	to pay attention [peɪ ə'tenʃn]	Please pay attention: this is important.	*aufpassen, achtgeben*
	to kiss [kɪs]	Isn't that sweet? He's kissing his girlfriend.	*(sich) küssen*

Unit 2

S. 21	**to guess** [ges]	I don't know the answer, but I can guess.	*raten, erraten*
	special ['speʃl]	A birthday is a special day.	*besonders, Spezial-*
	around [ə'raʊnd]	There are around 6 billion people in the world.	*ungefähr, zirka*
	foreign ['fɒrən]	⚠ *Aussprache!*	*ausländisch, fremd, Fremd-*
	menu ['menju:]	'What's on the menu?' – 'Pizza, pasta, ...'	*Speisekarte*
	to name [neɪm]	The parents named their daughter 'Rose'.	*benennen, nennen*
	area ['eəriə]	The national park covers a large area.	*Bereich, Gebiet*
S. 22	**subject** ['sʌbdʒɪkt]	I don't want to talk about that. Change the subject.	*Thema*
	to scan [skæn]	She scans the newspaper for jobs every day.	*absuchen, überfliegen*
	specific [spə'sɪfɪk]	'It costs about €50.' – 'Can you be more specific?'	*bestimmt, spezifisch*
	helmet ['helmɪt]	Always wear a helmet when you ride your moped.	*Helm*
	homesickness ['həʊmsɪknəs]	I get homesickness when I'm away from home.	*Heimweh*
	soldier ['səʊldʒə]	He is a soldier in the US army.	*Soldat/in*
	peacekeeping soldier ['pi:ski:pɪŋ səʊldʒə]	UN peacekeeping soldiers wear blue helmets.	*Soldat/in einer UN-Friedenstruppe*
	mission ['mɪʃn]	Are you ready for this dangerous mission?	*Auftrag, Einsatz, Mission*
	Afghanistan [æf'gænɪstɑ:n]		*Afghanistan*
	to feel/be homesick [ˌfi:l/bi 'həʊmsɪk]	I feel homesick. I want to go home.	*Heimweh haben*
	to miss sbŋsth [mɪs]	He misses his family when he's away from home.	*jdn/etw vermissen*
	sure [ʃʊə]	I'm not sure this is right. It could be wrong.	*sicher*
	to deal with sth ['di:l wɪð]	It's a difficult problem, but you have to deal with it.	*mit etw fertig werden, mit etw zurechtkommen*
	advice [əd'vaɪs]	Can you give me advice about what I should do?	*Rat, Ratschläge*
	Sudan [su'dɑ:n]		*Sudan*
	United Nations [juˌnaɪtɪd 'neɪʃnz]	192 countries are in the United Nations.	*Vereinte Nationen*

tʃ	dʒ	ʃ	ʒ	θ	ð	ŋ	s	z	v	w
chips	jet	ship	garage	thing	the	ring	ice	as	very	wet

	community service [kə'mju:nəti sɜ:vɪs]	Instead of joining the army, he did community service.	*Zivildienst*
	abroad [ə'brɔ:d]	Do you prefer holidays abroad, or in your own country?	*im Ausland*
	farmer ['fɑ:mə]	We need farmers to grow our food.	*Bauer/Bäuerin, Landwirt/in, Farmer/in*
	terrible ['terəbl]	I have a terrible headache: it's really bad.	*furchtbar, schrecklich*
	culture ['kʌltʃə]	He's interested in French culture: literature, art etc.	*Kultur*
	shock [ʃɒk]	It was a shock when my dad died.	*Schock*
	development [dɪ'veləpmənt]	Development will make people's lives better.	*Entwicklung*
	development worker [dɪ'veləpmənt wɜ:kə]	Liz is a development worker in poor countries.	*Entwicklungshelfer/in*
	luckily ['lʌkɪli]	Luckily he wasn't hurt in the accident.	*zum Glück*
	aspect ['æspekt]	What aspect of the film do you find most interesting?	*Seite, Aspekt*
	to be able to [bi 'eɪbl tə]	Are you able to help me? No, I can't.	*in der Lage sein, können*
	medic ['medɪk]	This man is hurt. He needs a medic.	*Arzt/Ärztin*
	military ['mɪlətri]	He's a military leader, a general.	*Militär*
	disaster [dɪ'zɑ:stə]	Hurricane Katrina was a disaster for the USA.	*Katastrophe*
	relief [rɪ'li:f]	The hungry people need relief quickly.	*Hilfe*
	health [helθ]	Her health is good. She isn't often ill.	*Gesundheit*
	experience [ɪk'spɪəriəns]	My holiday in Africa was an interesting experience.	*Erfahrung, Erlebnis*
S.23	**to mention** ['menʃn]	You didn't mention your name.	*erwähnen, (be)nennen*
	colleague ['kɒli:g]	This is my colleague, Sue. Sue works with me.	*Kollege/Kollegin*
	to focus on sth ['fəʊkəs ɒn]	We need to focus on the main problem.	*sich auf etw konzentrieren*
	unfriendly [ʌn'frendli]	'Go away!' – 'Don't be so unfriendly!'	*unfreundlich*
	exercise ['eksəsaɪz]	You need more exercise. Why don't you do a sport?	*Bewegung*
	to get (some) exercise [ˌget sʌm 'eksəsaɪz]	I get exercise every day. I swim or I go running.	*Sport treiben, trainieren, sich bewegen*
	assignment [ə'saɪnmənt]	Your next assignment is to shoot the president.	*Auftrag, Aufgabe*
	well-being ['welbi:ɪŋ]	Stress can affect your well-being.	*Wohlbefinden*
	mental ['mentl]	It's a difficult mental task: you have to think hard.	*geistig, mental*
	physical ['fɪzɪkl]	I like physical activities like sport or walking.	*körperlich, physisch*
	focus ['fəʊkəs]	A chess player needs lots of focus.	hier: *Konzentrationsfähigkeit*
S.24	**to sail** [seɪl]	I like to sail my boat on the sea at the weekend.	*segeln, (mit dem Schiff) fahren*
	the southern seas [ðə ˌsʌðən 'si:z]	I want to visit the southern seas between Australia and Polynesia.	*die Südsee*
	sight [saɪt]	The island was a beautiful sight.	*Anblick, Blick*
	at first sight [ət fɜ:st 'saɪt]	He loved her at first sight – as soon as he saw her.	*auf den ersten Blick*
	to marry ['mæri]	I can't marry you: I've already got a husband.	*heiraten*
	springer spaniel [ˌsprɪŋə 'spænjəl]	A springer spaniel is a type of dog.	*Englischer Springer Spaniel (Hunderasse)*
	board game ['bɔ:d geɪm]	Chess is a board game.	*Brettspiel*

i:	ɪ	e	æ	ɑ:	ɒ	ɔ:	ʊ	u:	ʌ	ɜ:	ə
see	sit	ten	bad	arm	got	saw	put	too	cut	bird	about

	foreigner ['fɒrənə]	I'm not a foreigner, I was born in this country.	*Ausländer/in*
	to be one's turn [bi wʌnz 'tɜ:n]	I'll make the tea. It's my turn.	*dran/an der Reihe sein*
	to toss [tɒs]	He tossed a ball in the air.	*werfen*
	coin [kɔɪn]	Have you got a 50-cent coin?	*Münze*
	heads [hedz]	It's heads: I win.	*(Münze:) Kopf*
	tails [teɪlz]	No, it's tails: you lose.	*(Münze:) Zahl*
	space [speɪs]	If you throw a six, you'll land on this space.	*(Brettspiel:) Feld*
	square [skweə]	Some squares on the board are green and some are orange.	*Quadrat, Feld, Platz*
	exchange [ɪks'tʃeɪndʒ]	I want to do an exchange with a British student.	*Austausch, Tausch*
	driving licence ['draɪvɪŋlaɪsns]	You can't drive. You don't have a driving licence.	*Führerschein*
	annoying [ə'nɔɪɪŋ]	You're very annoying. Please go away!	*lästig, ärgerlich*
	brand [brænd]	I only buy trainers from famous brands like Nike.	*Marke, Designerlabel*
	to promise ['prɒmɪs]	I promise to love you for ever.	*versprechen*
S. 25	**to invite** [ɪn'vaɪt]	I invited 50 guests to my birthday party.	*einladen*
	customer ['kʌstəmə]	There are 100 customers in the supermarket.	*Kunde/Kundin*
	to serve [sɜ:v]	Can you serve me, please? I want to buy this.	*servieren*
	pot [pɒt]	Would you like a pot of tea?	*Kanne*
	can [kæn]	A can of cola, please.	*Dose*
	curious ['kjʊəriəs]	Tell me what happened. I'm curious about it.	*neugierig*
	strange [streɪndʒ]	You won't believe it, it's a very strange story.	*seltsam, komisch*
	engaged [ɪn'geɪdʒd]	We're engaged. We're getting married in May.	*verlobt*
	divorced [dɪ'vɔ:st]	He's her ex-husband: they're divorced.	*geschieden*
	cell phone ['sel fəʊn]	Call me on my cell phone.	*Handy, Mobiltelefon*
	mobile (phone) [ˌməʊbaɪl 'fəʊn]	What's your mobile number?	*Handy, Mobiltelefon*
	wedding ['wedɪŋ]	There are three weddings in the church this Saturday.	*Hochzeit*
	to decline [dɪ'klaɪn]	Sorry, I have to decline. I can't come to your party.	*ablehnen*
	artist ['ɑ:tɪst]	He's a good artist: he paints great pictures.	*Künstler/in*
	photograph ['fəʊtəgrɑ:f]	That's me in the photograph.	*Foto(grafie)*
	to have sth in common [həv ɪn 'kɒmən]	They have a lot in common: they like the same things.	*etw gemeinsam haben*
	moonlit ['mu:nlɪt]	It's a moonlit night, so we can see clearly.	*im Mondschein*
	walk [wɔ:k]	Let's go for a walk in the park.	*Spaziergang*
	vegetarian [ˌvedʒə'teəriən]	Vegetarians don't eat meat.	*Vegetarier/in*
	pepper ['pepə]	Peppers grow on a bush. They can be green, red or yellow.	*Paprika*
	countryside ['kʌntrisaɪd]	I don't like the town. The countryside is better.	*Landschaft, Land*
	Tuscan ['tʌskən]		*toskanisch*
S. 26	**internship** ['ɪntɜ:nʃɪp]	I'm doing an internship in a company for six weeks.	*Praktikum*
	technician [tek'nɪʃn]	I want to be a technician: I'm interested in how things work.	*Techniker/in*
	passenger ['pæsɪndʒə]	The Airbus 380 is a passenger aircraft.	*Passagier-*

tʃ	dʒ	ʃ	ʒ	θ	ð	ŋ	s	z	v	w
chips	jet	ship	garage	thing	the	ring	ice	as	very	wet

	nickname ['nɪkneɪm]	He's called Steve but his nickname is 'Doc'.	*Spitzname*
	to found [faʊnd]	Bill Gates founded Microsoft in 1975.	*gründen*
	government ['gʌvənmənt]	The government runs the country.	*Regierung*
	minister ['mɪnɪstə]	The EU finance ministers are meeting in Brussels.	*Minister/in*
	to communicate [kə'mju:nɪkeɪt]	We communicate by email most of the time.	*kommunizieren, sich verständigen*
S. 27	**similar** ['sɪmələ]	It isn't quite the same, but it's similar.	*ähnlich*
	event [ɪ'vent]	The arrival of a baby is an important event for a family.	*Ereignis*
	translation [træns'leɪʃn]	You have to do a translation from English to German.	*Übersetzung*
	lyrics ['lɪrɪks]	I like this song but I don't understand the lyrics.	*(Lied-)Text*
	chancellor ['tʃɑ:nsələ]	Gerhard Schröder was chancellor until 2005.	*Kanzler/in*
	contest ['kɒntest]	It's a contest so there has to be a winner and a loser.	*Wettbewerb, Wettkampf*
T	**cloudy** ['klaʊdi]	It's cloudy, but it isn't raining yet.	*bewölkt*
	degree [dɪ'gri:]	The temperature was 12 degrees centigrade.	*Grad*
	to expect [ɪk'spekt]	I expect the train will come soon.	*erwarten*
	flight [flaɪt]	We're on flight LH702 from Berlin to Rome.	*Flug*
	key [ki:]	I can't find the key to the front door.	*Schlüssel*
S. 28	**to photograph** ['fəʊtəgrɑ:f]	He photographed lots of people at the party.	*fotografieren*
	to catch [kætʃ]	Catch the ball!	*fangen, fassen*
	to fight [faɪt]	Children! Don't fight in the car!	*kämpfen, bekämpfen, streiten*
	to seek [si:k]	Seek and you will find.	*suchen*
	title ['taɪtl]	What's the title of that book?	*Titel*
	currently ['kʌrəntli]	It's currently in cinemas all over Germany.	*aktuell, im Moment*

Unit 3

S. 29	**voluntary** ['vɒləntri]	I don't get paid: it's a voluntary job.	*freiwillig, ehrenamtlich, unentgeltlich*
	to mime [maɪm]	You're supposed to mime, so don't speak!	*pantomimisch darstellen*
S. 30	**volunteer** [ˌvɒlən'tɪə]	I work for free. I'm a volunteer, you see.	*ehrenamtliche/r Helfer/in, Freiwillige/r*
	musician [mju:'zɪʃn]	She's a musician. She sings and plays the piano.	*Musiker/in*
	style [staɪl]	I like different styles of music: indie, techno, R&B.	*Stil*
	to include [ɪn'klu:d]	We all need to work hard. That includes you, Sal.	*beinhalten, umfassen*
	disabled [dɪs'eɪbld]	I need the disabled toilets: I can't walk.	*behindert, Behinderten-*
	cash [kæʃ]	I don't have any cash, just my credit card.	*Bargeld*
	customer service [ˌkʌstəmə 's3:vɪs]	Phone customer service if you have a problem with our products.	*Kundendienst*
	poster ['pəʊstə]	The concert information is on the poster.	*Plakat*
	retail ['ri:teɪl]	I work in retail, in a shop.	*Einzelhandel*
	sales [seɪlz]	If you want to buy one, talk to the sales assistant.	*Verkauf, Vertrieb*

i:	ɪ	e	æ	ɑ:	ɒ	ɔ:	ʊ	u:	ʌ	ɜ:	ə
see	sit	ten	bad	arm	got	saw	put	too	cut	bird	about

survey ['sɜ:veɪ]	I'm doing a survey. Can I ask you some questions?	*Umfrage, Erhebung*
entry ['entri]	How much does entry to the disco cost?	*Eintritt, Zutritt*
payment ['peɪmənt]	I'd like to make a payment, please. Fifty euros.	*Zahlung*
to handle sth ['hændl]	He handles that camera very well.	*etw handhaben, mit etw umgehen*
steward [stju:əd]	Ask the steward, she'll show you the way.	*Ordner/in*
to direct sb [də'rekt]	Could you direct me to the toilets, please?	*jdm den Weg zeigen*
tent [tent]	When we go camping we stay in a tent.	*Zelt*
to put sth up [ˌpʊt 'ʌp]	They put up signs saying 'No parking'.	*etw aufstellen*
campsite ['kæmpsaɪt]	They stayed on a campsite in Italy.	*Campingplatz*
bacon ['beɪkən]	Bacon and eggs is a traditional English breakfast.	*Speck*
worth [wɜ:θ]	It's only a T-shirt. It isn't worth €100.	*wert, im Wert von*
meal [mi:l]	I eat three meals a day.	*Essen, Mahlzeit*
accommodation [əˌkɒmə'deɪʃn]	What accommodation do you like best: hotels or youth hostels?	*Unterkunft*
to camp [kæmp]	They camped in a field.	*zelten*
nearby ['nɪəbaɪ]	There isn't a shop nearby. The nearest one is 10 km away.	*in der Nähe*
to attend sth [ə'tend]	20,000 people attended the festival last year.	*in/zu etw gehen, bei etw anwesend sein*
to volunteer [ˌvɒlən'tɪə]	If you volunteer, you'll get a free ticket, but no money.	*ehrenamtlich tätig sein*
situation [ˌsɪtʃu'eɪʃn]	⚠ *Aussprache!*	*Situation*
to look sth up [ˌlʊk 'ʌp]	He didn't know the word, so he looked it up.	*etw (im Wörterbuch) nachschlagen*
to fit (sth) [fɪt]	I've got too many clothes. They don't fit in my bag.	*(zu/in etw) passen*
kind [kaɪnd]	What kind of food do you like best?	*Art*
curriculum vitae (CV) [kəˌrɪkjələm 'vi:taɪ]	*AE:* résumé	*Lebenslauf (BE)*
to apply [ə'plaɪ]	I want to apply for this job.	*sich bewerben*
education [ˌedʒu'keɪʃn]	You need a good education if you want a good job.	*(Schul-)Bildung*
primary school ['praɪməri sku:l]	Ben started primary school at the age of five.	*Grundschule*
secondary school ['sekəndri sku:l]	When he was 11, he went to secondary school.	*weiterführende Schule*
work placement ['wɜ:k pleɪsmənt]	Three students are doing work placements with us.	*Praktikum*
fluent ['flu:ənt]	His French is fluent because his mum is French.	*(bei Fremdsprachen:) fließend*
basic ['beɪsɪk]	My Italian is basic: I can't speak it well.	*hier: Grundkenntnisse*
reference ['refərəns]	We need a reference from your last employer.	*Referenz*
available [ə'veɪləbl]	Sorry, that book isn't available any longer.	*erhältlich*
on request [ɒn rɪ'kwest]	More information on request.	*auf Anfrage*
model ['mɒdl]	Use this letter as a model for your own letter.	*Muster, Vorbild*
S. 33 **event** [ɪ'vent]	He works at events like concerts and festivals.	*Veranstaltung*

tʃ	dʒ	ʃ	ʒ	θ	ð	ŋ	s	z	v	w
chips	jet	ship	garage	thing	the	ring	ice	as	very	wet

	security officer [sɪ'kjʊərəti ɒfɪsə]	The security officer checks if people are allowed into a building.	*Sicherheitsbedienstete/r*
	caterer ['keɪtərə]	The caterers are working in the kitchen.	*Lieferant von Speisen und Getränken, Caterer*
	entertainment [,entə'teɪnmənt]	He works in entertainment. He's a TV star.	*Unterhaltung, Entertainment*
	to unload [,ʌn'ləʊd]	Unload the boxes from the car and put them over there.	*abladen*
	truck [trʌk]	Put all the boxes on the truck and drive to London.	*Lastwagen*
	stage [steɪdʒ]	The rock star is on the stage.	*Bühne*
	stuff [stʌf]	Who put all this stuff here?	*Zeug, Kram*
	performer [pə'fɔːmə]	She's a performer – a singer and dancer.	*Mitwirkende/r*
	crew [kruː]	There isn't just one person, there's a whole crew of workers.	*Mannschaft*
	pie [paɪ]	This apple pie is still hot.	*Kuchen, Pastete*
	backstage [,bæk'steɪdʒ]	You might meet a rock star backstage.	*hinter der Bühne*
	pleased [pliːzd]	I'm pleased with the photo: it's good.	*froh, erfreut*
	smoothly [smuːðli]	It's all going smoothly – no problems.	*glatt*
	to solve [sɒlv]	Who can solve this problem for me?	*lösen*
	urgent ['ɜːdʒənt]	Phone the police quickly. It's urgent.	*dringend*
	pass [pɑːs]	Only people with a pass can come in.	*Pass*
	authorised ['ɔːθəraɪzd]	You aren't authorised to come in here. Stay out!	*befugt*
	valid ['vælɪd]	That ticket isn't valid: it's for yesterday.	*gültig*
S. 34	**to climb** [klaɪm]	Don't climb that tree: it's dangerous.	*klettern*
	fence [fens]	There's a fence between the two gardens.	*Zaun*
	ground [graʊnd]	The apples fell to the ground.	*Boden, Erde*
	to sign [saɪn]	Don't to forget to sign the letter with your name.	*unterschreiben, signieren*
	paramedic [,pærə'medɪk]	He's very ill. We need a paramedic.	*Sanitäter/in*
	to wave [weɪv]	Look, there's Ben. Wave to him!	*winken*
	piano [pi'ænəʊ]	I'd like to play an instrument – the piano, maybe.	*Klavier*
	organizer ['ɔːgənaɪzə]	There were too many people at the concert. The organizer made a mistake.	*Organisator/in, Veranstalter/in*
	canteen [kæn'tiːn]	You can get something to eat in the canteen.	*Kantine*
	option ['ɒpʃn]	⚠ *Aussprache!*	*Option, Wahlmöglichkeit*
	to chat [tʃæt]	Stop chatting and get on with your work!	*sich unterhalten, plaudern*

Unit 4

S. 37	**building** ['bɪldɪŋ]	There are shops, houses and other buildings in the street.	*Gebäude*
	pharmacy ['fɑːməsi]	I need some pills. Where's the nearest pharmacy?	*Apotheke*
	block of flats [blɒk əv 'flæts]	He lives on the 14th floor of a block of flats.	*Wohnblock, Mietshaus*
	concert hall ['kɒnsət hɔːl]	The Rolling Stones are playing in the concert hall.	*Konzertsaal*
	stadium ['steɪdiəm]	The football match is in the stadium.	*Stadion*

i:	ɪ	e	æ	ɑ:	ɒ	ɔ:	ʊ	u:	ʌ	ɜ:	ə
see	sit	ten	bad	arm	got	saw	put	too	cut	bird	about

underground ['ʌndəgraʊnd]	*AE:* subway	*U-Bahn (BE)*
T **platform** ['plætfɔ:m]	The train to Reading leaves from platform 1.	*Bahnsteig*
upstairs [ˌʌp'steəz]	The bedrooms are upstairs, not down here.	*oben*
noisy ['nɔɪzi]	It's so noisy here – my ears hurt!	*laut, lärmend*
ID [ˌaɪ 'di:]	Can I see your ID, please?	*Ausweis*
to borrow ['bɒrəʊ]	You can borrow my pen, but you must give it back.	*ausleihen*
reservation [ˌrezə'veɪʃn]	Crown Hotel? I'd like to make a reservation, please.	*Reservierung*
single room [ˌsɪŋgl 'ru:m]	I only need a single room: there's just me.	*Einzelzimmer*
to unscramble [ˌʌn'skræmbl]	I can't unscramble this anagram.	*entwirren*
S.38 **on the move** [ˌɒn ðə 'mu:v]	They're always on the move from town to town.	*in Bewegung, unterwegs*
courier ['kʊriə]	This letter needs to get there fast, so use a courier.	*Kurier*
to ride sth [raɪd]	I ride my bike to work.	*etw fahren*
to get around [ˌget ə'raʊnd]	She uses a moped to get around.	*herumkommen, sich fortbewegen*
tyre ['taɪə]	Mountainbikes usually have thick tyres.	*Reifen*
flat tyre [ˌflæt 'taɪə]	Oh, no! I've got a flat tyre on my bike.	*platter Reifen*
embassy ['embəsi]	He went to the embassy to get a new passport.	*Botschaft*
rickshaw ['rɪkʃɔ:]	A rickshaw is cheaper than a taxi but not as fast.	*Rikscha*
auto rickshaw ['ɔ:tə rɪkʃɔ:]	An auto rickshaw has a motor.	*Autorikscha, Motorikscha, Tuk-Tuk*
chaotic [keɪ'ɒtɪk]	There are no rules here, it's chaotic.	*chaotisch*
economic [ˌi:kə'nɒmɪk]	I like to read the economic and financial news.	*wirtschaftlich, Wirtschafts-*
activity [æk'tɪvəti]	There's a lot of activity here: it's very busy.	*Aktivität, hier: Betriebsamkeit*
guide [gaɪd]	The guide tells you about all the tourist attractions.	*Führer*
to argue ['ɑ:gju:]	Don't argue with me! I'm right and you're wrong!	*sich streiten*
to have a hard [həv ə hɑ:d 'taɪm]	I have a hard time listening to him, he's so boring.	*es schwer haben*
such (a) ['sʌtʃ ə]	I have such a lot of work to do. It will take hours.	*so, solch (eine/r/s)*
huge [hju:dʒ]	It's a huge city, much bigger than Berlin.	*riesig, groß*
stressed out [ˌstrest 'aʊt]	We're busy at work, so we're all stressed out.	*gestresst*
compliment ['kɒmplɪmənt]	Thanks for the compliment. That's nice of you!	*Kompliment*
relaxed [rɪ'lækst]	I'm feeling relaxed: everything will be OK.	*locker, entspannt*
atmosphere ['ætməsfɪə]	There's a nice, friendly atmosphere in this city.	*Atmosphäre*
rand [rænd]	⚠ *Aussprache!*	*Rand (südafrikanische Währung)*
ambassador [æm'bæsədə]	The US ambassador will meet the Queen tomorrow.	*Botschafter*
opposite ['ɒpəzɪt]	Black is the opposite of white.	*Gegenteil*
to highlight ['haɪlaɪt]	Use a pen to highlight important words.	*hervorheben*

tʃ	dʒ	ʃ	ʒ	θ	ð	ŋ	s	z	v	w
chips	jet	ship	garage	thing	the	ring	ice	as	very	wet

	organized ['ɔ:gənaɪzd]	Your desk is so organized: everything is in the right place.	*(gut) organisiert*
S.39	**column** ['kɒləm]	There are two columns in the table: left and right.	*Spalte*
	population [ˌpɒpju'leɪʃn]	The population of Germany is about 100 million.	*Bevölkerung*
	average ['ævərɪdʒ]	The average age in this class is 16.	*Durchschnitt(s-)*
	temperature ['temprətʃə]	⚠ *Aussprache!*	*Temperatur*
	billionaire [ˌbɪljə'neə]	He has $1,000,000,000, so he's a billionaire.	*Milliardär/in*
	traffic ['træfɪk]	There's a lot of traffic on the roads today.	*Verkehr*
	accident ['æksɪdənt]	Drive carefully, or you'll have an accident.	*Unfall*
	monitor ['mɒnɪtə]	The computer works, but the monitor is broken.	*Monitor*
S.40	**scientist** ['saɪəntɪst]	Albert Einstein was a scientist.	*(Natur-)Wissenschaftler/in*
	screen [skri:n]	Read the email on the screen, don't print it.	*Bildschirm*
	lens [lenz]	My glasses are broken: one lens has fallen out.	*Linse*
	contact lens ['kɒntækt lens]	I don't need glasses, I wear contact lenses.	*Kontaktlinse*
	to connect [kə'nekt]	Connect the words to make a sentence.	*verbinden*
	tiny ['taɪni]	It's very small – tiny, in fact.	*winzig, klein*
	to produce [prə'dju:s]	The farm produces chickens and eggs.	*produzieren, herstellen*
	transparent [træns'pærənt]	That white shirt is almost transparent: you can see through it.	*durchsichtig*
	semi- ['semi]	Half a circle is a semi-circle.	*halb-, semi-*
	circuit ['sɜ:kɪt]	This microchip contains an electrical circuit.	*Schaltung, Schaltkreis*
	width [wɪdθ]	The width of a hair is only about 0.025 mm.	*Breite, Stärke*
	scale [skeɪl]	I can't read the text. Please change it to a larger scale.	*Maßstab*
	vision ['vɪʒn]	He has lost most of his vision: he's almost blind.	*Sehvermögen, Blickfeld*
	to imagine [ɪ'mædʒɪn]	Imagine if we could fly.	*sich vorstellen*
	to turn [tɜ:n]	He turned and walked out of the room.	*sich drehen*
	direction [də'rekʃn]	Which direction? Left or right?	*Richtung*
	arrow ['ærəʊ]	Follow the arrows to find the station.	*Pfeil*
	subway ['sʌbweɪ]	*BE:* underground, tube	*U-Bahn (AE)*
S.41	**mile** [maɪl]	A mile is 1.609 kilometres.	*Meile*
	to turn right/left [tɜ:n 'raɪt/'left]	Turn right at the end of the street.	*rechts/links abbiegen*
T	**to miss sth** [mɪs]	We've missed it. We have to go back.	*etw verfehlen*
	to give sb directions [gɪv də'rekʃnz]	Could you give me directions to the post office, please?	*jdm den Weg zeigen/erklären*
S.42	**dish** [dɪʃ]	Spaghetti bolognaise is a favourite dish in England.	*Gericht*
	ingredient [ɪn'gri:diənt]	The ingredients include eggs, water, ...	*Zutat*
	appetizer ['æpɪtaɪzə]	I'll start with an appetizer, please.	*Appetithappen*
	main dish [ˌmeɪn 'dɪʃ]	They had fish for their main dish.	*Hauptgericht*
	side dish ['saɪd dɪʃ]	I'll have a green salad as a side dish.	*Beilage*
	dessert [dɪ'zɜ:t]	What's for dessert? Ice cream?	*Nachtisch, Dessert*
	course [kɔ:s]	It was a four-course meal.	*(Menü:) Gang*

i:	ɪ	e	æ	ɑ:	ɒ	ɔ:	ʊ	u:	ʌ	ɜ:	ə
see	sit	ten	bad	arm	got	saw	put	too	cut	bird	about

	strict [strɪkt]	Our teacher is strict: we have to work hard in class.	*streng*
	to divide [dɪ'vaɪd]	If we divide €30 between the six of us, we'll have €5 each.	*teilen, aufteilen*
	preparation [ˌprepə'reɪʃn]	Preparation before an exam is important.	*Vorbereitung*
	to deliver [dɪ'lɪvə]	Can you deliver a pizza to 13 Crown Road, please?	*liefern, anliefern*
	to prepare [prɪ'peə]	Prepare the meat before you cook it.	*(sich) vorbereiten*
	to peel [pi:l]	In Britain they peel potatoes before they cook them.	*schälen*
	to get to know sb [get tə 'nəʊ]	It has taken us five years to get to know our neighbours.	*jdn kennen lernen*
	chef [ʃef]	He works as a chef in a restaurant.	*Koch/Köchin*
	to train ['treɪn]	Josh trained as a music teacher.	*eine Ausbildung machen*
	cook [kʊk]	Five cooks work in the restaurant.	*Koch/Köchin*
	to overcook [ˌəʊvə'kʊk]	You've overcooked it: it tastes really bad!	*verbrennen*
	to throw sth away [ˌθrəʊ ə'weɪ]	Throw this old bread away, please.	*etw wegwerfen*
	crab [kræb]	Crabs live in the sea and on the beach.	*Krebs, Krabbe*
	lobster ['lɒbstə]	Lobsters live in the sea and are bigger than crabs.	*Hummer*
	shellfish ['ʃelfɪʃ]	Shellfish aren't fish, but they live in the sea.	*Schalentier*
	to time [taɪm]	You have to time it exactly.	*den richtigen Zeitpunkt abpassen*
	immediately [ɪ'mi:diətli]	Put it on the table immediately, while it's hot.	*sofort, unverzüglich*
	noodle ['nu:dl]	Noodles are popular in China and Japan.	*Nudel*
	applause [ə'plɔ:z]	After the concert there was lots of applause.	*Beifall, Applaus*
	variety [və'raɪəti]	Variety is important. You shouldn't eat the same foods all the time.	*Abwechslung*
	to prepare [prɪ'peə]	How do you prepare this fish?	*zubereiten*
	head [hed]	The head waiter tells the other waiters what to do.	*Chef-*
	instead [ɪn'sted]	There aren't any chips. Will you have salad instead?	*stattdessen*
	to represent [ˌreprɪ'zent]	The band will represent Germany in the Eurovision Song Contest.	*repräsentieren*
	to coordinate [kəʊ'ɔ:dɪneɪt]	We must coordinate our work so that we don't forget anything.	*koordinieren*
	dishwasher ['dɪʃwɒʃə]	Put those dirty plates in the dishwasher.	*Spülmaschine; Spüler/in*
	pan [pæn]	We use a lot of pans in the kitchen.	*schmecken*
S. 44	**napkin** ['næpkɪn]	*BE:* serviette	*Serviette (AE)*
	to order ['ɔ:də]	Waiter! We're ready to order, please.	*bestellen*
	rare [reə]	I like my steak rare, so don't cook it long.	*(Steak:) blutig*
	well-done [ˌwel 'dʌn]	I like my steak well-done, nice and brown.	*(Steak:) durch*
	bill [bɪl]	'Anything else, sir?' – 'Just the bill, please.'	*Rechnung*
	separate ['seprət]	Can we have three separate bills, please?	*getrennt*
	Enjoy your meal. [ɪn'dʒɔɪ jə mi:l]	Here you are, madam. Enjoy your meal.	*Guten Appetit.*

tʃ	dʒ	ʃ	ʒ	θ	ð	ŋ	s	z	v	w
chips	jet	ship	garage	thing	the	ring	ice	as	very	wet

Unit 5

S. 45	**questionnaire** [ˌkwestʃə'neə]	The hotel asks its guests to complete a questionnaire.	*Fragebogen*
	to compare [kəm'peə]	Compare the two cars: which one is faster?	*vergleichen*
	result [rɪ'zʌlt]	My exam results were very good.	*Ergebnis*
	optimistic [ˌɒptɪ'mɪstɪk]	I'm optimistic. I think everything will be OK.	*optimistisch*
	attitude ['ætɪtju:d]	You need to change your attitude to your schoolwork.	*Einstellung, Haltung*
	climate ['klaɪmət]	The climate in Europe is milder than in Africa.	*Klima*
	climate change ['klaɪmət tʃeɪndʒ]	How will climate change affect our grandchildren?	*Klimawandel*
	optimist ['ɒptɪmɪst]	⚠ *Aussprache (Betonung)!*	*Optimist/in*
	pessimist ['pesɪmɪst]	⚠ *Aussprache (Betonung)!*	*Pessimist/in*
	risk [rɪsk]	There is a risk that you might get hurt.	*Risiko*
	waterproof ['wɔ:təpru:f]	This jacket is waterproof, so I won't get wet.	*wasserdicht*
	qualification [ˌkwɒlɪfɪ'keɪʃn]	What's your qualification for this job?	*Qualifikation, Abschluss*
	sold out [ˌsəʊld 'aʊt]	The tickets for the football match are sold out.	*ausverkauft*
	There isn't any point in … [ðeər ˌɪznt eni 'pɔɪnt ɪn]	There isn't any point in doing that: it won't help.	*Es hat gar keinen Sinn …*
	hopefully ['həʊpfli]	Hopefully I'll pass my exams.	*hoffentlich*
	on sale [ɒn 'seɪl]	Are tickets for the concert still on sale?	*im Verkauf; zu kaufen*
S. 46	**essay** ['eseɪ]	Write an essay of about 200 words.	*Aufsatz*
	prediction [prɪ'dɪkʃn]	Make predictions about what will happen.	*Voraussage*
	not … either [nɒt … 'aɪðə]	Maybe I am fat, but you aren't so thin either.	*auch nicht, auch kein/e/n*
	realistic [ˌri:ə'lɪstɪk]	This portait isn't realistic: it doesn't look like you.	*realistisch, wirklichkeitsnah*
	to be addictive [bi ə'dɪktɪv]	Cigarettes are addictive .	*süchtig machen*
	illegal [ɪ'li:gl]	⚠ *Aussprache!*	*illegal*
	a shame [ə 'ʃeɪm]	It's a shame that he lost his money.	*schade, ein Jammer*
	pollution [pə'lu:ʃn]	Cars cause a lot of pollution in our cities.	*(Umwelt-)Verschmutzung*
	control [kən'trəʊl]	He lost control of his car.	*Kontrolle*
	phew! [fju:]	Phew! It's hot in here.	*puh!*
	to invent [ɪn'vent]	Charles Babbage invented the first computer.	*erfinden*
	atomic [ə'tɒmɪk]	The first atomic bomb fell on Hiroshima.	*Atom-*
	power ['paʊə]	Computers need power to run.	*hier: Energie, Strom*
	solar ['səʊlə]	Solar energy uses the sun.	*Sonnen-*
	human ['hju:mən]	The first human landed on the moon in 1969.	*Mensch*
	waste [weɪst]	Don't do it. It's a waste of time.	*Verschwendung*
	on average [ɒn 'ævərɪdʒ]	On average, women live longer than men.	*durchschnittlich*
S. 47	**speech** [spi:tʃ]	The minister gave a long and boring speech.	*Rede; gesprochene Sprache*
	imagination [ɪˌmædʒɪ'neɪʃn]	Science fiction writers need a lot of imagination.	*Phantasie*
	invention [ɪn'venʃn]	The internet may be the most important invention of the late 20th century.	*Erfindung*
	wasteful ['weɪstfl]	It's wasteful to throw things away if you can use them again.	*verschwenderisch*
	to turn out [ˌtɜ:n 'aʊt]	Everything turned out well in the end.	*ausgehen, sich herausstellen*

i:	ɪ	e	æ	ɑ:	ɒ	ɔ:	ʊ	u:	ʌ	ɜ:	ə
see	sit	ten	bad	arm	got	saw	put	too	cut	bird	about

	self-confident [ˌself ˈkɒnfɪdənt]	He's very self-confident. He thinks he can do anything.	*selbstbewusst*
	unnecessary [ʌnˈnesəsəri]	That comma is unnecessary: you don't need it.	*unnötig*
S. 48	**lifetime** [ˈlaɪftaɪm]	What exciting events will we see in our lifetime?	*Leben, Lebensdauer*
	definitely [ˈdefɪnətli]	It's definitely the best thing to do.	*bestimmt, absolut*
	to express [ɪkˈspres]	I'm only expressing my opinion.	*ausdrücken*
	view [vju:]	What's your view about it?	*Ansicht*
	to agree [əˈgri:]	I agree: you're right.	*zustimmen*
	to disagree [ˌdɪsəˈgri:]	I disagree: you're wrong.	*nicht zustimmen*
	programme [ˈprəʊgræm]	There was an interesting programme on TV.	*Sendung*
	documentary [ˌdɒkjuˈmentri]	It was a documentary about solar energy.	*Dokumentar-, Dokumentation*
	graph [grɑ:f]	This graph shows population changes in Europe.	*Diagramm*
T	**reason** [ˈri:zn]	What's the reason for the changes?	*Grund, Begründung*
S. 49	**respect** [rɪˈspekt]	I have a lot of respect for her. She's a good teacher.	*Respekt*
	dude [du:d]	Hey, dude! How's life?	*Typ, Kumpel*
	message [ˈmesɪdʒ]	Did you get my message about the party?	*Mitteilung, Botschaft*
	angry [ˈæŋgri]	Don't get angry with me: it isn't my fault.	*wütend, verärgert*
	depressing [dɪˈpresɪŋ]	This film is depressing. Please turn it off.	*deprimierend*
	thought [θɔ:t]	I write my thoughts in my diary every day.	*Gedanke*
	thought-provoking [ˈθɔ:t prəvəʊkɪŋ]	This book is very thought-provoking.	*zum Nachdenken anregend*
	pensioner [ˈpenʃənə]	Most people over 65 are pensioners.	*Rentner/in*
S. 50	**social** [ˈsəʊʃl]	I want to do a social job, with disabled people perhaps.	*sozial*
	career [kəˈrɪə]	It's a job, but is it really a career for life?	*Karriere, Beruf, Laufbahn*
	profile [ˈprəʊfaɪl]	Click here to change your profile.	*Profil*
	to note down [ˌnəʊt ˈdaʊn]	Note down the main points of the conversation.	*notieren, aufschreiben*
	caring [ˈkeərɪŋ]	He helps people because he's a caring person.	*liebevoll, sozial eingestellt*
	communication [kəˌmju:nɪˈkeɪʃn]	⚠ *Aussprache!*	*Kommunikation*
	to make a difference [meɪk ə ˈdɪfrəns]	I want to make a difference to people's lives.	*etwas bewirken*
	particularly [pəˈtɪkjələli]	AIDS is a big problem, particularly in poor countries.	*besonders*
	wealthy [ˈwelθi]	I have a bit of money, but I'm not really wealthy.	*wohlhabend, reich*
	creativity [ˌkri:eɪˈtɪvəti]	Creativity is useful in a lot of media jobs.	*Kreativität*
	ability [əˈbɪləti]	An ability to listen is important in this job.	*Fähigkeit*
	to organize [ˈɔ:gənaɪz]	You need to organize your work better.	*organisieren*
	care assistant [ˌkeər əˈsɪstənt]	The care assistant looks after the old man.	*Pflegeassistent/in*
	nursing home [ˈnɜ:sɪŋ həʊm]	There were 29 old people in the nursing home.	*Pflegeheim*
	the elderly [ði ˈeldəli]	When she was 75, she went into a home for the elderly.	*ältere Menschen*
	patient [ˈpeɪʃnt]	Be patient: I'll come as soon as I can.	*geduldig*

	duty ['dju:ti]	It's your duty to help these people.	*Aufgabe, Pflicht*
	resident ['rezɪdənt]	How many residents are there in the home?	*Bewohner*
	to feed [fi:d]	He can't feed himself, he's too ill.	*ernähren*
	trip [trɪp]	We're going on a two-week trip to Paris.	*Ausflug*
	borough ['bʌrə]	Lambeth is a borough of London.	*Bezirk*
	unemployment [ˌʌnɪm'plɔɪmənt]	Unemployment increases when people lose their jobs.	*Arbeitslosigkeit*
	serious ['sɪəriəs]	Don't laugh! It's a serious problem.	*ernst, ernsthaft*
	responsible [rɪ'spɒnsəbl]	She's a responsible person. She always does a good job.	*verantwortungsbewusst*
	carry out [ˌkæri 'aʊt]	He carries out his tasks without complaining.	*durchführen*
	to monitor ['mɒnɪtə]	We need to monitor the situation in case it changes.	*überwachen, kontrollieren*
	welfare ['welfeə]	I'm only interested in your welfare.	*Wohl*
	charity ['tʃærəti]	The Red Cross and Oxfam are large charities.	*gemeinnützige Organisation*
	fundraiser ['fʌndreɪzə]	I'm a fundraiser for Greenpeace.	*Spendensammler/in*
	to be responsible for sth [bi rɪ'spɒnsəbl fə]	The manager is responsible for the people in the office.	*für etw zuständig sein, für etw verantwortlich sein*
	to raise money [reɪz 'mʌni]	They raise money for poor people.	*Geld aufbringen,* hier: *sammeln*
	imaginative [ɪ'mædʒɪnətɪv]	That's a very imaginative idea. How did you think of it?	*phantasievoll, kreativ*
	to create [kri'eɪt]	We must create more jobs for young people.	*schaffen*
	income ['ɪnkʌm]	He lives on a low income: €20 a day.	*Einkommen*
	to assist [ə'sɪst]	How can we assist her to find a home?	*helfen, mithelfen, assistieren*
	press [pres]	I don't believe everything I read in the press.	*Presse*
	to attract [ə'trækt]	We need to attract the right people.	*anlocken, anziehen*
	donor ['dəʊnə]	Donors gave $200,000 to the victims.	*Spender/in*
	collection [kə'lekʃn]	The collection is for the Red Cross.	*Sammlung*
	to recruit [rɪ'kru:t]	The boss wants to recruit more workers.	*einstellen*
	to manage ['mænɪdʒ]	She manages 12 people.	*leiten, verwalten*
S. 51	**fortune teller** ['fɔ:tʃu:n telə]	She asked a fortune teller about her future.	*Wahrsager/in*
S. 52	**personnel officer** [ˌpɜ:sə'nel ɒfɪsə]	The personnel officer gave me an interview.	*Personalreferent/in, Personalchef/in*
	to show sb around [ˌʃəʊ ə'raʊnd]	First we'll show you around the company.	*jdn herumführen*
	employee [ɪm'plɔɪi:]	The company has 50 employees.	*Angestellte/r*
	workstation ['wɜ:k steɪʃn]	This is your new workstation. You've got a desk, a chair and a computer.	*Arbeitsplatz*
	senior ['si:niə]	Senior managers get paid more than the rest of us.	*leitende/r (Angestellte/r)*
T	**to introduce sb to sb** [ˌɪntrə'dju:s]	Let me introduce you: Lucy Jamieson – Ben Elton.	*jdn jdm vorstellen*
T	**to look after sb** [lʊk 'ɑ:ftə]	Can you look after the baby for me?	*sich um jdn kümmern*
T	**to settle in** ['setl ɪn]	It all seems strange now, but you'll soon settle in.	*sich eingewöhnen*
T	**ancient** ['eɪnʃənt]	I'm only 55. I'm not ancient!	*alt, uralt*
T	**managing director** [ˌmænɪdʒɪŋ də'rektə]	The managing director runs the company.	*Geschäftsführer/in*

i:	ɪ	e	æ	ɑ:	ɒ	ɔ:	ʊ	u:	ʌ	ɜ:	ə
see	sit	ten	bad	arm	got	saw	put	too	cut	bird	about

	experienced [ɪk'spɪəriənst]	Are you experienced, or is this your first job?	*erfahren*

Unit 6

S. 53	**network** ['netwɜːk]	The internet is a computer network.	*Netzwerk*
	face-to-face [ˌfeɪs tə 'feɪs]	Don't phone him. Talk to him face-to-face.	*persönlich*
	text message ['tekst mesɪdʒ]	Use your phone to send her a text message.	*SMS*
	invitation [ˌɪnvɪ'teɪʃn]	Did you get an invitation to the party?	*Einladung*
	to hurt [hɜːt]	Ouch! I've hurt my head!	*verletzen*
	feeling ['fiːlɪŋ]	He lost all the feeling in his left arm.	*Gefühl*
	mail-order company [meɪl ˌɔːdə 'kʌmpəni]	I bought this jacket from a mail-order company.	*Versandhandel*
S. 54	**confession** [kən'feʃn]	I have a confession to make: I did it.	*Geständnis*
	embarrassment [ɪm'bærəsmənt]	You can see his embarrassment. He's red in the face.	*Verlegenheit, Peinlichkeit, Ärgernis*
	to embarrass sb [ɪm'bærəs]	Mum! Don't embarrass me in front of my girlfriend!	*jdm peinlich sein, jdn bloßstellen*
	rude [ruːd]	≠ polite	*unverschämt, unhöflich*
	comment ['kɒment]	The teacher wrote a comment in my book.	*Bemerkung, Kommentar*
	to stick [stɪk]	Stick the picture on the wall, so we can all see it.	*kleben*
	printout ['prɪntaʊt]	I need a printout of that email, please.	*Ausdruck*
	locker ['lɒkə]	Swimmers can leave their clothes in the lockers.	*Spind*
	to sweep [swiːp]	Please sweep the floor. It's dirty.	*kehren, putzen*
	employer [ɪm'plɔɪə]	He's my employer. I work for him.	*Arbeitgeber/in*
	shy [ʃaɪ]	Don't be shy! Come over here and say hello.	*schüchtern*
	to receive [rɪ'siːv]	I've just received this fax from Belinda Jamieson.	*erhalten*
	hoax [həʊks]	It isn't real, it's a hoax.	*Streich, Jux*
	to be embarrassed [bi ɪm'bærəst]	When they laughed at him, he was embarrassed.	*sich schämen*
	to delete [dɪ'liːt]	Delete these old emails. We don't need them.	*löschen*
	occasionally [ə'keɪʒnəli]	I don't eat chips often, but occasionally I like them.	*gelegentlich, hin und wieder*
	particular [pə'tɪkjələ]	Are you looking for a particular style of shirt, sir?	*besondere/r/s, spezielle/r/s*
	complaint [kəm'pleɪnt]	I want to make a complaint about the bad food.	*Beschwerde, Reklamation*
	to forward ['fɔːwəd]	I want to see that email. Please forward it to me.	*weiterleiten*
	department [dɪ'pɑːtmənt]	There are five departments in the company.	*Abteilung*
	to drive sb crazy [draɪv 'kreɪzi]	Stop shouting, kids! You're driving me crazy.	*jdn in den Wahnsinn treiben*
	accidentally [ˌæksɪ'dentəli]	We weren't fighting: I hit him accidentally.	*versehentlich, zufällig*
	to complain [kəm'pleɪn]	If you don't like the food, complain to the chef.	*sich beschweren*
	to apologize [ə'pɒlədʒaɪz]	Don't apologize, it's OK.	*sich entschuldigen*
S. 55	**by mistake** [baɪ mɪ'steɪk]	I sent it to the wrong person by mistake.	*irrtümlich*

tʃ	dʒ	ʃ	ʒ	θ	ð	ŋ	s	z	v	w
chips	jet	ship	garage	thing	the	ring	ice	as	very	wet

	order ['ɔ:də]	Put these letters in the right order to make a word.	*Reihenfolge*
	suitable ['su:təbl]	Jeans aren't suitable for the office, Ms Smith.	*passend*
	to recognize ['rekəgnaɪz]	Oh, it's you! I didn't recognize you.	*erkennen, wiedererkennen*
	noticeboard ['nəʊtɪsbɔ:d]	He put a photo of me on the school noticeboard.	*Pinnwand*
	to brainstorm ['breɪnstɔ:m]	Let's try to brainstorm some good ideas.	*Ideen sammeln*
	to criticize ['krɪtɪsaɪz]	Don't criticize me! You're the one who's wrong.	*kritisieren*
	unfortunately [ʌn'fɔ:tʃənətli]	Unfortunately the weather was bad.	*leider, unglücklicherweise*
S. 56	**behaviour** [bɪ'heɪvjə]	Your behaviour in class is becoming a problem.	*Verhalten, Benehmen*
	item ['aɪtəm]	Have you paid for all the items in your bag?	*Artikel, Gegenstand, Ding*
	capital letter ['kæpɪtl letə]	Names always begin with a capital letter.	*Großbuchstabe*
	connection [kə'nekʃn]	I don't see the connection between these two things.	*Verbindung*
	spell checker ['spel tʃekə]	Use a spell checker before you send the email.	*Rechtschreibüberprüfung*
	upset [ˌʌp'set]	Don't get upset! Everybody makes mistakes.	*aufgeregt, verärgert*
	to offend [ə'fend]	You've offended her. You must say sorry.	*beleidigen*
	sense [sens]	What's the sense in standing here in the rain?	*Sinn*
	to make sense [meɪk 'sens]	It doesn't make sense to me. What's its meaning?	*Sinn haben/ergeben, einleuchten*
	to cool down [ˌku:l 'daʊn]	Stop shouting! Cool down, then talk to each other quietly about it.	*sich beruhigen*
	informal [ɪn'fɔ:ml]	It's just an informal conversation, not an interview.	*informell*
	tone [təʊn]	I don't like the tone of his email.	*Ton*
	voice [vɔɪs]	Belinda has a very loud voice.	*Stimme*
	to overdo [ˌəʊvə'du:]	That's enough: don't overdo it.	*übertreiben*
	to respect [rɪ'spekt]	You must respect your teachers.	*achten, respektieren*
	speed [spi:d]	'What speed are we doing?' – '80 kilometres an hour.'	*Geschwindigkeit*
	to break [breɪk]	Don't break the rules, or you're out.	*brechen*
	loser ['lu:zə]	In sport there's usually a winner and a loser.	*Verlierer/in*
	Get a life! [ˌget ə 'laɪf]	You're so boring. Get a life!	*Werd' endlich erwachsen!*
	Accounts [ə'kaʊnts]	Amy is good with numbers. She'll be useful in Accounts.	*Buchhaltung*
	criticism ['krɪtɪsɪzəm]	I accept your criticism: I was wrong.	*Kritik*
	to quit [kwɪt]	I don't like this job. I quit!	*aufhören, aussteigen*
	recipient [rɪ'sɪpiənt]	She sent the same email to 40 recipients.	*Empfänger/in*
S. 57	**to network** ['netwɜ:k]	He only goes to parties to network with 'important' people.	*vernetzen, Kontakte knüpfen*
	to keep in touch [ˌki:p ɪn 'tʌtʃ]	Keep in touch with us when you're in the USA.	*in Kontakt bleiben*
	explanation [ˌeksplə'neɪʃn]	What's your explanation for this mistake, Ben?	*Erklärung, Erläuterung*
	crash course ['kræʃ kɔ:s]	I need to learn French quickly, so I'll do a crash course.	*Schnellkurs*
	potential [pə'tenʃl]	⚠ *Aussprache!*	*Potential*
	visible ['vɪzəbl]	It isn't visible. I can't see it at all.	*sichtbar*

	excellent ['eksələnt]	≈ very good	*hervorragend*
	feature ['fi:tʃə]	What are the main features of this software?	*Merkmal, Eigenschaft*
S.58	**contact** ['kɒntækt]	Do you have any business contacts?	*hier: Kontaktperson*
	gear [gɪə]	We need a lot of gear for the camping trip.	*Ausrüstung*
	credit ['kredɪt]	I have € 2500 credit on my Visa card.	*Guthaben*
	clothing ['kləʊðɪŋ]	≈ clothes	*Kleidung*
	to sign up [ˌsaɪn 'ʌp]	If you want to use Facebook, you need to sign up.	*sich anmelden*
	to add [æd]	How can I add photos to my Facebook page?	*hinzufügen*
	seller ['selə]	Learn how to make money as an eBay seller.	*Verkäufer/in*
	to attach [ə'tætʃ]	I forgot to attach the photos to the email.	*beifügen, anhängen*
	file [faɪl]	There are 2,500,000 files on your computer.	*Datei*
	to look forward to sth [ˌlʊk 'fɔ:wəd tə]	I'm looking forward to the party next week.	*sich auf etw freuen*
S.59	**to tick off** [ˌtɪk 'ɒf]	Tick off the things on the list as you pack them.	*abhaken*
	voicemail ['vɔɪsmeɪl]	Please leave a message on my voicemail.	*Anrufbeantworter, Voicemail*
	to update [ˌʌp'deɪt]	Don't forget to update the letter before you send it.	*aktualisieren, auf den neusten Stand bringen*
	budget ['bʌdʒɪt]	There's only $500 left in the budget for this project.	*Budget, Etat, Haushalt*
	to mark [mɑ:k]	Mark the message 'important' if you want everyone to read it.	*kennzeichnen*
	to keep on top of things [ki:p ɒn ˌtɒp əv 'θɪŋz]	She's a good worker: she always keeps on top of things.	*den Überblick haben/ behalten*
S.60	**to break into** ['breɪk ɪntə]	Police? Someone is trying to break into my flat.	*einbrechen in*
	to replace [rɪ'pleɪs]	If you lose your ticket, we can't replace it.	*ersetzen, austauschen*
	to advise [əd'vaɪz]	What do you advise me to do?	*beraten, raten*
	art [ɑ:t]	I'm good at art. I draw good pictures.	*Kunst; Grafik, Illustration*
	fault [fɔ:lt]	There's something wrong with this phone. It must have a fault.	*Fehler, Defekt*
	support [sə'pɔ:t]	With support, blind people can lead a happy life.	*Unterstützung, Betreuung*
	after-sales support [ˌɑ:ftə seɪlz sə'pɔ:t]	If you have a problem, phone after-sales support.	*Nachverkaufsunterstützung, Support*
	common ['kɒmən]	Smith is a common surname: many people have it.	*häufig, weit verbreitet*
	insurance [ɪn'ʃʊərəns]	You need insurance in case you lose your things.	*Versicherung*
	properly ['prɒpəli]	That's not good enough. Do it properly!	*richtig*
	to service ['sɜ:vɪs]	I work in a garage: I service cars.	*warten*
	to combine [kəm'baɪn]	He combined sport and business by becoming a football manager.	*kombinieren*
	to develop [dɪ'veləp]	It took us three years to develop this software.	*entwickeln*

Unit 7

S.61	**job-seeker** ['dʒɒbsiːkə]	Are you a job-seeker, or are you still at school?	*Arbeitssuchende/r*
	score [skɔː]	What was your score in the test?	*Ergebnis, Punktestand*
	carefully ['keəfəli]	Read the text carefully so you don't miss anything.	*hier: aufmerksam*
	to sort through sth ['sɔːt θruː]	Sort through these emails to find the important ones.	*etw durchsehen*
	to succeed [sək'siːd]	If you don't try, you won't succeed.	*gelingen, Erfolg haben*
	to fail [feɪl]	They lost all their money when the business failed.	*versagen, scheitern*
	to work out [ˌwɜːk 'aʊt]	Can you work out the answer to the question?	*herausfinden*
	power tool ['paʊə tuːl]	Many power tools have batteries these days.	*Elektrowerkzeug*
	reaction [ri'ækʃn]	What was his reaction to the news?	*Reaktion*
	drawing ['drɔːɪŋ]	She's good at drawing. That picture really looks like me, doesn't it?	*Zeichnen*
	painting ['peɪntɪŋ]	Do you think Picasso was good at painting? This picture looks silly to me.	*Malen*
	musical instrument [ˌmjuːzɪkl 'ɪnstrəmənt]	A piano is a musical instrument.	*Musikinstrument*
	to go together (well) [gəʊ təˌgeðə 'wel]	Do you think that red and green go together well?	*(gut) zueinander passen*
	material [mə'tɪəriəl]	What material is this wall made of?	*Material*
	fabric ['fæbrɪk]	She bought some fabric to make a dress.	*Stoff, Gewebe*
	construction [kən'strʌkʃn]	I like building things, so I want to work in construction.	*Baugewerbe*
	manufacturing [ˌmænju'fæktʃərɪŋ]	Bosch and VW are both manufacturing companies.	*Fertigung(sindustrie)*
	transport ['trænspɔːt]	The transport minister wants to build more roads.	*Verkehrswesen*
	performing arts [pə'fɔːmɪŋ 'ɑːts]	I want to be an actor: I've always loved the performing arts.	*darstellende Künste*
S.62	**classmate** ['klɑːsmeɪt]	Sue and her classmates will have exams soon.	*Klassenkamerad/in*
	traineeship [treɪ'niːʃɪp]	After college I want to do a traineeship in industry.	*Ausbildungsplatz*
	to line sth up [ˌlaɪn 'ʌp]	My dad is going to line up a job for me.	*etw organisieren*
	sales assistant ['seɪlz əsɪstənt]	≈ shop assistant	*Verkäufer/in*
	part-time [ˌpɑːt'taɪm]	I only work part-time: 20 hours a week.	*Teilzeit-*
	to take sb on [ˌteɪk 'ɒn]	He needs a job. Will you take him on?	*jdn einstellen*
	management ['mænɪdʒmənt]	The management wants us to work more hours.	*Geschäftsführung, Verwaltung, Management*
	therapy ['θerəpi]	She has tried different therapies for her health problems.	*Therapie*
	after all [ˌɑːftər 'ɔːl]	Don't be angry with her. After all, she's only a child.	*doch*
	to make sth up [ˌmeɪk 'ʌp]	It isn't true. You made it up!	*etw erfinden, sich etw ausdenken*
	to escape [ɪ'skeɪp]	They ran inside to escape from the rain.	*entkommen, entfliehen*
	nasty ['nɑːsti]	I'm not stupid: that was a nasty thing to say.	*gemein*

iː	ɪ	e	æ	ɑː	ɒ	ɔː	ʊ	uː	ʌ	ɜː	ə
see	sit	ten	bad	arm	got	saw	put	too	cut	bird	about

	mystery shopper [ˌmɪstri ˈʃɒpə]	Is that man a normal customer, or a mystery shopper?	*Testkäufer/in*
	to employ [ɪmˈplɔɪ]	Our business employs 2,500 people.	*beschäftigen, einstellen*
	to evaluate [ɪˈvæljueɪt]	'How do you evaluate the situation?' – 'It looks bad.'	*bewerten, beurteilen*
	satisfying [ˈsætɪsfaɪɪŋ]	I find my job satisfying: it's interesting and fun.	*befriedigend, zufriedenstellend*
	varied [ˈveərid]	The plants in the garden are varied, not all the same.	*abwechslungsreich*
S.63	**speech bubble** [ˈspiːtʃ bʌbl]	Read the speech bubbles in the cartoon.	*Sprechblase*
	school leaver [ˈskuːl liːvə]	Many school leavers will soon start their first job.	*Schulabgänger/in*
	position [pəˈzɪʃn]	We think you're the best person for this position.	*Stelle, Position*
	necessary [ˈnesəsəri]	I don't enjoy doing it, but it's necessary.	*nötig, notwendig*
	awful [ˈɔːfl]	The film wasn't just bad, it was awful.	*schrecklich, fürchterlich*
S.64	**enthusiastic** [ɪnˌθjuːziˈæstɪk]	'Oh, no! Chips again.' – 'Can't you be more enthusiastic?'	*begeistert*
T	**relevant** [ˈreləvənt]	I don't see how that is relevant here. Please explain.	*wichtig, relevant*
	interview [ˈɪntəvjuː]	I have to go for an interview on Tuesday.	*Vorstellungsgespräch*
	to rush into doing sth [ˌrʌʃ ɪntə ˈduːɪŋ]	Don't rush into it. Take your time.	*etw überstürzt tun*
	to be keen on sth [bi ˈkiːn ɒn]	I'm not keen on bananas. I prefer apples.	*auf etw versessen sein*
	to be a good match for sth [bi ə ˌgʊd ˈmætʃ fə]	This job is a good match for your interests.	*gut zu etw passen*
	challenging [ˈtʃælɪndʒɪŋ]	It's a challenging job: it won't be easy.	*fordernd, anspruchsvoll*
	responsibility [rɪˌspɒnsəˈbɪləti]	It's your responsibility to get there on time.	*Verantwortung*
	pay [peɪ]	Your pay will be €600 a week.	*Lohn, Gehalt*
	to lead [liːd]	This path doesn't lead anywhere. It just stops.	*führen*
	knowledge [ˈnɒlɪdʒ]	I don't have much knowledge of computers.	*Wissen, Kenntnisse*
	technique [tekˈniːk]	This is a good technique for answering difficult questions.	*Methode, Technik*
	promotion [prəˈməʊʃn]	We're going to give you a promotion.	*Beförderung, Aufstieg*
	decision [dɪˈsɪʒn]	Yes or no? It's your decision.	*Entscheidung, Entschluss*
S.65	**apprenticeship** [əˈprentɪʃɪp]	Your apprenticeship will last three years.	*Ausbildung(splatz)*
	automated [ˈɔːtəmeɪtɪd]	It's all automated. No people are needed.	*automatisiert*
	to predict [prɪˈdɪkt]	Can you predict what will happen next?	*voraussagen, vorhersehen*
	certain [ˈsɜːtn]	You may be right, but I'm not certain.	*sicher*
	complex [ˈkɒmpleks]	This is a complex problem: there are a lot of things to think about.	*komplex*
	button [ˈbʌtn]	Press this button to start the machine.	*Knopf*
	numerical [njuːˈmerɪkl]	It's a numerical code: there are no letters in it.	*numerisch, digital*
	vehicle [ˈviːəkl]	Cars, trains and motorbikes are vehicles.	*Fahrzeug*
	spacecraft [ˈspeɪskrɑːft]	The astronauts will travel to Mars in this spacecraft.	*Raumschiff*
	machinist [məˈʃiːnɪst]	A machinist uses a machine to make metal parts.	*Maschinist/in*
	to operate [ˈɒpəreɪt]	How do I operate this machine?	*bedienen*

tʃ	dʒ	ʃ	ʒ	θ	ð	ŋ	s	z	v	w
chips	jet	ship	garage	thing	the	ring	ice	as	very	wet

	machinery [mə'ʃi:nəri]	JCB and Liebherr make earth-moving machinery.	*Maschinen*
	engineer [ˌendʒɪ'nɪə]	These engineers designed the bridge.	*Ingenieur/in*
	car manufacturing [ˌkɑ: mænju'fæktʃərɪŋ]	Ford is a car manufacturing company.	*Automobilbau*
	to install [ɪn'stɔ:l]	Do you want me to install the software on this computer?	*installieren*
	range [reɪndʒ]	There is a range of sports magazines in the shop.	*Reihe, Auswahl*
	power generation ['paʊə dʒenəreɪʃn]	Wind and solar are 'clean, green' forms of power generation.	*Stromerzeugung*
	lighting ['laɪtɪŋ]	It's too dark. We need better lighting.	*Beleuchtung*
	heating ['hi:tɪŋ]	It's cold in here. Maybe the heating isn't working.	*Heizung*
	to require [rɪ'kwaɪə]	This software requires Windows 7 or later.	*erfordern, brauchen*
	unlikely [ʌn'laɪkli]	It may happen, but it's unlikely.	*unwahrscheinlich*
	out of date [ˌaʊt əv 'deɪt]	The software is out of date. You need the new version.	*überholt, veraltet*
S.66	**job interview** ['dʒɒb ɪntəvju:]	The company asked him to come for a job interview.	*Vorstellungsgespräch*
	to run out of time [ˌrʌn aʊt əf 'taɪm]	We've run out of time: we have to go now.	*keine Zeit mehr haben*
	to get a haircut [ˌget ə 'heəkʌt]	Your hair is too long. Get a haircut.	*sich die Haare schneiden lassen*
	location [ləʊ'keɪʃn]	'What's your location?' – 'I'm at the railway station.'	*Ort, Stelle*
S.67	**to sink** [sɪŋk]	The boat sank slowly to the bottom of the sea.	*sinken, untergehen*
	desert island [ˌdezət 'aɪlənd]	Nobody lives here: it's a desert island.	*einsame Insel*
	shelter ['ʃeltə]	We must find some shelter from the rain.	*Unterkunft*
	fishing ['fɪʃɪŋ]	He likes fishing but he doesn't eat fish.	*Angeln*
	to be useless at doing sth [bi 'ju:sləs ət]	I'm useless at doing this. Why don't you do it?	*zu etw nicht zu gebrauchen sein*
	chocolate bar ['tʃɒklət bɑ:]	If you're hungry, have a chocolate bar.	*Schokoriegel*
F	**cabin** ['kæbɪn]	I'm cold out here on deck. Can I go in the cabin?	*Kabine*
	panel ['pænl]	The panel will now ask you some questions.	*Gremium*
	to suggest [sə'dʒest]	I suggest that we have coffee now.	*vorschlagen*
	to reject [rɪ'dʒekt]	They rejected the idea because it was silly.	*ablehnen*
	suggestion [sə'dʒestʃən]	What do we do now? Any suggestions?	*Vorschlag*
	to back sth up [ˌbæk 'ʌp]	Can you back that up with some facts?	*etw untermauern, rechtfertigen, begründen*

Unit 8

S.69	**youth** [ju:θ]	There's nothing wrong with modern youth: we're just young people.	*Jugend, Jugendlicher*
	crime [kraɪm]	The police say crime is worse than ever.	*Kriminalität; Verbrechen, Straftat*
	shoplifting ['ʃɒplɪftɪŋ]	Shoplifting costs this shop €1000 every week.	*Ladendiebstahl*
	to steal [sti:l]	Help! He's stealing my car!	*stehlen*
	possession [pə'zeʃn]	Possession of illegal drugs is very serious.	*Besitz*
	vandalism ['vændəlɪzəm]	Is graffiti vandalism or art?	*Vandalismus*

i:	ɪ	e	æ	ɑ:	ɒ	ɔ:	ʊ	u:	ʌ	ɜ:	ə
see	sit	ten	bad	arm	got	saw	put	too	cut	bird	about

	drunk driving [ˌdrʌŋk 'draɪvɪŋ]	Drunk driving is dangerous. Please take a taxi home from the party.	*Alkohol am Steuer*
	telephone harassment [ˌtelɪfəʊn 'hærəsmənt]	Stop calling me! This is telephone harrassment.	*Telefonterror*
	character assassination ['kærəktər əsæsɪneɪʃn]	This newspaper story is character assassination, not news.	*Rufmord*
	assault [ə'sɔ:lt]	During the assault, three boys hit him on the head.	*Körperverletzung; Angriff, Überfall*
	substance ['sʌbstəns]	Cannabis is an illegal substance in most countries.	*Substanz, Stoff*
	lie [laɪ]	That's a lie! It isn't true.	*Lüge*
	to insult [ɪn'sʌlt]	'You're stupid!' – 'Don't insult me!'	*beleidigen, beschimpfen*
	beer [bɪə]	'Would you like a beer?' – 'No thanks, I don't drink alcohol.'	*Bier*
	wheel [wi:l]	A bicycle has two wheels.	*Rad,* hier: *Lenkrad*
	property ['prɒpəti]	That bag isn't your property, it's mine.	*Eigentum*
	quotation [kwəʊ'teɪʃn]	'Is that really what he said?' – 'Yes. It's a direct quotation.'	*Zitat*
	to rob [rɒb]	The two boys robbed the old lady and took her money.	*rauben, berauben, ausrauben*
	guilty ['gɪlti]	Don't lie. You did it. We know you're guilty.	*schuldig*
	innocent ['ɪnəsnt]	I didn't do it. I'm innocent.	*unschuldig*
	to commit (a crime) [kəˌmɪt ə 'kraɪm]	They committed 20 crimes before the police found them.	*(eine Straftat) begehen*
	honest ['ɒnɪst]	I never lie. I'm very honest.	*ehrlich*
	victim ['vɪktɪm]	The victim had to go to hospital.	*Opfer*
	witness ['wɪtnəs]	She saw it all. She's a witness.	*Zeuge/Zeugin*
	bystander ['baɪstændə]	I didn't do anything. I was just a bystander.	*Zuschauer/in*
	judge [dʒʌdʒ]	The judge listened to both sides.	*Richter/in*
	probation [prə'beɪʃn]	You'll get two years on probation.	*Bewährung*
	probation officer [prə'beɪʃn ɒfɪsə]	He has to see a probation officer every day.	*Bewährungshelfer/in*
	prison ['prɪzn]	The judge sent him to prison for three months.	*Gefängnis*
	prison officer ['prɪzn ɒfɪsə]	The prison officer talked with the criminals.	*Gefängniswärter/in*
S.70	**bullying** ['bʊliɪŋ]	Many students have problems with bullying.	*Mobben, Tyrannisieren*
	bully ['bʊli]	Leave him alone, you bully!	*Mobber/in, Tyrann/in*
	to target sb ['tɑ:gɪt]	They only target kids who are smaller than them.	*auf jdn zielen, es auf jdn absehen*
	minority [maɪ'nɒrəti]	Only a minority of young women are happy with how they look.	*Minderheit*
	to involve [ɪn'vɒlv]	This doesn't involve you. Keep out of it!	*betreffen*
	biography [baɪ'ɒgrəfi]	⚠ *Aussprache!*	*Biografie*
	except for [ɪk'sept fə]	Why so sad? Except for you, everyone is happy.	*außer*
	suicide ['su:ɪsaɪd]	He's dead. The police say it was suicide, not murder.	*Selbstmord*
	to act [ækt]	Don't act like an idiot!	*sich benehmen, sich verhalten*
	gay [geɪ]	Yes, I'm gay. Do you have a problem with that?	*schwul*
	to call sb names [ˌkɔ:l 'neɪmz]	If you call her names, she'll probably hit you.	*jdn beleidigen, jdn beschimpfen*

tʃ	dʒ	ʃ	ʒ	θ	ð	ŋ	s	z	v	w
chips	jet	ship	garage	thing	the	ring	ice	as	very	wet

	to repeat [rɪ'pi:t]	Could you repeat that? I didn't hear you.	*wiederholen*
	to treat sb tri:t]	You should treat your girlfriend better. She's nice.	*jdn behandeln*
	to get in trouble [ˌget ɪn 'trʌbl]	Careful! You'll get in trouble with the teacher.	*Ärger bekommen, in Schwierigkeiten geraten*
	to hurt sb [hɜ:t]	Ouch! You hurt me!	*jdm wehtun, jdn verletzen*
	Sincerely yours, [sɪn'sɪəli jɔ:z]	*BE:* Yours sincerely,	*Mit freundlichen Grüßen (AE)*
S. 71	**to ignore** [ɪg'nɔ:]	Just ignore him and maybe he'll be quiet.	*ignorieren, nicht beachten*
	depressed [dɪ'prest]	You look depressed. Is something wrong?	*niedergeschlagen, deprimiert*
S. 72	**crime scene** ['kraɪm si:n]	The police found the knife at the crime scene.	*Tatort*
T	**Goodness!** ['gʊdnəs]	Goodness! Is it really that late?	*Meine Güte!*
	to hurry up [ˌhʌri 'ʌp]	Hurry up! We'll miss the film.	*sich beeilen*
	the cops [ðə 'kɒps]	Quick, run. They've called the cops!	*die Bullen*
	light [laɪt]	He was wearing a light blue jacket.	*hell*
	skin [skɪn]	'White' people's skin isn't actually white.	*Haut*
	curly ['kɜ:li]	You used to have curly hair. Now it's straight.	*lockig*
	bald [bɔ:ld]	My dad had lots of hair, but now he's bald.	*kahl, glatzköpfig*
F	**nose** [nəʊz]	Too much alcohol gives you a red nose.	*Nase*
	corpulent ['kɔ:pjələnt]	She's corpulent – fat, in fact.	*korpulent*
	bank robber ['bæŋk rɒbə]	We're bank robbers: give us the money!	*Bankräuber/in*
T	**athletic** [æθ'letɪk]	She's quite athletic: she can run very fast.	*sportlich*
	muscle ['mʌsl]	He's strong. Look at those muscles!	*Muskel(n)*
	leather ['leðə]	Leather jackets are usually expensive.	*Leder*
	mask [mɑ:sk]	I didn't see his face. He wore a mask, you see.	*Maske*
S. 73	**number plate** ['nʌmbə pleɪt]	The car had a French number plate.	*Nummernschild*
	broken ['brəʊkən]	My foot is broken, so I can't run.	*gebrochen, kaputt*
S. 74	**to pay** [peɪ]	It always pays to work hard.	*sich auszahlen*
	tap [tæp]	What's wrong with the tap? No water is coming out.	*Wasserhahn*
	to break [breɪk]	Cheap tools always break after a while.	*kaputtgehen*
	DIY store [ˌdi: aɪ 'waɪ stɔ:]	Dad's going to the DIY store to buy a hammer.	*Baumarkt*
	detective [dɪ'tektɪv]	The store detective saw her take the clothes without paying.	*Detektiv*
	to attack [ə'tæk]	A man attacked him with a knife.	*angreifen*
	compensation [ˌkɒmpən'seɪʃn]	I want €10,000 compensation for this mistake!	*Entschädigung, Schadenersatz*
	fine [faɪn]	He must pay a €200 fine.	*Geldstrafe*
	to shoplift ['ʃɒplɪft]	If you shoplift, we will call the police.	*Ladendiebstahl begehen*
	thief [θi:f]	Stop the thief! He took my money!	*Dieb/in*
	greedy ['gri:di]	You don't need that much, you're just greedy.	*gierig, habgierig*
S. 75	**glasses** ['glɑ:sɪz]	I can't read this without my glasses.	*Brille*
	to rewrite [ˌri:'raɪt]	Rewrite this sentence using a verb from the box.	*umformulieren*
S. 76	**trial** ['traɪəl]	The murder trial lasted for six weeks.	*Gerichtsverhandlung, Prozess*
	fairy tale ['feəri teɪl]	Little Emma likes to hear a fairy tale when she goes to bed.	*Märchen*

iː	ɪ	e	æ	ɑː	ɒ	ɔː	ʊ	uː	ʌ	ɜː	ə
see	sit	ten	bad	arm	got	saw	put	too	cut	bird	about

	to pretend [prɪ'tend]	I know you heard me. Don't pretend that you didn't.	*vorgeben, sich ausgeben als*
	to survive [sə'vaɪv]	She's very sick, but she will survive.	*überleben*
	woodsman ['wʊdzmən]	A woodsman cuts down trees.	*Waldarbeiter*
	to cut open [ˌkʌt 'əʊpən]	He cut open the bag to get the money.	*aufschneiden*
	belly ['beli]	My belly hurts after all that food.	*Bauch*
	to pull sb/sth out [ˌpʊl 'aʊt]	He was nearly dead when they pulled him out of the sea.	*jdn/etw herausziehen*
	stone [stəʊn]	They threw stones at the police car.	*Stein*
	to sew [səʊ]	She can sew well. She makes her own dresses.	*nähen*
	to sew sth up [ˌsəʊ 'ʌp]	I can't wear these trousers until I sew them up.	*etw zunähen*
	according to [ə'kɔːdɪŋ tə]	According to Bill, the story isn't true.	*nach, gemäß, zufolge*
	to let sb out [ˌlet 'aʊt]	Hey! Let me out of this room!	*hier: jdn entlassen*
	Little Red Riding-Hood [ˌlɪtl red 'raɪdɪŋ hʊd]	Rotkäppchen	
	jury ['dʒʊəri]	There were 12 men and women in the jury.	*die Geschworenen*
	member of the jury [ˌmembər əv ðə 'dʒʊəri]	The press can't talk to members of the jury.	*Geschworene/r*
	court [kɔːt]	We'll find out in court who is telling the truth.	*Gericht*
	vote [vəʊt]	Let's have a vote. Who's for the idea and who's against it?	*Abstimmung*
	either ... or [ˌaɪðə ... 'ɔː]	We can play either football or hockey.	*entweder ... oder*
	to attempt [ə'tempt]	Don't attempt to run. You won't get far.	*versuchen*
	punishment ['pʌnɪʃmənt]	Your punishment is to go to prison for 12 years.	*Bestrafung, Strafe*
	dance of joy [ˌdɑːns əv 'dʒɔɪ]	He was so happy, he did a dance of joy.	*Freudentanz*
	traumatized ['trɔːmətaɪzd]	After the awful class, the teacher felt traumatized.	*traumatisiert*
	enormous [ɪ'nɔːməs]	The dog is enormous. It's as big as a small horse.	*enorm*
	trouble ['trʌbl]	There will be trouble when Mum hears about this!	*Ärger, Schwierigkeiten*
	to examine [ɪg'zæmɪn]	The doctor has examined her. She's OK.	*untersuchen*
	to perform [pə'fɔːm]	We're going to perform a musical.	*aufführen, spielen*

Unit 9

S. 77	**percentage** [pə'sentɪdʒ]	What percentage of teenagers use drugs?	*Anteil, Prozentsatz*
	contract ['kɒntrækt]	Your contract says that you have to clean this office every week.	*Vertrag*
	invoice ['ɪnvɔɪs]	You don't need to pay now. I'll send you an invoice.	*Rechnung*
	service ['sɜːvɪs]	Our cleaning service costs €20 an hour.	*Dienstleistung*
	to charge (a price) [tʃɑːdʒ]	If you aren't happy with your meal, we won't charge you for it.	*(einen Preis) verlangen, berechnen*
	discount ['dɪskaʊnt]	I can give you a 15% discount if you buy 12 bottles.	*Rabatt, Nachlass*
S. 78	**action** ['ækʃn]	Enough talking! It's time to take action.	*Handlung, Handeln, Aktion, Action*
	role-playing game [ˌrəʊl pleɪɪŋ 'geɪm]	RuneScape is an online role-playing game.	*Rollenspiel*
	to recommend [ˌrekə'mend]	Can you recommend a good restaurant around here?	*empfehlen*

tʃ chips	dʒ jet	ʃ ship	ʒ garage	θ thing	ð the	ŋ ring	s ice	z as	v very	w wet

	costume ['kɒstjuːm]	He's going to the party in a Spiderman costume.	*Kostüm*
	host [həʊst]	This is a wonderful party. You're a great host!	*Gastgeber/in, Moderator/in*
	delicious [dɪ'lɪʃəs]	Mmm! This food is delicious.	*lecker*
	to hire sb ['haɪə]	They even hired waiters to bring the guests drinks.	*jdn beauftragen*
	decoration [ˌdekə'reɪʃn]	It isn't real fruit, it's just for decoration.	*Dekoration, Schmuck*
	to clean up [ˌkliːn 'ʌp]	Who's going to clean up after the party?	*aufräumen, saubermachen*
	murder mystery [ˌmɜːdə 'mɪstri]	The party will have a murder mystery theme.	*Krimi*
	detective [dɪ'tektɪv]	My name is Detective Schmidt. I'm with Interpol.	*(Kriminal-)Polizist/in*
	to murder ['mɜːdə]	You murdered her with a knife, didn't you?	*ermorden*
	the Roaring Twenties [ðə ˌrɔːrɪŋ 'twentiz]	My great-grandmother was a young girl in the Roaring Twenties.	*die Wilden Zwanziger*
	to decorate ['dekəreɪt]	Can we help you decorate the Christmas tree?	*dekorieren, schmücken*
	trivia ['trɪviə]	She knows trivia like the name of every US president.	*wissenswerte Kleinigkeiten*
	prize [praɪz]	I've won a prize! A holiday in Spain!	*Preis*
S. 79	**to add up** [ˌæd 'ʌp]	I've added up the money, but we're still €15 short.	*zusammenrechnen*
	optional ['ɒpʃənl]	⚠ *Aussprache!*	*optional*
S. 80	**barbecue** ['bɑːbɪkjuː]	The weather's nice. Let's have a barbecue in the garden.	*Grill(party)*
	vampire ['væmpaɪə]	⚠ *Aussprache!*	*Vampir/in*
	speaker ['spiːkə]	There's no music coming out of that speaker.	*Lautsprecher*
	buyer ['baɪə]	I've found a buyer for my bike. He'll give me €50.	*Käufer/in*
T	**to lend** [lend]	Can you lend me €10? I'll give it back.	*leihen*
	to store [stɔː]	My iPod can store 20,000 songs.	*speichern*
	effective [ɪ'fektɪv]	This medicine isn't very effective. I still feel ill.	*effektiv*
	use [juːs]	I made good use of my French when I was on holiday in France.	*Gebrauch*
	to turn sth on [ˌtɜːn 'ɒn]	How do I turn this camera on?	*etw anschalten*
	volume ['vɒljuːm]	It's too loud. Turn down the volume.	*Lautstärke*
	to scream [skriːm]	Katie, don't scream! It hurts my ears.	*schreien*
	to get damaged [get 'dæmɪdʒd]	If it gets damaged, you'll have to pay for it.	*beschädigt werden*
	amplifier ['æmplɪfaɪə]	I need a new amplifier for my music system.	*Verstärker*
	cable ['keɪbl]	Is this the cable from the TV?	*Kabel*
	unit ['juːnɪt]	It's a camera, TV and computer, all in one unit.	*Einheit, Gerät, Element*
	console ['kɒnsəʊl]	I got a video game console for Christmas.	*Konsole*
T	**indicator** ['ɪndɪkeɪtə]	The indicator shows that there isn't any power.	*Anzeige*
	control [kən'trəʊl]	It's too hot. The temperature control doesn't work.	*Regler*
	to plug sth in [ˌplʌg 'ɪn]	It won't work unless you plug it in, silly!	*etw anschließen, einstecken*
	to type (in) [ˌtaɪp 'ɪn]	Type in your name and password.	*(ein)tippen*
	zone [zəʊn]	What zone are we in? Western Europe or Central Europe?	*Bereich*
S. 81	**to pass sth** [pɑːs]	We're lost. We've passed this house three times.	*an etw vobeigehen/-fahren*

i:	ɪ	e	æ	ɑ:	ɒ	ɔ:	ʊ	u:	ʌ	ɜ:	ə
see	sit	ten	bad	arm	got	saw	put	too	cut	bird	about

	cash [kæʃ]	We don't take credit cards. You have to pay cash.	*bar*
	clerk [klɑ:k]	The clerk in the store was very helpful.	*Verkäufer/in*
	to stick sth out [ˌstɪk 'aʊt]	Don't stick your arm out of the car window.	*etw hinausstecken*
	presentation [ˌprezn'teɪʃn]	I have to give a presentation in front of the class.	*Präsentation, Vortrag*
	to research [rɪ'sɜ:tʃ]	You can use the internet to research the answers.	*recherchieren*
	introduction [ˌɪntrə'dʌkʃn]	Start your talk with an introduction.	*Einleitung*
	to move on (to sth) [ˌmu:v 'ɒn]	Then you can move on to the main part of your talk.	*weitergehen, (zu etw) übergehen*
	conclusion [kən'klu:ʒn]	In conclusion, we have seen that ...	*Schluss*
S. 82	**to pack** [pæk]	It's nearly time to go. Have you packed your bag?	*packen, einpacken*
	suitcase ['su:tkeɪs]	This suitcase is too small for all my holiday clothes.	*Koffer*
	size [saɪz]	What size T-shirt is that, medium or large?	*Größe*
	sunglasses ['sʌnglɑ:sɪz]	The sun is very bright. I need my sunglasses.	*Sonnenbrille*
	riddle [maɪk 'rɪdl]	This riddle is very difficult.	*Rätsel*
	to point [pɔɪnt]	I can't see it. Can you point to it, please?	*zeigen*
	empty ['empti]	The bag is empty. There's nothing in it.	*leer*
T	**waist** [weɪst]	I'm fatter than I was. My waist is 95 cm.	*Taille*
	baggy ['bægi]	'This shirt is too baggy.' – 'No, that's the style.'	*weit (geschnitten)*
	to suit sb [su:t]	Green suits you. You should wear it more often.	*(Kleider:) jdm stehen*
	cash desk ['kæʃ desk]	I want to buy this, but I can't find the cash desk.	*Kasse*
	changing room ['tʃeɪndʒɪŋ ru:m]	Clothes shops usually have a changing room.	*Umkleidekabine*
	to try sth on [ˌtraɪ 'ɒn]	I want to try on these trousers before I buy them.	*etw anprobieren*
S. 83	**to shop** [ʃɒp]	Do you often shop in this supermarket?	*einkaufen*
	tight [taɪt]	This T-shirt is too tight. I can't put it on.	*eng*
	item of clothing [ˌaɪtəm əv 'kləʊðɪŋ]	Buy two items of clothing and get the third free!	*Kleidungsstück*
S. 84	**unappetizing** [ʌn'æpətaɪzɪŋ]	This food looks unappetizing. I'm not going to eat it.	*unappetitlich*
	tasteless ['teɪstləs]	Clean water is tasteless.	*geschmacklos*
	crowd [kraʊd]	There was a crowd of about 100 people in the park.	*Menge*
	crowded ['kraʊdɪd]	This disco is crowded. There isn't room to dance.	*überfüllt*
	narrow ['nærəʊ]	The street is narrow. There isn't room to park.	*eng*
	to present [prɪ'zent]	They presented their new car at the Motor Show.	*vorstellen, präsentieren*
	to advertise ['ædvətaɪz]	We'll advertise the job in the newspaper.	*bewerben, Werbung machen für*
	target group ['tɑ:gɪt gru:p]	Our target group for this product is teenagers 13–16.	*Zielgruppe*
	billboard ['bɪlbɔ:d]	She saw her face 5 metres high on a billboard.	*Werbetafel*

tʃ	dʒ	ʃ	ʒ	θ	ð	ŋ	s	z	v	w
chips	jet	ship	garage	thing	the	ring	ice	as	very	wet

Unit 10

S.85	**conference** ['kɒnfərəns]	200 business people were at the conference.	*Konferenz*
	to work overtime [ˌwɜːk 'əʊvətaɪm]	I have to work overtime this weekend.	*Überstunden machen*
	to sort [sɔːt]	Please sort these T-shirts into small, medium and large.	*sortieren*
	mail [meɪl]	Do you get a lot of mail from fans?	*Post*
	to greet sb [griːt]	Who will greet the Queen when she gets off the plane?	*jdn begrüßen*
S.86	**corporation** [ˌkɔːpə'reɪʃn]	Microsoft is a very large corporation.	*Konzern, Gesellschaft*
	to move [muːv]	The family moved from Berlin to Munich.	*umziehen*
	almost ['ɔːlməʊst]	She's almost 17. Her birthday is next week.	*fast, beinah*
	animated film [ˌænɪmeɪtɪd 'fɪlm]	It isn't an animated film. It has live actors.	*Zeichentrickfilm, Animationsfilm*
	successful [sək'sesfl]	The film was successful: it made lots of money.	*erfolgreich*
	sensation [sen'seɪʃn]	⚠ *Aussprache!*	*Sensation*
	breakthrough ['breɪkθruː]	He was already 45 when he had his Hollywood breakthrough.	*Durchbruch*
	Snow White ['snəʊ waɪt]	Schneewittchen	
	dwarf, dwarves [dwɔːf, dwɔːvz]	He's only 1.4 metres tall, almost a dwarf.	*Zwerg, Zwerge*
	length [leŋθ]	Four hours? There aren't many films of that length.	*Länge*
	to realise sth ['rɪəlaɪz]	Few people are able to realise their dreams.	*etw verwirklichen, umsetzen*
	amusement [ə'mjuːzmənt]	Disneyland is an amusement park.	*Vergnügung*
	box office ['bɒks ɒfɪs]	The film made a lot of money at the box office.	*(Theater-, Kino-)Kasse*
	to earn [ɜːn]	I earn €500 a week in my job.	*verdienen, einbringen, einspielen*
	gigantic [dʒaɪ'gæntɪk]	King Kong is a film about a gigantic gorilla.	*riesig*
	branch [brɑːntʃ]	Would you like to work at our Berlin branch, Mr Schmidt?	*Zweig, Sparte (eines Unternehmens)*
	resort [rɪ'zɔːt]	For our next holiday we're going to a resort in Spain.	*Urlaubsort, Ferienanlage*
	cruise [kruːz]	They went on a two-week cruise on a big ship.	*Kreuzfahrt*
	to publish ['pʌblɪʃ]	The company publishes several magazines.	*verlegen, veröffentlichen*
	worldwide ['wɜːldwaɪd]	It isn't just a problem in Germany. It's a worldwide problem.	*weltweit*
	publisher ['pʌblɪʃə]	'Who is the book's publisher?' – 'Cornelsen.'	*Verleger/in, Verlag*
	parent company [ˌpeərənt 'kʌmpəni]	Our small company belongs to a big parent company.	*Muttergesellschaft*
	success [sək'ses]	The party was a success. We all loved it.	*Erfolg*
S.87	**half, halves** [hɑːf, hɑːvz]	Somebody has eaten half of this chocolate bar.	*Hälfte, Hälften*
	genius ['dʒiːniəs]	Einstein was a genius.	*Genie*
	producer [prə'djuːsə]	She works as a film producer in Hollywood.	*Produzent/in, Hersteller/in*
	ownership ['əʊnəʃɪp]	Car ownership in Germany is much higher than in the USA.	*Besitz*
	production [prə'dʌkʃn]	Production of the new car will start next year.	*Produktion, Herstellung*
	creation [kri'eɪʃn]	Did the creation of the world really take God seven days?	*Schöpfung*
	creator [kri'eɪtə]	J.K. Rowling was the creator of Harry Potter.	*Schöpfer/in*

i:	ɪ	e	æ	ɑ:	ɒ	ɔ:	ʊ	u:	ʌ	ɜ:	ə
see	sit	ten	bad	arm	got	saw	put	too	cut	bird	about

	inventor [ɪn'ventə]	Rudolf Diesel was the inventor of the diesel engine.	*Erfinder/in*
	keyboard ['ki:bɔ:d]	This computer doesn't have a keyboard, you just touch the screen.	*Tastatur*
	receptionist [rɪ'sepʃənɪst]	The receptionist will show you to my office.	*Empfangsmitarbeiter/in*
	developer [dɪ'veləpə]	Our software developers are working on a new game.	*Entwickler/in*
S.88	**reception** [rɪ'sepʃn]	Please go to reception first.	*Empfang, Rezeption*
	caller ['kɔ:lə]	Someone phoned you. I didn't get the caller's name.	*Anrufer/in*
	to put sb through [ˌpʊt 'θru:]	I'll put you through to Mr Jones now.	*(Telefon:) jdn durchstellen*
	intern ['ɪntɜ:n]	I'm an intern, so they don't pay me to work here.	*Praktikant/in*
S.89	**drawer** [drɔ:]	The diary is in the top drawer of my desk.	*Schublade*
	envelope ['envələʊp]	Do you have an envelope for this letter, please?	*Briefumschlag*
	shelf, shelves [ʃelf, ʃelvz]	There were ten books on the shelf.	*Regal, Regale*
	finance ['faɪnæns]	⚠ *Aussprache!*	*Finanz-*
	floor [flɔ:]	He works on the fourth floor of the building.	*Stockwerk, Etage*
	brochure ['brəʊʃə]	This brochure will tell you about the company.	*Prospekt, Werbebroschüre*
S.90	**to get rid of sth** [get 'rɪd əv]	Get rid of those old clothes. You don't need them.	*etw loswerden*
	auction ['ɔ:kʃn]	She paid €5 for the skateboard in an eBay auction.	*Versteigerung, Auktion*
	to auction (off) [ˌɔ:kʃn 'ɒf]	They auctioned off the furniture they didn't want.	*versteigern*
	laser pointer ['leɪzə pɔɪntə]	Never point a laser pointer at someone's eyes. You could make them blind.	*Lichtzeiger, Laserpointer*
	shocked [ʃɒkt]	I was shocked to hear that news story.	*schockiert*
	to join [dʒɔɪn]	Would you like to join our club?	*beitreten, mitmachen, eintreten in*
	firm [fɜ:m]	Our firm sells computer systems.	*Firma*
	consulting [kən'sʌltɪŋ]	If you need business advice, go to a consulting firm.	*Beratung*
S.91	**to specialize in sth** ['speʃəlaɪz ɪn]	We specialize in website design: that's all we do.	*sich auf etw spezialisieren*
	founding ['faʊndɪŋ]	Since the company's founding in 1975, it has done well.	*Gründung*
S.92	**puzzle** ['pʌzl]	There is a difficult puzzle in this magazine.	*Rätsel*
	package ['pækɪdʒ]	Please take this package to the post office.	*Paket*
	industrial park [ɪnˌdʌstriəl 'pɑ:k]	There were lots of businesses in the industrial park.	*Industriegebiet*
	label ['leɪbl]	The address is on the label.	*Etikett*
	to figure out [ˌfɪgər 'aʊt]	Can you figure out the answer?	*herausfinden*
	nappy ['næpi]	The baby's nappy needs changing.	*Windel*
	hairpiece ['heəpi:s]	The old man is bald so he wears a hairpiece.	*Toupet, Haarteil*
	rose [rəʊz]	There are a lot of roses in the park.	*Rose*
	gardener ['gɑ:dnə]	She pays a gardener to look after her garden.	*Gärtner/in*
	secretary ['sekrətri]	I'm Mr Smith's secretary. Sorry, you can't see him now.	*Sekretär/in*
	mail room ['meɪl rʊm]	Take these letters to the mail room.	*Poststelle*

	attendant [ə'tendənt]	The old man has a personal attendant to look after him.	*Bedienstete/r*
	to be located [bi ləʊ'keɪtɪd]	'Where is your office located?' – 'On the fourth floor.'	*sich befinden, liegen*

Unit 11

S. 93	**environment** [ɪn'vaɪrənmənt]	The Green party wants to help the environment.	*Umwelt*
	sweets [swi:ts]	Young children eat too many sweets.	*Süßigkeiten*
	organic [ɔ:'gænɪk]	Organic farms don't use dangerous chemicals.	*Bio-*
	dried [draɪd]	There isn't any fresh milk, just this dried milk.	*getrocknet, Trocken-*
	nut [nʌt]	There aren't many nuts in this fruit and nut mixture.	*Nuss*
	oil [ɔɪl]	Oh no! There's oil on the ground under my car.	*Öl*
	engine ['endʒɪn]	≈ motor	*Motor*
	two-stroke engine [ˌtu: strəʊk 'endʒɪn]	The old moped had a two-stroke engine.	*Zweitaktmotor*
	deposit [dɪ'pɒzɪt]	There's a 10-cent deposit on this bottle.	*Pfand*
	carton ['kɑ:tn]	A carton of milk, please.	*Karton*
	...-flavoured ['fleɪvəd]	It's banana-flavoured milk.	*mit ...-Geschmack*
	container [kən'teɪnə]	Boxes and bottles are types of container.	*Behältnis*
	recyclable [ˌri:'saɪkləbl]	Glass bottles are recyclable.	*recyclebar*
S. 94	**street light** ['stri:t laɪt]	This road is too dark at night. Why aren't there any street lights?	*Straßenlaterne*
	wasteland ['weɪstlænd]	There are no houses here, it's just wasteland.	*Ödland, unbebautes Gelände*
	housing estate ['haʊzɪŋ ɪsteɪt]	We live on a big housing estate. There are 500 houses.	*Wohnsiedlung*
	rubbish ['rʌbɪʃ]	We can't use this. It's just rubbish.	*Müll, Abfall*
	shopping trolley ['ʃɒpɪn trɒli]	They took a shopping trolley from the supermarket.	*Einkaufswagen*
	figure ['fɪgə]	I can't see them clearly. They're just dark figures.	*Gestalt*
	back [bæk]	Can you take this heavy box? My back hurts.	*Rücken*
	spade [speɪd]	A spade is a useful tool in the garden.	*Spaten*
	pickaxe ['pɪkæks]	I need a pickaxe to break this hard earth.	*Pickel*
	urban ['ɜ:bən]	I live in an urban area, not in the country.	*städtisch, urban, Stadt-*
	pile [paɪl]	His dirty clothes are in a pile on his bedroom floor.	*Haufen, Stapel*
	garden bed ['gɑ:dn bed]	Look at the nice flowers in that garden bed.	*Beet*
	onion ['ʌnjən]	No onion in my salad, thanks. It's too strong for me.	*Zwiebel*
	cabbage ['kæbɪdʒ]	Cabbage is a round, green vegetable.	*Kohl*
	to plant [plɑ:nt]	They planted 200 trees in the park.	*pflanzen*
	local ['ləʊkl]	I'm not local. I'm just here on holiday.	*örtlich, ansässig*
	to wake up [ˌweɪk 'ʌp]	Wake up! It's almost 9 o'clock.	*aufwachen*
	leaflet ['li:flət]	Please read this leaflet about the environment.	*Flugblatt, Handzettel*
	letterbox ['letəbɒks]	Put the letters in the letterbox.	*Briefkasten*
	to garden ['gɑ:dn]	She likes to garden in her free time.	*gärtnern*
	peaceful ['pi:sfl]	It's so peaceful here: nice and quiet.	*friedlich*
	unused [ˌʌn'ju:zd]	This land is unused, so it's OK to play here.	*ungenutzt*

	to grow sth [grəʊ]	She grows fruit and vegetables in her garden.	*etw anbauen*
	to care about sth ['keər əbaʊt]	I don't care about that, it isn't my problem.	*sich um etw kümmern, scheren*
	anonymous [ə'nɒnɪməs]	It's an anonymous letter. I don't know who sent it.	*anonym*
	to feel [fiːl]	I don't feel that this is a good idea.	*glauben, der Ansicht sein*
	council ['kaʊnsl]	He phoned the council about his neighbours' music.	*Stadtrat, Bezirksrat*
	property developer [ˌprɒpəti dɪ'veləpə]	A property developer is going to build some houses here.	*Immobilienfirma*
	soil [sɔɪl]	Plants need soil to grow in.	*Erde, Boden*
	vandal ['vændl]	Vandals broke the glass.	*Vandale*
	councillor ['kaʊnsələ]	The city councillors decided to sell the park.	*(Stadt-, Bezirks-)Ratsmitglied*
	trespasser ['trespəsə]	No trespassers! This is my land.	*Eindringling, Unbefugte/r*
	rather than ['rɑːðə ðən]	Let's have chips rather than potatoes.	*statt*
	to pick [pɪk]	Please don't pick the fruit.	*pflücken, ernten*
	to value ['væljuː]	He values the time he spends with his family.	*schätzen*
	at first [ət 'fɜːst]	It was difficult at first. After that it became easier.	*zunächst*
	to vandalize ['vændlaɪz]	Hey! Don't vandalize that bus stop!	*verwüsten*
	a laugh [ə 'lɑːf]	We weren't really fighting: it was just a laugh.	*ein Spaß*
	nowadays ['naʊədeɪz]	Years ago, kids were polite. Nowadays they aren't.	*heutzutage, jetzt*
	to wreck [rek]	That garden was nice. Now you've wrecked it.	*zerstören*
	gang [gæŋ]	Teenage gangs are a problem in some towns.	*Bande*
	to visualize ['vɪʒuəlaɪz]	Try to visualize the word if you want to learn it.	*bildlich umsetzen*
S. 95	**natural** ['nætʃrəl]	Wood is a natural material.	*natürlich*
	man-made ['mænmeɪd]	Most things in the city are man-made.	*künstlich hergestellt*
	to contain [kən'teɪn]	Does this bread contain salt?	*enthalten*
S. 96	**community** [kə'mjuːnəti]	We are all part of a community.	*Gemeinde, Gemeinschaft*
	environmental [ɪnˌvaɪrən'mentl]	Greenpeace is an environmental organization.	*Umwelt-*
	to aim [eɪm]	We aim to change the world.	*beabsichtigen, anstreben*
	background ['bækgraʊnd]	Who is he? You don't know anything about his background.	*Herkunft*
	educational [ˌedʒu'keɪʃənl]	It isn't just a holiday: it's educational too.	*Ausbildungs-*
	carpentry ['kɑːpəntri]	I'm learning carpentry because I like working with wood.	*Tischlern, Zimmerhandwerk*
	cultivation ['kʌltɪveɪʃn]	Before cultivation, this farm was a wood.	*Kultivierung*
	roof [ruːf]	Put a roof on to keep the rain and snow out.	*Dach*
	wall [wɔːl]	Why don't we put a picture on the wall?	*Wand, Mauer*
	tank [tæŋk]	Is there any water in the tank?	*Tank*
	to hold [həʊld]	We could hold a party in the street.	*abhalten*
	space [speɪs]	It's a small room. There isn't space for 50 people.	*Platz*
	to relax [rɪ'læks]	Relax! It's time to stop work.	*sich entspannen, sich erholen*
	surroundings [sə'raʊndɪŋz]	We live in beautiful surroundings by the sea.	*Umgebung*
S. 97	**bush** [bʊʃ]	That rose bush needs some water.	*Busch*
	fertilizer ['fɜːtəlaɪzə]	Without fertlizer, the vegetables will be small.	*Dünger*

tʃ	dʒ	ʃ	ʒ	θ	ð	ŋ	s	z	v	w
chips	jet	ship	garage	thing	the	ring	ice	as	very	wet

	pesticide ['pestɪsaɪd]	Use pesticide to kill the insects.	*Schädlingsbekämpfungs-mittel*
	tidy ['taɪdi]	His room is always tidy.	*sauber*
	to remove [rɪ'mu:v]	Please remove your hat when you enter the church.	*entfernen*
	leaf, leaves [li:f, li:vz]	The leaves fall from the trees in autumn.	*(Laub-)Blatt, Blätter*
	litter ['lɪtə]	It is forbidden to drop litter on the street.	*Abfall*
	arborist ['ɑ:bərɪst]	The arborist says that these trees are sick.	*Baumpfleger/in*
	surgeon ['sɜ:dʒən]	The surgeon had to cut off his arm.	*Chirurg/in*
	to climb up [ˌklaɪm 'ʌp]	Can you climb up the tree?	*hochklettern, erklimmen*
	height [haɪt]	My height is 1.67 metres.	*Höhe*
	forestry ['fɒrɪstri]	The forestry company has 2 million hectares of trees.	*Forstwirtschaft*
	to protect [prə'tekt]	We need to protect nature.	*schützen*
	to cut down (a tree) [ˌkʌt 'daʊn]	I cut down the tree because it was too big.	*(einen Baum) fällen*
	walking trail ['wɔ:kɪŋ treɪl]	The walking trail goes around the mountain.	*Wanderweg*
	ranger ['reɪndʒə]	The ranger works in the forest.	*Förster/in, Waldhüter/in*
	to prevent [prɪ'vent]	How can we prevent this problem in the future?	*verhüten, verhindern*
	damage ['dæmɪdʒ]	Vandals often do a lot of damage.	*Schaden*
	wildlife ['waɪldlaɪf]	You can see wildlife in the park if you are quiet.	*Tierwelt*
	to observe [əb'zɜ:v]	He observed a family of elephants for several weeks.	*beobachten*
	record ['rekɔ:d]	She keeps a record of what she buys every week.	*Aufzeichnung, Dokumentation*
T	**lonely** ['ləʊnli]	Aren't you lonely, living here by yourself?	*einsam*
	hard hat [ˌhɑ:d 'hæt]	The builders have to wear hard hats.	*Helm*
	brilliant ['brɪliənt]	A party? What a brilliant idea!	*toll, super*
	binoculars [bɪ'nɒkjələz]	Binoculars make things look much closer.	*Fernglas*
	chainsaw ['tʃeɪnsɔ:]	I need a chainsaw to cut this thick piece of wood.	*Kettensäge*
	gloves [glʌvz]	My hands are warm in these gloves.	*Handschuhe*
	ladder ['lædə]	The shelf is too high. I need a ladder to get the book.	*Leiter*
	lawnmower ['lɔ:nməʊə]	A lawnmower is a machine for cutting grass.	*Rasenmäher*
	wheelbarrow ['wi:lbærəʊ]	Use the wheelbarrow to move those heavy stones.	*Schubkarre*
S. 98	**thumb** [θʌm]	We have four fingers and a thumb on each hand.	*Daumen*
	supplier [sə'plaɪə]	The shop gets these paints from a special supplier.	*Lieferant, Anbieter*
	to process ['prəʊses]	The computer processes the data very quickly.	*bearbeiten*
	order ['ɔ:də]	I'd like to make an order for 50 exercise books, please.	*Auftrag, Bestellung*
	recording [rɪ'kɔ:dɪŋ]	Listen to the recording as many times as you want.	*Aufnahme*
	goods [gʊdz]	We'll send you the goods within 14 days.	*Ware(n)*
	packing list ['pækɪŋ lɪst]	Check the packing list. Have we forgotten anything?	*Packliste, Versandliste*

i:	ɪ	e	æ	ɑ:	ɒ	ɔ:	ʊ	u:	ʌ	ɜ:	ə
see	sit	ten	bad	arm	got	saw	put	too	cut	bird	about

	to select [sɪ'lekt]	Select the one that you want.	*wählen, auswählen*
	warehouse ['weəhaʊs]	We don't keep them in the shop. They're in the warehouse.	*Lager*
	to seal [si:l]	Seal the box so that nobody can open it.	*zukleben*
	despatch [dɪ'spætʃ]	Despatch is normally the day after we receive your order.	*Versand*
	despatch note [dɪ'spætʃ nəʊt]	You have to send a despatch note with the package.	*Versandanzeige, Warenbegleitschein*
	live [lɪv]	You can't send live animals by post.	*lebend, lebendig*
T	**order processing** [ˌɔ:də 'prəʊsesɪŋ]	Order processing can take up to five days.	*Auftragsabwicklung, -bearbeitung*
	plant nursery ['plɑ:nt nɜ:səri]	You can buy young plants from a plant nursery.	*Gärtnerei*
	pot [pɒt]	This plant is too big for this little pot.	*Topf*
	seed [si:d]	Put the seeds in the soil, add water and wait 14 days.	*Samen*
	to label ['leɪbl]	Label these things so that we know what they are.	*kennzeichnen, etikettieren*
	tray [treɪ]	There are 50 small plants in this tray.	*Wanne*
	greenhouse ['gri:nhaʊs]	A greenhouse is made of glass or plastic.	*Gewächshaus, Treibhaus*
	to enter ['entə]	Enter your email address in the box, then click 'Next'.	*(Computer:) eingeben*
S. 99	**to strike** [straɪk]	The terrorists struck the railway station.	*schlagen, zuschlagen*
	bright [braɪt]	That's a really bright T-shirt! I need my sunglasses!	*(Farbe:) leuchtend*
	to sow [səʊ]	Sow the flower seeds in the garden in April–May.	*säen, aussäen*
	drum [drʌm]	The oil was in a large drum.	*Fass*
	patch (of land) [pætʃ]	There's a patch of grass between the two houses.	*Stück (Land)*

Test 3

S. 100	**appearance** [ə'pɪərəns]	Can you describe the man's appearance?	*Aussehen, Erscheinungsbild*

Unit 12

S. 101	**happiness** ['hæpinəs]	Isn't happiness more important than money?	*Glück*
	survey-taker ['sɜ:veɪ teɪkə]	1000 survey-takers answered the questions.	*Befragte/r*
	to die [daɪ]	We know that we're all going to die one day.	*sterben*
	infancy ['ɪnfənsi]	In poor countries, many children die in infancy.	*Säuglingsalter*
	flavour ['fleɪvə]	'What flavour is your ice-cream?' – 'Banana.'	*Geschmack, Aroma*
	childhood ['tʃaɪldhʊd]	Did you have a happy childhood?	*Kindheit*
	to scare sb [skeə]	The mouse scared the elephant.	*jdn erschrecken, jdm Angst machen*
	adolescence [ˌædə'lesns]	Adolescence can be difficult, for both teenagers and parents.	*Jugend, Pubertät*
	nervous ['nɜ:vəs]	She's nervous about her exams.	*nervös*
	adulthood ['ædʌlthʊd]	When you reach adulthood, you'll have to get a job.	*Erwachsenenalter*
	to fall in love [ˌfɔ:l ɪn 'lʌv]	He fell in love with his best friend's girlfriend.	*sich verlieben*
	to neglect [nɪ'glekt]	Don't neglect your schoolwork.	*vernachlässigen*

tʃ	dʒ	ʃ	ʒ	θ	ð	ŋ	s	z	v	w
chips	jet	ship	garage	thing	the	ring	ice	as	very	wet

	to imitate ['ɪmɪteɪt]	Don't imitate the teacher, she'll see you!	*imitieren, nachmachen*
S.102	**drop-out** ['drɒpaʊt]	I'm not a drop-out, I'm just taking a year off.	*(Schul-, Uni-)Abbrecher/in*
	to divorce [dɪ'vɔːs]	They divorced and found new partners.	*sich scheiden lassen*
	miserable ['mɪzrəbl]	You look miserable. Is something wrong?	*elend*
	to drop out (of school) [ˌdrɒp aʊt əv 'skuːl]	He dropped out of school and got a job.	*(die Schule) abbrechen*
	diploma [dɪ'pləʊmə]	You need a diploma to do this job.	*Abschluss*
	therefore ['ðeəfɔː]	There isn't a bus, therefore we'll have to walk.	*deshalb, daher*
	profession [prə'feʃn]	It isn't just a job, it's a profession.	*Beruf*
	to study ['stʌdi]	He studied languages at university.	*lernen, studieren*
	to manage ['mænɪdʒ]	It was difficult, but she managed to do it.	*gelingen, es schaffen*
	PhD [ˌpiː eɪtʃ 'diː]	What year did you get your PhD, Dr Smith?	*Doktortitel*
	passion ['pæʃn]	Football is a passion for him: he loves it.	*Leidenschaft*
	academic [ˌækə'demɪk]	She works at the university as an academic.	*Akademiker/in*
	to separate ['sepəreɪt]	My parents have separated, but they haven't divorced yet.	*(sich) trennen*
	to quit school [ˌkwɪt 'skuːl]	She quit school before her exams.	*die Schule schmeißen*
S.103	**precision** [prɪ'sɪʒn]	Precision is needed to make very small machines.	*Präzision, Präzisions-*
	to fill an order [ˌfɪl ən 'ɔːdə]	We can't fill the order. We don't have the goods.	*einen Auftrag ausführen*
	surgical ['sɜːdʒɪkl]	It's a surgical instrument used in hospitals.	*chirurgisch*
	pharmaceutical [ˌfɑːmə'suːtɪkl]	The pharmaceutical industry makes medicines.	*Pharma-, pharmazeutisch*
	machine operator [məˌʃiːn 'ɒpəreɪtə]	I'm a machine operator: I drive a big tractor.	*Maschinenführer/in*
	nurse [nɜːs]	The nurse gave the patient some pills.	*Krankenschwester, Krankenpfleger*
	in italics [ɪn ɪ'tælɪks]	The sentences in this column are in italics.	*kursiv*
S.104	**to save sb** [seɪv]	Save me! I can't swim!	*jdn retten*
	gerbil ['dʒɜːbɪl]	It isn't a rat or a mouse, it's a gerbil.	*Rennmaus*
	temperature ['temprətʃə]	You have a high temperature. You must be ill.	*Fieber*
	to take sb's temperature [teɪk 'temprətʃə]	Nurse, please take the patient's temperature.	*bei jdm Fieber messen*
	to strike [straɪk]	A piece of glass struck him on the arm.	*treffen*
	lightning ['laɪtnɪŋ]	There was a lot of lightning during the storm.	*Blitz*
	to be trapped [bi 'træpt]	I can't get out of here: I'm trapped!	*in der Falle sitzen*
	attraction [ə'trækʃn]	⚠ *Aussprache!*	*Attraktion*
	fish tank ['fɪʃ tæŋk]	There are 20 goldfish in the big fish tank.	*Aquarium*
	clue [kluː]	I don't know who did it, but this could be a clue.	*Anhaltspunkt, Hinweis*
S.105	**magic show** [ˌmædʒɪk 'ʃəʊ]	There was an exciting magic show at the children's party.	*Zaubervorstellung*
	bartender ['bɑːtendə]	Bartender! Another beer, please.	*Barkeeper*
	doorman ['dɔːmən]	I'm the doorman, sir. You can't come in the club.	*Türsteher*
	breadcrumbs ['bredkrʌmz]	When you cut the bread, you left breadcrumbs on the table.	*Brotkrümel, Brösel*
S.106	**to chase** [tʃeɪs]	That dog always chases cats.	*jagen, nachjagen*
	to shoot [ʃuːt]	They shot the film in New Zealand.	*(Film:) drehen; fotografieren*

	viewer ['vju:ə]	Young viewers under 12 should not watch this film.	*Zuschauer/in*
	to pan [pæn]	The camera slowly panned across the desert.	*(Kamera:) schwenken*
	to slow sth down [,sləʊ 'daʊn]	Downloading films slows down my internet connection.	*etw verlangsamen, bremsen*
	shot [ʃɒt]	This next shot was taken later in the day.	*(Film:) Einstellung, Szene*
	function ['fʌŋkʃn]	This camera has a lot of different functions.	*Funktion*
	to reduce [rɪ'dju:s]	You'll have to reduce the size of the photo.	*verringern, mindern, reduzieren*
	quality ['kwɒləti]	Is the quality of the photo high enough?	*Qualität*
S. 107	**close-up** ['kləʊs ʌp]	Can we have a close-up of the actor's face, please?	*Nahaufnahme*
	wide [waɪd]	How wide is your TV screen?	*breit, weit, groß*
	wide shot [,waɪd 'ʃɒt]	You can hardly see the man's face in this wide shot.	*Totale*
	humorous ['hju:mərəs]	It's a humorous story: it makes people laugh.	*witzig, humorvoll*
S. 108	**astrological sign** [æstrə'lɒdʒɪkl 'saɪn]	There are 12 astrological signs in the zodiac.	*Sternzeichen*
	lion ['laɪən]	The lions ate the elephant.	*Löwe*
	bull [bʊl]	Careful! There's a bull in that field.	*Stier*
	virgin ['vɜ:dʒɪn]	Jesus' mother was the Virgin Mary.	*Jungfrau*
	scales [skeɪlz]	According to the scales, your weight is 55 kg.	*Waage*
	archer ['ɑ:tʃə]	Robin Hood was an archer.	*Bogenschütze/-in*
	ram [ræm]	A ram is a male sheep.	*Widder*
	twins [twɪnz]	My brother and I are twins. We're both 30.	*Zwillinge*
	carrier ['kæriə]	He works as a newspaper carrier every morning before school.	*Träger/in*
	goat [gəʊt]	There were goats and cows on the farm.	*Ziege, Bock*
	scorpion ['skɔ:pjən]	In the desert, you have to be careful of scorpions.	*Skorpion*
	characteristic [,kærəktə'rɪstɪk]	⚠ *Aussprache!*	*Merkmal, Eigenschaft*
	analytical [,ænə'lɪtɪkl]	Analytical people like to solve problems.	*analytisch*
	courageous [kə'reɪdʒəs]	It was courageous to help your friend against those two bigger boys.	*mutig*
	communicative [kə'mju:nɪkətɪv]	He isn't communicative. He prefers not to talk.	*kommunikativ*
	determined [dɪ'tɜ:mɪnd]	I'm determined to do this. Don't try to stop me.	*entschlossen*
	emotional [ɪ'məʊʃənl]	⚠ *Aussprache!*	*emotional, gefühlsbetont*
	generous ['dʒenərəs]	'Here's €100.' – 'That's very generous of you.'	*großzügig*
	loyal ['lɔɪəl]	⚠ *Aussprache!*	*loyal, treu*
	rebellious [rɪ'beljəs]	She's a rebellious child. She never does what I want.	*rebellisch*
	sensitive ['sensətɪv]	Don't be so sensitive. It was just a joke.	*sensibel*
	unpredictable [,ʌnprɪ'dɪktəbl]	The weather's unpredictable. I don't know if it will rain.	*unberechenbar*
	horoscope ['hɒrəskəʊp]	Have you read your horoscope in today's newspaper?	*Horoskop*
	romance [rəʊ'mæns]	Paris is a great city for romance.	*Romanze*
	full moon [,fʊl 'mu:n]	It's easy to see tonight: there's a full moon.	*Vollmond*

tʃ	dʒ	ʃ	ʒ	θ	ð	ŋ	s	z	v	w
chips	jet	ship	garage	thing	the	ring	ice	as	very	wet

Unit 13

S. 109	**flag** [flæg]	That's the German flag on the Reichstag building.	*Flagge*
	capital ['kæpɪtl]	Berlin is the capital of Germany.	*Hauptstadt*
	border ['bɔ:də]	This is the border between France and Italy.	*Grenze*
	official language [əˌfɪʃl 'læŋgwɪdʒ]	English and Welsh are the official languages of Wales.	*Amtssprache*
	star [stɑ:]	Look at all the stars in the night sky!	*Stern*
S. 110	**to search for sth** ['sɜ:tʃ fə]	They're searching for a nice house that isn't too expensive.	*nach etw suchen*
	to further one's career [ˌfɜ:ðə wʌnz kə'rɪə]	I'm doing this training to further my career.	*beruflich weiterkommen*
	desperately ['despərətli]	With two minutes left, the score was 1:1. Both teams tried desperately to win.	*verzweifelt*
	builder ['bɪldə]	He's a builder. He builds houses.	*Bauunternehmer/in, Bauarbeiter/in*
	to persuade sb [pə'sweɪd]	I'm going. Don't try to persuade me to stay.	*jdn überzeugen, überreden*
	adaptation [ˌædæp'teɪʃn]	There will be a period of adaptation to your new job.	*Anpassung, Umstellung*
	royal ['rɔɪəl]	The Queen is the head of the British royal family.	*königlich*
	infirmary [ɪn'fɜ:mri]	≈ hospital	*Krankenhaus*
	to be/go short of sth [bi 'ʃɔ:t əv]	I'm short of money. Could you give me €50?	*nicht genug von etw haben*
	resource [rɪ'sɔ:s]	⚠ *Aussprache!*	*Mittel, Ressource*
	to break sth [breɪk]	Sorry! I've just broken a glass.	*etw kaputtmachen*
	replacement [rɪ'pleɪsmənt]	That was the last glass. We don't have a replacement.	*Ersatz*
	ambitious [æm'bɪʃəs]	I'm ambitious: I want a better job.	*ehrgeizig*
	degree [dɪ'gri:]	She has a degree in French and English.	*Hochschulabschluss*
	senior ['si:niə]	I'm the senior manager. Do as I say.	*leitend*
	staff nurse ['stɑ:f nɜ:s]	I want to see the staff nurse, not a student.	*Stationsschwester*
	emergency [ɪ'mɜ:dʒənsi]	It's an emergency. Phone the police!	*Notfall*
	ward [wɔ:d]	There are 20 patients in this ward of the hospital.	*(Kranken-)Station*
	close [kləʊs]	Bill is a close friend of mine.	*eng*
	bunch [bʌntʃ]	They're a nice bunch of kids.	*(von Menschen) Gruppe, Haufen*
	to settle down [ˌsetl 'daʊn]	I want to see the world before I settle down.	*sesshaft werden, eine Familie gründen*
	broad [brɔ:d]	≠ narrow	*breit, groß*
	range [reɪndʒ]	He has tried a range of different jobs.	*Spannbreite, Umfang*
	dead end [ˌded 'end]	We can't go further: it's a dead end.	
S. 111	**job opportunity** [dʒɒb ˌɒpə'tju:nəti]	I'm looking for a job opportunity in marketing.	*offene Stelle*
	to return [rɪ'tɜ:n]	≈ go back	*zurückkehren*
	equipped [ɪ'kwɪpt]	The school is equipped with good computers.	*ausgestattet*
	rather ['rɑ:ðə]	I would rather work in a big company.	*eher*
S. 112	**lift** [lɪft]	Can I get a lift to Stuttgart in your car?	*Mitfahrgelegenheit*

i:	ɪ	e	æ	ɑ:	ɒ	ɔ:	ʊ	u:	ʌ	ɜ:	ə
see	sit	ten	bad	arm	got	saw	put	too	cut	bird	about

	to get casual jobs [get ˌkæʒuəl 'dʒɒbz]	We can get casual jobs as waiters or shop assistants.	*jobben*
	to busk [bʌsk]	She often busks in the city with her saxophone.	*Straßenmusik machen*
	to run out of sth [ˌrʌn 'aʊt əv]	We can't buy it: we've run out of money.	*etw nicht mehr haben*
	hostel ['hɒstl]	It's fun to stay in a hostel on holiday.	*(Jugend-)Herberge*
	to afford sth [ə'fɔ:d]	Can we afford it, or is it too expensive?	*sich etw leisten können*
S. 113	**hospital porter** [ˌhɒspɪtl 'pɔ:tə]	A hospital porter will move the beds.	*Pflegekraft*
	handkerchief ['hæŋkətʃɪf]	⚠ *Aussprache!*	*Taschentuch*
	cold [kəʊld]	It's raining. You'll get a cold if you go out in a T-shirt.	*Erkältung*
	to turn sth off [ˌtɜ:n 'ɒf]	Please turn off the TV if you aren't watching it.	*etw ausschalten*
	difficulty ['dɪfɪkəlti]	We're having difficulty with this exercise. What's the answer?	*Schwierigkeit*
	communication difficulties [kəˌmju:nɪ'keɪʃn dɪfɪkəltiz]	They have communication difficulties because he can't hear well.	*Verständigungs-schwierigkeiten*
	misunderstanding [ˌmɪsʌndə'stændɪŋ]	It was just a misunderstanding. I understand now.	*Missverständnis*
	to confirm [kən'fɜ:m]	I think this answer is right. Ask the teacher to confirm it.	*bestätigen*
	to catch sth [kætʃ]	Sorry, I didn't catch that. What did you say?	*etw hören, verstehen*
S. 114	**paraphrase** ['pærəfreɪz]	I don't understand that word. Could you paraphrase it?	*umschreiben*
	to realise ['rɪəlaɪz]	I didn't realise that you were German. Your English is very good.	*bemerken*
	lost property office [ˌlɒst 'prɒpəti ɒfɪs]	'I've lost my bag.' – 'Go to the lost property office.'	*Fundbüro*
S. 115	**confusion** [kən'fju:ʒn]	Why the confusion? The answer is clear.	*Verwirrung*
	to cause [kɔ:z]	Bad weather caused the train to be late.	*verursachen*
S. 116	**health care** ['helθ keə]	I would like to work in health care.	*Gesundheitswesen, medizinische Versorgung*
	health services officer [ˌhelθ sɜ:vɪsɪz 'ɒfɪsə]	The health services officer welcomed the patient.	*Kaufmann/-frau im Gesundheitswesen*
	identity card [aɪ'dentəti kɑ:d]	The police officer asked for his identity card.	*Personalausweis*
	patient ['peɪʃnt]	⚠ *Aussprache!*	*Patient/in*
	operation [ˌɒpə'reɪʃn]	⚠ *Aussprache!*	*Operation*
	form [fɔ:m]	The form contains a lot of information about me.	*Formular*
	to fill in [ˌfɪl 'ɪn]	Fill in your name and address, please.	*ausfüllen*
	medical insurance [ˌmedɪkl ɪn'ʃʊərəns]	You need a doctor. Do you have medical insurance?	*Krankenversicherung*
	medical assistant [ˌmedɪkl ə'sɪstənt]	A medical assistant helps a doctor.	*Medizinische/r Fachangestellte/r*
	surgery ['sɜ:dʒəri]	It's a small surgery with two doctors.	*Arztpraxis*
	to swipe (a chip card) [swaɪp]	I need to swipe your card to see your details on the computer.	*(eine Chipkarte) durchziehen*
	practice ['præktɪs]	How many doctors work at this practice?	*Praxis*
	examination [ɪgˌzæmɪ'neɪʃn]	You have to take off your shirt for the examination.	*Untersuchung*

tʃ	dʒ	ʃ	ʒ	θ	ð	ŋ	s	z	v	w
chips	jet	ship	garage	thing	the	ring	ice	as	very	wet

	minor ['maɪnə]	It's only a minor problem.	*kleiner*
	sample ['sɑ:mpl]	I need to take a sample of your blood.	*Probe*
	administrative [əd'mɪnɪstrətɪv]	I have an administrative job, in the office.	*Verwaltungs-*
	medical supply company [ˌmedɪkl sə'plaɪ kʌmpəni]	We buy bandages from a medical supply company.	*Unternehmen für Sanitätsbedarf*
	dull [dʌl]	≈ boring	*langweilig*
	dental assistant [ˌdentl ə'sɪstənt]	The dental assistant will clean your teeth.	*Zahnmedizinische/r Fachangestellte/r*
	dentist ['dentɪst]	A dentist works with people's teeth.	*Zahnarzt/-ärztin*
	treatment ['tri:tmənt]	How much will the treatment cost?	*Behandlung*
	to fetch [fetʃ]	Please fetch the next patient.	*holen*
	waiting room ['weɪtɪŋ ru:m]	There are three people in the doctor's waiting room.	*Wartezimmer*
	to hand [hænd]	Please hand me the photo.	*überreichen, (über)geben*
	file [faɪl]	All your information is in the file.	*(Patienten-)Akte*
	to pass [pɑ:s]	Could you pass me the bottle of water, please?	*reichen, geben*
	X-ray ['eksreɪ]	He may have broken his finger. He needs an X-ray.	*Röntgen*
	tooth, teeth [tu:θ, ti:θ]	Adults have 32 teeth, if they haven't lost any.	*Zahn, Zähne*
	to disinfect [ˌdɪsɪn'fekt]	Disinfect the instruments after the operation.	*desinfizieren*
	surface ['sɜ:fɪs]	We have to clean all the surfaces before we paint.	*Oberfläche*
	to sterilise ['sterəlaɪz]	Sterilise the baby's bottle to kill any bacteria.	*sterilisieren*
	dentures ['dentʃəz]	She needed dentures after she lost all her teeth.	*Gebiss, Zahnersatz*
	laboratory [lə'bɒrətri]	The laboratory will test the blood.	*Labor*
	quality ['kwɒləti]	She has good qualities: she's friendly and helpful.	*Eigenschaft*
	to require [rɪ'kwaɪə]	I'm fine. I don't require any help, thanks.	*verlangen*
	manner ['mænə]	He has a nice manner with the children.	*Art (des Umgangs)*
	coordination [kəʊˌɔ:dɪ'neɪʃn]	⚠ *Aussprache!*	*Koordination*
	hand-to-eye coordination [ˌhænd tə 'aɪ kəʊɔ: dɪneɪʃn]	You need good hand-to-eye coordination to play tennis.	*Hand-Auge-Koordination*
	data entry ['deɪtə entri:]	You mustn't make mistakes in a data entry job.	*Dateneingabe*
	thoroughness ['θʌrənəs]	Thoroughness is important: don't forget anything.	*Hochwasser, Überschwemmung*

Unit 14

S. 117	**flood** [flʌd]	After the flood, the whole house was wet.	*Hochwasser, Überschwemmung*
	birth [bɜ:θ]	The birth went well. Mother and baby are both OK.	*Geburt*
	to give birth [gɪv 'bɜ:θ]	She gave birth to a healthy baby girl.	*gebären, ein Kind zur Welt bringen*
	robbery ['rɒbəri]	They took €100,000 in the robbery.	*Raub, Raubüberfall*
	power failure ['paʊə feɪljə]	I can't use my computer. We've had a power failure.	*Stromausfall*
	ambulance ['æmbjələns]	I think she's broken her leg. Call an ambulance.	*Krankenwagen, Rettungswagen*

i:	ɪ	e	æ	ɑ:	ɒ	ɔ:	ʊ	u:	ʌ	ɜ:	ə
see	sit	ten	bad	arm	got	saw	put	too	cut	bird	about

	fire brigade ['faɪə brɪgeɪd]	Help! Fire! Call the fire brigade!	*Feuerwehr*
	to lose one's cool [ˌlu:z wʌnz 'ku:l]	Think clearly and don't lose your cool.	*die Fassung verlieren*
	first-aid kit [ˌfɜ:st'eɪd kɪt]	I've cut my hand. Where's the first-aid kit?	*Verbandskasten*
	germ [dʒɜ:m]	There are dangerous germs in that dirty water.	*Keim*
	wound [wu:nd]	There was lots of blood from the wound in his head.	*Wunde*
	to cover ['kʌvə]	Cover the milk to keep it fresh.	*abdecken, bedecken*
	bandage ['bændɪdʒ]	⚠ *Aussprache!*	*Bandage*
	to tape a bandage [ˌteɪp ə 'bændɪdʒ]	Tape a bandage around his hand.	*einen Verband anlegen*
	injured ['ɪndʒəd]	'Are you injured?' – 'No, I'm OK.'	*verletzt*
	joint [dʒɔɪnt]	Your fingers have three joints but your thumbs only have two.	*Gelenk*
	to wrap [ræp]	Wrap the baby in something warm. It's cold out here.	*einwickeln, hier: verbinden*
	to hold sth in place [ˌhəʊld ɪn 'pleɪs]	We need to hold it in place, or it will fall off.	*etw fixieren*
	swelling ['swelɪŋ]	Put ice on your foot to reduce the swelling.	*Schwellung*
	pain [peɪn]	I didn't feel much pain when I broke my arm.	*Schmerz*
	tweezers ['twi:zəz]	She used tweezers to get the little piece of metal out of his eye.	*Pinzette*
	painkiller ['peɪnkɪlə]	Take two painkillers with water every eight hours.	*Schmerzmittel, -tabletten*
	gauze bandage ['gɔ:z bændɪdʒ]	Put a gauze bandage on the wound.	*Mullbinde*
	elastic bandage [ɪˌlæstɪk 'bændɪdʒ]	I'll put an elastic bandage round your knee so you can walk.	*elastische Binde*
	latex glove ['leɪteks glʌvz]	Wear latex gloves to keep the blood off your hands.	*Latexhandschuh*
	scissors ['sɪzəz]	I need a pair of scissors to cut this paper.	*Schere*
	instant cold pack [ˌɪnstənt 'kəʊld pæk]	An instant cold pack will make your knee feel better.	*Kältekompresse*
	plaster ['plɑ:stə]	I've cut my finger. Can I have a plaster, please?	*Pflaster*
	antiseptic liquid [æntiˌseptɪk 'lɪkwɪd]	Antiseptic liquid will kill the bacteria.	*Desinfektionslösung*
	adhesive tape [əd'hi:sɪv teɪp]	It won't fall off if you put adhesive tape on it.	*Heftpflaster*
S. 118	**Ferris wheel** ['ferɪs wi:l]	The London Eye is one of the world's largest Ferris wheels.	*Riesenrad*
	passenger ['pæsɪndʒə]	There were 350 passengers on the aircraft.	*Passagier/in, Fahrgast*
	to trap sb [træp]	They shut the door and trapped him in the room.	*jdn einschließen*
	to break out [ˌbreɪk 'aʊt]	He was able to break out of the police station.	*ausbrechen*
	control room [kən'trəʊl rʊm]	Phone the control room and tell them to stop the turbine.	*Steuerraum, Leitstand*
	to lower ['ləʊə]	They lowered James Bond from a helicopter.	*abseilen, herunterlassen*
	rope [rəʊp]	We can't climb down the mountain without a rope.	*Seil*
	to rescue ['reskju:]	It took five hours to rescue everyone from the sea.	*retten*

tʃ	dʒ	ʃ	ʒ	θ	ð	ŋ	s	z	v	w
ch**ips**	**j**et	**sh**ip	gara**g**e	**th**ing	**th**e	ri**ng**	i**c**e	a**s**	**v**ery	**w**et

	via ['vaɪə]	We can communicate via email.	*über, mittels*
	intercom ['ɪntəkɒm]	Please ring the door bell and speak into the intercom.	*Gegensprechanlage*
	to restore [rɪ'stɔː]	It took 10 hours to restore power to the building.	*wiederherstellen*
S. 119	**dispatcher** [dɪ'spætʃə]	Phone 112 and answer the dispatcher's questions.	*Disponent/in*
	fire fighter ['faɪə faɪtə]	By the time the fire fighters arrived, the fire was big.	*Feuerwehrmann/frau*
	civil defence [ˌsɪvl dɪ'fens]	After the flood, civil defence workers saved many lives.	*Zivilschutz*
	rescuer ['reskjuːə]	I'd like to thank my rescuers for saving my life.	*Retter/in*
	electrician [ɪˌlek'trɪʃn]	We don't have any power in the building. Call an electrician.	*Elektriker/in*
T	**to put out (a fire)** [ˌpʊt 'aʊt]	It was only a small fire, so it was easy to put it out.	*(ein Feuer) löschen*
	control [kən'trəʊl]	Without the computer we have no control of the robot.	*Steuerung*
	emergency control [ɪ'mɜːdʒənsi kəntrəʊl]	If the machine won't stop, use the emergency control system.	*Notsteuerung*
	contactor ['kɒntæktə]	Use the contactor to turn off the motor.	*Schalter*
	to improvise ['ɪmprəvaɪz]	We don't have the right equipment, but we can improvise.	*improvisieren*
	rescue squad ['reskjuː skwɒd]	Don't worry. The rescue squad will be there soon.	*Rettungskommando, -trupp*
	in case [ɪn 'keɪs]	Take a coat in case the weather is cold.	*falls*
	dizzy ['dɪzi]	I felt dizzy when I looked down at the ground far below.	*schwindlig*
	to vomit ['vɒmɪt]	I feel sick. Where's the bathroom? I'm going to vomit.	*sich erbrechen*
	ride [raɪd]	There are a lot of different rides at Disneyland.	*Fahrt*
	fire extinguisher ['faɪər ɪkstɪŋgwɪʃə]	Point the fire extinguisher at the centre of the fire.	*Feuerlöscher*
	complication [ˌkɒmplɪ'keɪʃn]	It should be easy, but there are complications.	*Komplikation*
	tragedy ['trædʒədi]	After another tragedy on our roads, four people are dead.	*Tragödie*
S. 120	**rural** ['rʊərəl]	It's a rural area. There aren't many buildings here.	*ländlich*
	crossroad ['krɒsrəʊd]	At the crossroad, do I turn left, right, or go straight ahead?	*Kreuzung*
	landmark ['lændmɑːk]	The church is a good landmark: you can see it for miles.	*Orientierungspunkt*
	condition [kən'dɪʃn]	He's in a bad condition. He's very ill.	*Zustand; Leiden, Beschwerden*
	level ['levl]	You have a high level of alcohol in your blood.	*Niveau*
	consciousness ['kɒnʃəsnəs]	I lost consciousness, so I don't know what happened next.	*Bewusstsein*
	breathing ['briːðɪŋ]	After he had run for an hour, his breathing was very loud.	*Atmung*
	circulation [ˌsɜːkjə'leɪʃn]	Cold or blue fingers are a sign of bad circulation.	*Kreislauf*

iː	ɪ	e	æ	ɑː	ɒ	ɔː	ʊ	uː	ʌ	ɜː	ə
see	sit	ten	bad	arm	got	saw	put	too	cut	bird	about

Word list Unit 14

	pulse [pʌls]	'How do I know if she's dead?' – 'Can you feel a pulse?'	*Puls*
	conscious ['kɒnʃəs]	Can you hear me? Are you conscious?	*bei Bewusstsein*
T	**motorway** ['məʊtəweɪ]	The motorway is a lot quicker than the smaller roads.	*Autobahn*
S. 121	**ridiculous** [rɪ'dɪkjələs]	Take off that silly hat! You look ridiculous.	*lächerlich, lachhaft*
	to lock sth in sth [lɒk]	I can't get my keys, I've locked them in the house.	*etw in etw einschließen*
	to hit sb [hɪt]	Don't drive so fast. You'll hit someone.	*hier: jdn anfahren*
	to hallucinate [hə'luːsɪneɪt]	There isn't a green elephant. You're hallucinating.	*halluzinieren*
	to roast [rəʊst]	Roast the chicken for 2–3 hours at 180°C.	*braten*
	turkey ['tɜːki]	A turkey is a much larger bird than a chicken.	*Truthahn*
	deer [dɪə]	The deer in the park are beautiful, but they eat the young trees.	*Reh*
	back seat [ˌbæk 'siːt]	There were five of us in the car: two in the front and three on the back seat.	*Rücksitz*
	to scrape [skreɪp]	Somebody has scraped the paint on my car.	*kratzen*
	chimpanzee [ˌtʃɪmpæn'ziː]	⚠ *Aussprache!*	*Schimpanse*
	baseball bat ['beɪsbɔːl bæt]	In baseball, you use a baseball bat to hit the ball.	*Baseballschläger*
	to arrest sb [ə'rest]	The police arrested the criminal.	*jdn verhaften*
	to misuse [ˌmɪsjuːs]	Don't misuse the library. If you want to chat, go outside.	*missbrauchen, zweckentfremden*
S. 122	**to take a test** [ˌteɪk ə 'test]	You can take the driving test at the age of 18.	*eine Prüfung ablegen*
	to pass a test [ˌpɑːs ə 'test]	If you pass the test, you can drive a car.	*eine Prüfung bestehen*
	to fail a test [ˌfeɪl ə 'test]	Many people fail the test and have to take it again.	*eine Prüfung nicht bestehen*
	to celebrate ['selɪbreɪt]	Let's go to a restaurant to celebrate your birthday.	*feiern*
	to forgive [fə'gɪv]	'I'm sorry.' – 'That's OK. I forgive you.'	*verzeihen*
S. 123	**panic attack** [ˌpænɪk ə'tæk]	You're having a panic attack. Try to breathe slowly.	*Panikattacke*
S. 124	**stereotype** ['steriətaɪp]	'All Italians love pasta.' – 'That's just a stereotype.'	*Klischee*
T	**chopsticks** ['tʃɒpstɪks]	Can you eat Chinese food with chopsticks?	*Stäbchen*
	individual [ˌɪndɪ'vɪdʒuəl]	We're not the same: we're all individuals.	*Individuum*
	sunrise ['sʌnraɪz]	Sunrise tomorrow is at 5.35 a.m.	*Sonnenaufgang*
	sunset ['sʌnset]	Sunset is at 8.30 p.m.	*Sonnenuntergang*
	stinky ['stɪŋki]	Your socks are stinky. Please put your shoes on!	*stinkend*
	lunchroom ['lʌntʃrʊm]	Don't eat your sandwiches in class. Go to the lunchroom.	*Kantine, Mensa*
	patience ['peɪʃns]	You must work harder. I'm losing patience with you.	*Geduld*
	custom ['kʌstəm]	In English-speaking countries, the custom is to give presents on 25 December.	*Gepflogenheit, Brauch*
	to choke [tʃəʊk]	Don't put all that food in your mouth at once. You'll choke.	*ersticken*

tʃ	dʒ	ʃ	ʒ	θ	ð	ŋ	s	z	v	w
chips	jet	ship	garage	thing	the	ring	ice	as	very	wet

Unit 15

S. 125	**globalization** [ˌgləʊbəlaɪ'zeɪʃn]	Do you think that globalization will make all countries the same?	*Globalisierung*
	consumer [kən'sjuːmə]	We're all consumers: we all buy things.	*Verbraucher/in*
	trainers ['treɪnəz]	Alex runs in Nike trainers.	*Turnschuhe*
	watch [wɒtʃ]	What's the time? I'm not wearing my watch.	*(Armband)uhr*
S. 126	**buzzword** ['bʌzwɜːd]	It's a popular buzzword, but I don't think it means much.	*Schlagwort*
	instant(ly) ['ɪnstəntli]	I can't give you an instant answer. I'll tell you later, OK?	*augenblicklich, sofort(ig)*
	relative ['relətɪv]	'Do you have any relatives in Britain?' – 'Yes, my sister.'	*Verwandte/r*
	instant messaging [ˌɪnstənt 'mesɪdʒɪŋ]	Instant messaging is much faster than email.	*Nachrichtensofortversand, Instant Messaging*
	powerful ['paʊəfl]	Is China more powerful than the USA?	*mächtig*
	meanwhile ['miːnwaɪl]	Jim went into the shop and bought some food. Meanwhile, we waited outside.	*unterdessen*
	unfair [ˌʌn'feə]	Hey! You've got more than me. It's unfair.	*ungerecht*
	power ['paʊə]	The US president has more power than anyone else.	*Macht*
	originally [ə'rɪdʒənəli]	Originally I wanted to be a doctor, but then I became a teacher instead.	*ursprünglich*
	to be well off [bi ˌwel 'ɒf]	We used to be poor, but now we're well off.	*gut dran sein*
	potential [pə'tenʃl]	It's a potential problem, but maybe it won't happen.	*potenziell*
	suit [suːt]	Aren't you going to wear a suit to the job interview?	*Anzug, Kostüm*
	beef [biːf]	Beef is meat from cows.	*Rindfleisch*
	wine [waɪn]	Do you prefer white wine, rosé or red?	*Wein*
	to admit [əd'mɪt]	I must admit, I'm not very good at maths.	*zugeben, eingestehen*
	to exist [ɪg'zɪst]	Elves and dragons don't exist.	*existieren*
S. 127	**to benefit from sth** ['benɪfɪt frəm]	It's bad luck for them, but luckily we can benefit from it.	*von etw profitieren*
	trade [treɪd]	I'll give you €200 for your old moped. That's a fair trade, isn't it?	*Handel*
	amazing [ə'meɪzɪŋ]	That is a surprise to me. In fact, I find it amazing.	*erstaunlich*
	law [lɔː]	Murder is against the law, of course.	*Gesetz*
	fashionable ['fæʃnəbl]	Is that a new dress? It's very fashionable.	*in Mode, modisch*
	limited ['lɪmɪtɪd]	His interests are limited. He's only interested in football and girls.	*beschränkt, begrenzt*
	surprising [sə'praɪzɪŋ]	The way the film ended was surprising. I didn't expect it.	*überraschend*
	latest ['leɪtɪst]	Have you seen his latest film? It only came out last week.	*neueste/r/s*
	to be based in ... [bi 'beɪst ɪn]	The British government is based in London.	*seinen Sitz in ... haben*
	fairness ['feənəs]	I'd like to see more fairness in sport.	*Gerechtigkeit*
	agency ['eɪdʒənsi]	The CIA is a US intelligence agency.	*Agentur*
	decade ['dekeɪd]	Which decade was he born in? The 1980s?	*Jahrzehnt*

S. 128	**taste** [teɪst]	Dark chocolate has a bitter taste, don't you think?	*Geschmack*
	yummy ['jʌmi]	That ice cream is really yummy! You should try some.	*lecker*
	bite [baɪt]	Can I just have a little bite of your sandwich?	*Happen, Biss*
	cocoa ['kəʊkəʊ]	To make chocolate, you need cocoa, milk and sugar.	*Kakao*
	Côte d' Ivoire [ˌkot div'war]	⚠ *Aussprache! (französisch)*	*Elfenbeinküste*
	employment agent [ɪm'plɔɪmənt eɪdʒənt]	The employment agent will find you a job.	*Arbeitsvermittler/in*
	cotton ['kɒtn]	My T-shirt is made of cotton.	*Baumwolle*
	hut [hʌt]	We stayed in a small round hut in the African village.	*Hütte*
	field [fi:ld]	The cows are eating grass in the field.	*Feld*
	slave [sleɪv]	The boss owns the workers: they are really just slaves.	*Sklave/Sklavin*
	slavery ['sleɪvəri]	Slavery is illegal all over the world, but it still exists.	*Sklaverei*
	labour ['leɪbə]	Farm labour can be very hard work.	*Arbeit*
	wage [weɪdʒ]	We want a fair wage for a fair day's work.	*Lohn*
	talk [tɔ:k]	My talk is about Fairtrade and how it can change people's lives.	*Vortrag*
	to give a talk [gɪv ə 'tɔ:k]	I have to give a talk to my class about globalization.	*einen Vortrag halten*
	plantation [plæn'teɪʃn]	The farmer grows bananas on a large plantation.	*Plantage*
S. 129	**competitive** [kəm'petətɪv]	If our prices are too high, we won't be competitive.	*konkurrenzfähig*
	profit ['prɒfɪt]	⚠ *Aussprache!*	*Gewinn, Profit*
	to boycott ['bɔɪkɒt]	Do you think we should boycott products from countries we don't like?	*boykottieren*
	protest ['prəʊtest]	⚠ *Aussprache!*	*Protest*
S. 130	**by sea** [baɪ 'si:]	Did you fly or did you go by sea?	*auf dem Seeweg*
	freight [freɪt]	The aircraft is carrying freight, not passengers.	*Fracht*
	forwarder ['fɔ:wədə]	The forwarder will collect the boxes at 3 o'clock.	*Spediteur, Transportunternehmen*
	HGV (heavy goods vehicle) [ˌhevi gʊdz 'vi:əkl]	There were HGVs, buses and cars on the road.	*LKW*
	port operative ['pɔ:t ɒpərətɪv]	I'm a port operative. I load containers onto ships.	*Hafenarbeiter/in*
	stevedore ['sti:vədɔ:]	≈ port operative	*Hafenarbeiter/in*
	customs ['kʌstəmz]	Why didn't customs find the illegal drugs?	*Zoll*
	customs officer ['kʌstəmz ɒfɪsə]	The customs officer asked me to open my suitcase.	*Zollbeamter/-beamtin*
	merchant navy [ˌmɜ:tʃənt 'neɪvi]	He worked in the merchant navy for 20 years and saw many different countries.	*Handelsmarine*
	merchant naval rating [ˌmɜ:tʃənt neɪvl 'reɪtɪŋ]	A merchant naval rating works on a cargo or passenger ship.	*Matrose der Handelsmarine*
	galley ['gæli]	A galley is a ship's 'kitchen'.	*Kombüse*
	cargo ['kɑ:gəʊ]	The ship has a cargo of cocoa and bananas.	*Fracht, Ladung*
	crane [kreɪn]	A crane lifts the containers onto the ship.	*Kran*

tʃ	dʒ	ʃ	ʒ	θ	ð	ŋ	s	z	v	w
chips	jet	ship	garage	thing	the	ring	ice	as	very	wet

forklift truck [ˌfɔːklɪft 'trʌk]	Those boxes are heavy. You'll need a forklift truck to lift them.	*Gabelstapler*
efficient [ɪ'fɪʃnt]	⚠ *Aussprache!*	*effizient*
depot ['depəʊ]	⚠ *Aussprache!*	*Lager, Depot*
distribution [ˌdɪstrɪ'bjuːʃn]	I work in distribution. We send goods to customers.	*Versand*
to inspect [ɪn'spekt]	I need to inspect your bags, madam. Please open them so I can see inside.	*überprüfen, kontrollieren*
duty ['djuːti]	You'll have to pay duty on that alcohol, sir.	*Zollgebühr(en)*
Easter bunny [ˌiːstə 'bʌni]	My girlfriend gave me an Easter bunny, but I hate chocolate.	*Osterhase*
logistics [lə'dʒɪstɪks]	Logistics is all about efficient transport of goods.	*Logistik*
T **to turn up** [ˌtɜːn 'ʌp]	I don't know where it is, but I'm sure it will turn up.	*auftauchen, erscheinen*
reference number ['refərəns nʌmbə]	Each customer has a reference number on our computer system.	*Referenz*
to shine [ʃaɪn]	The sun is shining. It's a beautiful day.	*scheinen*
S. 131 **sack** [sæk]	⚠ *Aussprache!*	*Sack*
bean [biːn]	Green beans are my favourite vegetable.	*Bohne*
to make a living [meɪk ə 'lɪvɪŋ]	She makes a living as a taxi driver.	*den Lebensunterhalt verdienen*
to come up to sb [ˌkʌm 'ʌp tə]	A man came up to me in the street and asked me for money.	*auf jdn zukommen*
advantage [əd'vɑːntɪdʒ]	One advantage of learning English is that you can use it in many countries.	*Vorteil*

Alphabetisches Wörterverzeichnis

Dieses Wörterverzeichnis enthält alle Wörter aus **Keep Going** in alphabetischer Reihenfolge. Hier sind jedoch die Wörter, die zum Grundwortschatz gehören, nicht aufgeführt.

T = das Wort befindet sich im *Transcript* (Hörübung). **F** = das Wort befindet sich in den *Files*.

A

ability Fähigkeit *50*
able, to be ~ to in der Lage sein, können *22*
abroad im Ausland *22*
academic Akademiker/in *102*
accident Unfall *39*
accidentally versehentlich, zufällig *54*
accomodation Unterkunft *30*
according to nach, gemäß, zufolge *76*
Accounts Buchhaltung *56*
to act sich benehmen, sich verhalten *70*
action Handlung, Handeln, Aktion, Action *78*
activity Aktivität; hier: Betriebsamkeit *38*
adaptation Anpassung, Umstellung *110*
to add hinzufügen *58;* **to add up** zusammenrechnen *79*
addicted süchtig *12*
addictive, to be ~ süchtig machen *46*
adhesive tape Heftpflaster *117*
administrative Verwaltungs- *116*
to admit zugeben, eingestehen *126*
adolescence Jugend, Pubertät *101*
adult erwachsen, Erwachsene/r *10*
adulthood Erwachsenenalter *101*
advantage Vorteil *131*
adventure Abenteuer *8*
to advertise bewerben, Werbung machen für *84*
advertisement Anzeige, Inserat *9*
advice Rat, Ratschläge *22*
to advise beraten, raten *60*
to afford sth sich etw leisten können *112*
Afghanistan Afghanistan *22*
afraid, I'm ~ ... Leider ... *18*
after all doch *62*
after-sales support Nachverkaufsunterstützung, Kundendienst, Support *60*
agency Agentur *127*
aggressive aggressiv *15*
to agree zustimmen *48*
to aim beabsichtigen, anstreben *96*
alcohol Alkohol *14*
to allow erlauben, gestatten *10;* **to be allowed to do sth** etw tun dürfen *10*
almost fast, beinah *86*
amazing erstaunlich *127*
ambassador Botschafter *38*
ambitious ehrgeizig *110*
ambulance Krankenwagen, Rettungswagen *117*
amplifier Verstärker *80*
amusement Vergnügung *86*
analytical analytisch *108*
T **ancient** alt, uralt *52*
angry wütend, verärgert *49*
animated film Zeichentrickfilm, Animationsfilm *86*
annoying lästig, ärgerlich *24*
anonymous anonym *94*
antiseptic liquid Desinfektionslösung *117*
to apologize sich entschuldigen *54*
appearance Aussehen, Erscheinungsbild *100*
appetizer Appetithappen *42*
to applaud applaudieren, Beifall klatschen *43*
applause Beifall, Applaus *42*
to apply sich bewerben *32*
appointment Termin *18*
apprenticeship Ausbildung(splatz) *65*
arborist Baumpfleger/in *97*
archer Bogenschütze/-in *108*
area Bereich, Gebiet *21*
to argue sich streiten *38*
around ungefähr, zirka *21*
to arrest sb jdn verhaften *121*
arrow Pfeil *40*
art Kunst; Grafik, Illustration *60*
artist Grafiker/in, Zeichner/in *9;* Künstler/in *25*
aspect Seite, Aspekt *22*
assault Körperverletzung; Angriff, Überfall *69*
assignment Auftrag, Aufgabe *23*
to assist helfen, mithelfen, assistieren *50;* **to assist sb with sth** jdm bei etw helfen *17*
astrological sign Sternzeichen *108*
at first zunächst *94;* **at first sight** auf den ersten Blick *24*
at least zumindest, wenigstens *12*
T **athletic** sportlich *72*
atmosphere Atmosphäre *38*
atomic Atom- *46*
to attach beifügen, anhängen *58*
to attack angreifen *74*
to attempt versuchen *76*
to attend sth in/zu etw gehen, bei etw anwesend sein *30*
attendant Bedienstete/r *92*
attention Aufmerksamkeit *20;* **to pay attention** aufpassen, achtgeben *20*
attitude Einstellung, Haltung *45*
to attract anlocken, anziehen *50*
attraction Attraktion *104*
auction Versteigerung, Auktion *90*
to auction (off) versteigern *90*
authorised befugt *33*
automated automatisiert *65*
auto rickshaw Autorikscha, Motorikscha, Tuk-Tuk *38*
available erhältlich *32*
average Durchschnitt(s-) *39;* **on average** durchschnittlich *46*
awful schrecklich, fürchterlich *63*

B

back Rücken *94;* **back seat** Rücksitz *121*
to back sth up etw untermauern, rechtfertigen, begründen *67*
background Hintergrund *11;* Herkunft *96*
backstage hinter der Bühne *33*
bacon Speck *30*
T **baggy** weit (geschnitten) *82*
bald kahl, glatzköpfig *72*
bandage Bandage *117*
bank robber Bankräuber/in *72*
barbecue Grill(party) *80*
bartender Barkeeper *105*
baseball bat Baseballschläger *121*
based, to be ~ in ... seinen Sitz in ... haben *127*
beach umbrella Sonnenschirm *11*
bean Bohne *131*
to beat (sb) (jdn) schlagen *12*
beef Rindfleisch *126*
beer Bier *69*
behaviour Verhalten, Benehmen *56*
belly Bauch *76*
to belong to sb jdm gehören *18*
to benefit from sth von etw profitieren *127*
bill Rechnung *44*
billboard Werbetafel *84*
billion Milliarde *9*
billionaire Milliardär/in *39*
bin Mülleimer *17*

T **binoculars** Fernglas *97*
biography Biografie *70*
birth Geburt *117;*
to give birth gebären, ein Kind zur Welt bringen *117*
bite Happen, Biss *128*
blind blind *12*
block of flats Wohlblock, Mietshaus *37*
board game Brettspiel *24*
border Grenze *109*
borough Bezirk *50*
T **to borrow** ausleihen *37*
box office (Theater-, Kino-)Kasse *86*
to boycott boykottieren *129*
bracket Klammer *10*
to brainstorm Ideen sammeln *55*
branch Zweig, Sparte (eines Unternehmens) *86*
brand Marke, Designerlabel *24*
breadcrumbs Brotkrümel, Brösel *105*
break Pause *14*
to break brechen *56;* kaputtgehen *74;* **to break sth** etw kaputtmachen *110;*
to break down kaputtgehen *17;*
to break into einbrechen in *60;*
to break out ausbrechen *118*
breakthrough Durchbruch *86*
breath Atem *6;* **breath of fire** die Fähigkeit, Feuer zu speien *6*
to breathe atmen *8;*
to breathe fire Feuer speien *8*
breathing Atmung *120*
briefcase Aktentasche *18*
bright intelligent, aufgeweckt *14;* (Farbe:) leuchtend *99*
T **brilliant** genial, glänzend *14;* toll, super *97*
broad breit, groß *110*
brochure Prospekt, Werbebroschüre *89*
broken gebrochen, kaputt *73*
budget Budget, Etat, Haushalt *59*
to build bauen, aufbauen, errichten *6*
builder Bauunternehmer/in, Bauarbeiter/in *110*
building Gebäude *37*
bull Stier *108*
bully Mobber/in, Tyrann/in *70*
bullying Mobben, Tyrannisieren *70*
bunch (von Menschen) Gruppe, Haufen *110*
bush Busch *97*
businesswoman Geschäftsfrau *16*
to busk Straßenmusik machen *112*
button Knopf *65*
buyer Käufer/in *80*
buzzword Schlagwort *126*
by mistake irrtümlich *55;*
by sea auf dem Seeweg *130*
bystander Zuschauer/in *69*

C
cabbage Kohl *94*
T **cabin** Kabine *67*
cable Kabel *80*
to call nennen *12;*
to call sb names jdn beleidigen, jdn beschimpfen *70*
caller Anrufer/in *88*
calm ruhig *15*
to camp zelten *30*
campsite Campingplatz *30*
can Dose *25*
canteen Kantine *34*
capital Hauptstadt *109;*
capital letter Großbuchstabe *56*
captain Kapitän/in *15*
car manufacturing Automobilbau *65*
cardboard Pappe *14*
to care about sth sich um etw kümmern, scheren *94*
care assistant Pflegeassistent/in *50*
career Karriere, Beruf, Laufbahn *50*
carefully sorgfältig *15;* aufmerksam *61*
cargo Fracht, Ladung *130*
caring liebevoll, sozial eingestellt *50*
carpentry Tischlern, Zimmerhandwerk *96*
carpet Teppich *17*
carrier Träger/in *108*
to carry out durchführen *50*
carton Karton *93*
T **case, in ~** falls *119*
cash Bargeld *30;* bar *81;*
T **cash desk** Kasse *82;*
cash register Registrierkasse *18*
casual, to get ~ jobs jobben *112*
to catch fangen, fassen *28;* **to catch sth** etw hören, verstehen *113*
category Kategorie, Klasse *10*
caterer Lieferant von Speisen und Getränken, Caterer *33*
to cause verursachen *115*
to celebrate feiern *122*
cell phone Handy, Mobiltelefon *25*
certain sicher *65*
certificate Zeugnis, Zertifikat, Diplom *17*
chainsaw Kettensäge *97*
T **challenging** fordernd, anspruchsvoll *64*
chancellor Kanzler/in *27*
changing room Umkleidekabine *82*
chaotic chaotisch *38*
character Charakter, (Film-, Roman-) Figur, Person *6;* **character assassination** Rufmord *69*
characteristic Merkmal, Eigenschaft *108*
to charge (a price) (einen Preis) verlangen, berechnen *77*
charity gemeinnützige Organisation *50*
to chase jagen, nachjagen *106*
to chat sich unterhalten, plaudern *34*
to check überprüfen *17*
chef Koch/Köchin *42*
childhood Kindheit *101*
chimpanzee Schimpanse *121*
F **chocolate bar** Schokoriegel *67*
choice Wahl, Auswahl *15*
to choke ersticken *124*
T **chopsticks** Stäbchen *124*
circuit Schaltung, Schaltkreis *40*
circulation Kreislauf *120*
civil defence Zivilschutz *119*
class Kurs *17;*
classmate Klassenkamerad/in *62*
to clean up aufräumen, saubermachen *78*
clerk Verkäufer/in *81*
clever klug, schlau, clever *6*
to click klicken, anklicken *10*
climate Klima *45;*
climate change Klimawandel *45*
to climb klettern *34;* **to climb up** hochklettern, erklimmen *97*
close eng *110*
close-up Nahaufnahme *107*
clothing Kleidung *58*
T **cloudy** bewölkt *27*
clue Anhaltspunkt, Hinweis *104*
coach Trainer/in *14*
cocoa Kakao *128*
coin Münze *24*
cold Erkältung *113*
colleague Kollege/Kollegin *23*
collection Sammlung *50*
college Berufsschule *16*
column Spalte *39*
to combine kombinieren *60*
to come up to sb auf jdn zukommen *131;* **to come true** wahr werden *14*
comment Bemerkung, Kommentar *54*
to commit (a crime) (eine Straftat) begehen *69*
common häufig, weit verbreitet *60;*
to have sth in common etw gemeinsam haben *25*
to communicate kommunizieren, sich verständigen *26*
communication Kommunikation *50;*
communication difficulties Verständigungsschwierigkeiten *113*
communicative kommunikativ *108*
community Gemeinde, Gemeinschaft *96;*
community service Zivildienst *22*
company Gesellschaft, Firma *9*
to compare vergleichen *45*
compensation Entschädigung, Schadenersatz *74*
competition Wettbewerb *14*
competitive konkurrenzfähig *129*
to complain sich beschweren *54*
complaint Beschwerde, Reklamation *54*
complex komplex *65*

A–Z word list

complicated kompliziert 8
complication Komplikation 119
compliment Kompliment 38
concert hall Konzertsaal 37
conclusion Schluss 81
condition Zustand; Leiden, Beschwerden 120
conference Konferenz 85
confession Geständnis 54
to confirm bestätigen 113
confusion Verwirrung 115
to connect verbinden 40
connection Verbindung 56
conscious bei Bewusstsein 120
consciousness Bewusstsein 120
console Konsole 80
construction Baugewerbe 61
consulting Beratung 90
consumer Verbraucher/in 125
contact Kontakt, Kontaktperson 58; **contact lens** Kontaktlinse 40
T **contactor** Schalter 119
to contain enthalten 95
container Behältnis 93
contest Wettbewerb, Wettkampf 27
contract Vertrag 77
T **control** Kontrolle 46; Regler 80; Steuerung 119; **control room** Steuerraum, Leitstand 118
conversation Gespräch, Unterhaltung 19
cook Koch/Köchin 42
cool, to lose one's ~ die Fassung verlieren 117
to cool down sich beruhigen 56
cooperative kooperativ 15
to coordinate koordinieren 42
coordination Koordination 116
T **(the) cops** die Bullen 72
to copy abschreiben, kopieren 7
corner Ecke 10
corporation Konzern, Gesellschaft 86
T **corpulent** korpulent 72
costume Kostüm 78
cotton Baumwolle 128
council Stadtrat, Bezirksrat 94
councillor (Stadt-, Bezirks-) Ratsmitglied 94
countryside Landschaft, Land 25
courageous mutig 108
courier Kurier 38
course (Menü:) Gang 42
court Spielfeld 14; Gericht 76
to cover abdecken, bedecken 117
crab Krebs, Krabbe 42
crane Kran 130
crash course Schnellkurs 57
to create schaffen 50
creation Schöpfung 9
creative kreativ 9
creativity Kreativität 87
creator Schöpfer/in 87
credit Guthaben 58
crew Mannschaft 33
crime Kriminalität; Verbrechen, Straftat 69; **crime scene** Tatort 72
criminal Verbrecher/in, Kriminelle/r 8
criticism Kritik 56
to criticize kritisieren 55
crossroad Kreuzung 120
crowd Menge 84
crowded überfüllt 84
cruise Kreuzfahrt 86
cultivation Kultivierung 96
culture Kulture 22
curious neugierig 25
curly lockig 72
current aktuell 16; **currently** aktuell, im Moment 28
curriculum vitae (CV) Lebenslauf 32
custom Gepflogenheit, Brauch 124
customer Kunde/Kundin 25; **customer service** Kundendienst 30
customs Zoll 130; **customs officer** Zollbeamter/-beamtin 130
to cut down (a tree) (einen Baum) fällen 97; **to cut open** aufschneiden 76

D

daily routine Tagesablauf 16
damage Schaden 97
damaged, to get ~ beschädigt werden 80
dance of joy Freudentanz 76
darkness Dunkelheit, Finsternis 6
data entry Dateneingabe 116
date, out of ~ überholt, veraltet 65
dead end Sackgasse 110
to deal with sth mit etw fertig werden, mit etw zurechtkommen 22
decade Jahrzehnt 127
decision Entscheidung, Entschluss 64
to decline ablehnen 25
to decorate dekorieren, schmücken 78
decoration Dekoration, Schmuck 78
deer Reh 121
defender Verteidiger/in 15
definitely bestimmt, absolut 48
T **degree** Grad 27; Hochschulabschluss 110
to delete löschen 54
delicious lecker 78
to deliver liefern, anliefern 42
delivery Lieferung 43
dental assistant Zahnmedizinische/r Fachangestellte/r 116
dentist Zahnarzt/-ärztin 116
dentures Gebiss, Zahnersatz 116
department Abteilung 54
deposit Pfand 93
depot Lager, Depot 130
depressed niedergeschlagen, deprimiert 71
depressing deprimierend 49
F **desert island** einsame Insel 67
to design entwerfen, gestalten, konstruieren, bauen 10
despatch Versand 98; **despatch note** Versandanzeige, Warenbegleitschein 98
desperately verzweifelt 110
dessert Nachtisch, Dessert 42
detail Detail, Einzelheit 9
detective Detektiv 74; (Kriminal-) Polizist/in 78
determined entschlossen 108
to develop entwickeln 60
developer Entwickler/in 87
development Entwicklung 22; **development worker** Entwicklungshelfer/in 22
to die sterben 101
difference Unterschied 14; **to make a difference** etwas bewirken 50
difficulty Schwierigkeit 113
diploma Abschluss 102
to direct sb jdm den Weg zeigen 30
direction Richtung 40; **to give sb directions** jdm den Weg zeigen/erklären 41
disabled behindert, Behinderten- 30
to disagree nicht zustimmen 48
disaster Katastrophe 22
discount Rabatt, Nachlass 77
to discuss besprechen, erörtern, diskutieren 18
dish Gericht 42; **dishes** Geschirr 43; **dishwasher** Spülmaschine; Spüler/in 42
to disinfect desinfizieren 116
dispatcher Disponent/in 119
display Anzeige, Display 10
distribution Versand 130
to divide teilen, aufteilen 42
to divorce sich scheiden lassen 102
divorced geschieden 25
DIY store Baumarkt 74
T **dizzy** schwindlig 119
documentary Dokumentar-, Dokumentation 48
donor Spender/in 50
doorman Türsteher 105
dragon Drachen 6
to draw sth up etw aufstellen, entwerfen, aufsetzen 16
drawer Schublade 89
dried getrocknet, Trocken- 93
drill Bohrer 18
to drive sb crazy jdn in den Wahnsinn treiben 54
driving licence Führerschein 24
drop-out (Schul-, Uni-)Abbrecher/in 102
to drop out (of school) (die Schule) abbrechen 102
drug Droge 14
drum Fass 99
drunk driving Alkohol am Steuer 69
dude Typ, Kumpel 49
dull langweilig 116
duty Aufgabe, Pflicht 50; Zollgebühr(en) 130
dwarf, dwarves Zwerg, Zwerge 86

E

to earn verdienen, einbringen, einspielen *86*
Easter bunny Osterhase *130*
economic wirtschaftlich, Wirtschafts- *38*
education (Schul-)Bildung *32*
educational Ausbildungs- *96*
effective effektiv *80*
efficient effizient *130*
either ... or entweder ... oder *76*
elastic bandage elastische Binde *117*
(the) elderly ältere Menschen *50*
electrician Elektriker/in *119*
electricity Elekrizität *6*
elf Kobold, Elfe *6*
to embarrass sb jdm peinlich sein, jdn bloßstellen *54*
embarrassed, to be ~ sich schämen *54*
embarrassment Verlegenheit, Peinlichkeit, Ärgernis *54*
embassy Botschaft *38*
emergency Notfall *110;*
T **emergency control** Notsteuerung *119*
emotional emotional, gefühlsbetont *108*
empire Reich *6*
to employ beschäftigen, einstellen *62*
employee Angestellte/r *52*
employer Arbeitgeber/in *54*
employment agent Arbeitsvermittler/in *128*
empty leer *82*
to empty leeren *17*
engaged verlobt *25*
engine Motor *93;* **two-stroke engine** Zweitaktmotor *93*
engineer Ingenieur/in *65*
to enjoy sth etw genießen, gern haben *20*
Enjoy your meal. Guten Appetit. *44*
enormous enorm *76*
to enter (Computer:) eingeben *98*
entertainment Unterhaltung, Entertainment *33*
enthusiastic begeistert *64*
entry Eintritt, Zutritt *30*
envelope Briefumschlag *89*
environment Umwelt, Umfeld, Umgebung *93*
environmental Umwelt- *96*
equipment Geräte *17*
equipped ausgestattet *111*
to escape entkommen, entfliehen *62*
especially besonders, eigens, extra *10*
essay Aufsatz *46*
to evaluate bewerten, beurteilen *62*
event Ereignis *27;* Veranstaltung *33*
examination Untersuchung *116*
to examine untersuchen *76*
excellent hervorragend *57*
except for außer *70*
exchange Austausch, Tausch *24*
exercise Bewegung *23;* **to get (some) exercise** Sport treiben, trainieren, sich bewegen *23*
exercise machine Trainings-/Fitnessgerät *18*
to exist existieren *126*
T **to expect** erwarten *27*
experience Erfahrung, Erlebnis *22*
experienced erfahren *52*
explanation Erklärung, Erläuterung *57*
to express ausdrücken *48*
expression Ausdruck *17*
extremely äußerst *6*

F

fabric Stoff, Gewebe *61*
face-to-face persönlich *53*
factor Faktor *7*
to fail versagen, scheitern *61;* **to fail a test** eine Prüfung nicht bestehen *122*
fairness Gerechtigkeit *127*
fairy tale Märchen *76*
to fall over hinfallen *12;* **to fall in love** sich verlieben *101*
fame Ruhm *14*
farmer Bauer/Bäuerin, Landwirt/in, Farmer/in *22*
fashionable in Mode, modisch *127*
fault Fehler, Defekt *60*
favourite Lieblings- *6*
feature Merkmal, Eigenschaft *57*
to feed ernähren *50*
to feel glauben, der Ansicht sein *94*
feeling Gefühl *53*
female weiblich *14*
fence Zaun *34*
Ferris wheel Riesenrad *118*
fertilizer Dünger *97*
to fetch holen *116*
field Feld *128*
to fight kämpfen, bekämpfen, streiten *28*
figure Gestalt *94*
to figure out herausfinden *92*
file Datei *58;* (Patienten-)Akte *116*
to fill in ausfüllen *116;* **to fill an order** einen Auftrag ausführen *103*
finally zuletzt, endlich *11*
finance Finanz- *89*
fine Geldstrafe *74*
fire brigade Feuerwehr *117;* **fire extinguisher** Feuerlöscher *119;* **fire fighter** Feuerwehrmann/frau *119*
firm Firma *90*
first aid Erste Hilfe *17;* **first-aid kit** Verbandskasten *117*
fish tank Aquarium *104*
F **fishing** Angeln *67*
to fit (sth) (zu/in etw) passen *31*
to fix sth etw reparieren, flicken *17*
flag Flagge *109*
flat, block of ~s Wohlblock, Mietshaus *37*
flat tyre platter Reifen *38*
flavour Geschmack, Aroma *101;* **...-flavoured** mit ...-Geschmack *93*
T **flight** Flug *27*
flood Hochwasser, Überschwemmung *117*
floor Fußboden *17;* Stockwerk, Etage *89*
fluent (bei Fremdsprachen:) fließend *32*
focus hier: Konzentrationsfähigkeit *23*
to focus on sth sich auf etw konzentrieren *23*
to follow folgen *14*
(the) following (der/die/das) folgende *10*
foreground Vordergrund *11*
foreign ausländisch, fremd, Fremd- *21*
foreigner Ausländer/in *24*
forest Wald *6*
forestry Forstwirtschaft *97*
to forgive verzeihen *122*
forklift truck Gabelstapler *130*
form Formular *116*
fortune teller Wahrsager/in *51*
to forward weiterleiten *54*
forwarder Spediteur, Transportunternehmen *130*
to found gründen *26*
founding Gründung *91*
(for) free kostenlos, gratis *10*
freight Fracht *130*
full moon Vollmond *108*
function Funktion *106*
fundraiser Spendensammler/in *50*
to further one's career beruflich weiterkommen *110*

G

galley Kombüse *130*
gaming console Spielkonsole *9*
gang Bande *94*
gap Lücke *10*
to garden gärtnern *94*
garden bed Beet *94*
gardener Gärtner/in *92*
gauze bandage Mullbinde *117*
gay schwul *70*
gear Ausrüstung *58*
generous großzügig *108*
genius Genie *87*
gentle sanft *15*
gerbil Rennmaus *104*
germ Keim *117*
to get around herumkommen, sich fortbewegen *38*
to get to know kennen lernen *42*
to get up aufstehen *20*
giant Riese *15*
gift Geschenk *11*
gigantic riesig *86*
gist das Wesentliche *14*
to give sth up etw aufgeben, mit etw aufhören *14;* **to give a talk** einen Vortrag halten *128;*

- **to give birth** gebären, ein Kind zur Welt bringen *117*; **to give sb directions** jdm den Weg zeigen/erklären *41*
- **glasses** Brille *75*
- **globalization** Globalisierung *125*
- **gloves** Handschuhe *97*
- **to go together (well)** (gut) zueinander passen *61*
- **goalkeeper** Torwart/in *15*
- **goat** Ziege, Bock *108*
- T **Goodness!** Meine Güte! *72*
- **goods** Ware(n) *98*
- **government** Regierung *26*
- **graph** Diagramm *48*
- **greedy** gierig, habgierig *74*
- **greenhouse** Gewächshaus, Treibhaus *98*
- **to greet sb** jdn begrüßen *85*
- **ground** Boden, Erde *34*
- **to grow** wachsen *9*; **to grow sth** etw anbauen *94*
- **to guess** raten, erraten *21*
- **guide** Führer *38*
- **guilty** schuldig *69*
- **guy** Typ, Kumpel *6*
- **gym** Fitness-Studio *17*
- **gymnastics** Turnen *13*

H

- **haircut, to get a ~** sich die Haare schneiden lassen *66*
- **hairpiece** Toupet, Haarteil *92*
- **half, halves** Hälfte, Hälften *87*
- **to hallucinate** halluzinieren *121*
- **to hand** überreichen, (über)geben *116*
- **hand-to-eye coordination** Hand-Auge-Koordination *116*
- **handkerchief** Taschentuch *113*
- **to handle sth** etw handhaben, mit etw umgehen *30*
- **happiness** Glück *101*
- **hard: to have a ~ time doing sth** es schwer haben *38*
- T **hard hat** Helm *97*
- **to have sth in common** etw gemeinsam haben *25*
- **head** Chef- *42*
- **heading** Überschrift *14*
- **heads** (Münze:) Kopf *24*
- **health** Gesundheit *22*; **health care** Gesundheitswesen, medizinische Versorgung *116*
- **health services officer** Kaufmann/-frau im Gesundheitswesen *116*
- **healthy** gesund *13*
- **heating** Heizung *65*
- **height** Höhe *97*
- **helmet** Helm *22*
- **herd** Herde *10*
- **HGV (heavy goods vehicle)** LKW *130*
- **hidden** verborgen, versteckt *10*
- **to highlight** hervorheben *38*
- **to hire sb** jdn einstellen *17*; jdn beauftragen *78*
- **to hit sb** hier: jdn anfahren *121*; **to hit sb off the road** jdn von der Straße drängen *12*
- **hoax** Streich, Jux *54*
- **to hold** halten, abhalten, veranstalten *16*; abhalten *96*; **to hold sth in place** etw fixieren *117*
- **home** Zuhause, Wohnung, Haus *14*
- **homeless** obdachlos *14*
- **homesick, to feel/be ~** Heimweh haben *22*
- **homesickness** Heimweh *22*
- **honest** ehrlich *69*
- **hopefully** hoffentlich *45*
- **horoscope** Horoskop *108*
- **hospital porter** Pflegekraft *113*
- **host** Gastgeber/in, Moderator/in *78*
- **hostel** (Jugend-)Herberge *112*
- **housing estate** Wohnsiedlung *94*
- **huge** riesig, groß *38*
- **human** Mensch *46*
- **humorous** witzig, humorvoll *107*
- T **to hurry up** sich beeilen *72*
- **to hurt** verletzen *53*; **to hurt sb** jdm wehtun, jdn verletzen *70*; **to hurt oneself** sich wehtun *12*
- **hut** Hütte *128*

I

- T **ID** Ausweis *37*
- **to identify** herausfinden, erkennen, identifizieren *18*
- **identity card** Personalausweis *116*
- **to ignore** ignorieren, nicht beachten *71*
- **illegal** illegal *46*
- **imagination** Phantasie *47*
- **imaginative** phantasievoll, kreativ *50*
- **to imagine** sich vorstellen *40*
- **to imitate** imitieren, nachmachen *101*
- **immediately** sofort, unverzüglich *42*
- **to improve** verbessern, (sich) bessern *14*
- T **to improvise** improvisieren *119*
- T **in case** falls *119*; **in italics** kursiv *103*; **in total** insgesamt *14*
- **to include** beinhalten, umfassen *30*
- **income** Einkommen *50*
- **independent** unabhängig *15*
- T **indicator** Anzeige *80*
- T **individual** Individuum *124*
- **industrial park** Industriegebiet *92*
- **industry** Branche *9*
- **infancy** Säuglingsalter *101*
- **infirmary** Krankenhaus *110*
- **informal** informell *56*
- **information** Angaben, Informationen *7*
- **informed, to keep sb ~** jdn auf dem laufenden halten *17*
- **ingredient** Zutat *42*
- **injured** verletzt *117*
- **innocent** unschuldig *69*
- **to inspect** überprüfen, kontrollieren *130*
- **to install** installieren *65*
- **instant cold pack** Kältekompresse *117*
- **instant messaging** Nachrichten-sofortversand *126*
- **instant(ly)** augenblicklich, sofort(ig) *126*
- **instead** stattdessen *42*
- **instructions** Anleitung *19*
- **instructor** Lehrer/in, Trainer/in *14*
- **to insult** beleidigen, beschimpfen *69*
- **insurance** Versicherung *60*
- **intelligence** Intelligenz *7*
- **intelligent** intelligent *6*
- **intercom** Gegensprechanlage *118*
- **intern** Praktikant/in *88*
- **internship** Praktikum *26*
- T **interview** Vorstellungsgespräch *64*
- T **to introduce sb to sb** jdn jdm vorstellen *52*
- **introduction** Einleitung *81*
- **to invent** erfinden *46*
- **invention** Erfindung *47*
- **inventor** Erfinder/in *87*
- **invitation** Einladung *53*
- **to invite** einladen *25*
- **invoice** Rechnung *77*
- **to involve** betreffen *70*
- **italics, in ~** kursiv *103*
- **item** Artikel, Gegenstand, Ding *56*; **item of clothing** Kleidungsstück *83*
- **Ivory Coast** Elfenbeinküste *128*

J

- **job interview** Vorstellungsgespräch *66*; **job opportunity** offene Stelle *111*; **job-seeker** Arbeitssuchende/r *61*
- **to join** beitreten, mitmachen, eintreten in *90*
- **joint** Gelenk *117*
- **to joke** scherzen *15*
- **judge** Richter/in *69*
- **jury** die Geschworenen *76*; **member of the jury** Geschworene/r *76*

K

- **karate** Karate *13*
- T **keen, to be ~ on sth** auf etw versessen sein *64*
- **to keep in touch** in Kontakt bleiben *57*; **to keep on top of things** den Überblick haben/behalten *59*; **to keep sb informed** jdn auf dem laufenden halten *17*
- T **key** Schlüssel *27*; **keyboard** Tastatur *87*
- **kind** Art *31*
- **to kiss** (sich) küssen *20*
- **know, to get to ~ sb** jdn kennen lernen *42*
- T **knowledge** Wissen, Kenntnisse *64*

L

- **label** Etikett *92*
- **to label** kennzeichnen, etikettieren *98*
- **laboratory** Labor *116*
- **labour** Arbeit *128*
- **ladder** Leiter *97*

laugh, a ~ ein Spaß *94*
lake See *6*
lamb Lamm *43*
landmark Orientierungspunkt *120*
laser pointer Lichtzeiger, Laserpointer *90*
to last dauern *14*
latest neueste/r/s *127*
latex glove Latexhandschuh *117*
to laugh lachen *15*
law Gesetz *127*
lawnmower Rasenmäher *97*
T **to lead** führen *64*
leader Führer/in *12*
leaf, leaves (Laub-)Blatt, Blätter *97*
leaflet Flugblatt, Handzettel *94*
T **leather** Leder *72*
leisure Freizeit *16*
T **to lend** leihen *80*
length Länge *86*
lens Linse *40*
to let sb out hier: jdn entlassen *76*
letterbox Briefkasten *94*
level Niveau *120*
lie Lüge *69*
life, Get a ~! Werd' endlich erwachsen! *56*
lifesaving Lebensrettung *17*
lifetime Leben, Lebensdauer *48*
lift Mitfahrgelegenheit *112*
light Licht, Lampe, Leuchte *6;* hell *72*
lighting Beleuchtung *65*
lightning Blitz *104*
limited beschränkt, begrenzt *127*
to line sth up etw organisieren *62*
lion Löwe *108*
litter Abfall *97*
Little Red Riding-Hood Rotkäppchen *76*
live lebend, lebendig *98*
living, to make a ~ den Lebensunterhalt verdienen *131*
lobster Hummer *42*
local örtlich, ansässig *94*
located, to be ~ sich befinden, liegen *92*
location Ort, Stelle *66*
to lock sth in sth etw in etw einschließen *121*
locker Spind *54*
logistics Logistik *130*
lonely einsam *97T*
T **to look after sb** sich um jdn kümmern *52;* **to look forward to sth** sich auf etw freuen *58;* **to look sth up** etw (im Wörterbuch) nachschlagen *31*
to lose one's cool die Fassung verlieren *117*
loser Verlierer/in *56*
lost property office Fundbüro *114*
to lower abseilen, herunterlassen *118*
loyal loyal, treu *108*
luckily zum Glück *22*
lunchroom Kantine, Mensa *124*
lyrics (Lied-)Text *27*

M

machine operator Maschinenführer/in *103*
machinery Maschinen *65*
machinist Maschinist/in *65*
mad, to be ~ about sth nach etw verrückt sein *14*
magic show Zaubervorstellung *105;* **magic wand** Zauberstab *6*
mail Post *85;* **mail room** Poststelle *92*
mail-order company Versandhandel *53*
main dish Hauptgericht *42*
to maintain warten, unterhalten *17*
to make a difference etwas bewirken *50;* **to make a living** den Lebensunterhalt verdienen *131;* **to make sense** Sinn haben/ergeben, einleuchten *56;* **to make sth up** etw erfinden, sich etw ausdenken *62;* **to make sure** sicherstellen, gewährleisten *17*
male männlich *14*
man-made künstlich hergestellt *95*
to manage leiten, verwalten *50;* gelingen, es schaffen *102*
management Geschäftsführung, Verwaltung, Management *62*
manager Geschäftsführer/in, Leiter/in *19*
T **managing director** Geschäftsführer/in *52*
manner Art (des Umgangs) *116*
manufacturing Fertigung(sindustrie) *61*
to mark kennzeichnen *59*
to marry heiraten *24*
T **mask** Maske *72*
T **match, to be a good ~ for sth** gut zu etw passen *64*
to match zuordnen *17*
material Material *61*
meal Essen, Mahlzeit *30*
to mean bedeuten, heißen *8*
meaning Bedeutung *17*
meanwhile unterdessen *126*
medal Medaille *14*
medic Arzt/Ärztin *22*
medical assistant Medizinische/r Fachangestellte/r *116;* **medical insurance** Krankenversicherung *116;* **medical supply company** Unternehmen für Sanitätsbedarf *116*
medicine Arznei, Medizin *6*
member Mitglied *14;* **member of the jury** Geschworene/r *76*
membership Mitgliedschaft *17*
mental geistig, mental *23*
to mention erwähnen, (be)nennen *23*
menu Speisekarte *21*
merchant naval rating Matrose der Handelsmarine, Schiffsmechaniker/in *130;* **merchant navy** Handelmarine *130*
message Mitteilung, Botschaft *49*
T **mile** Meile *41*
military Militär *22*
to mime pantomimisch darstellen *29*
minister Minister/in *26*
minor kleiner *116*
minority Minderheit *70*
miserable elend *102*
to miss sb/sth jdn/etw vermissen *22;*
T **to miss sth** etw verfehlen *41*
mission Auftrag, Einsatz, Mission *22*
mistake, by ~ irrtümlich *55*
misunderstanding Missverständnis *113*
to misuse missbrauchen, zweckentfremden *121*
mixed gemischt *14*
mobile (phone) Handy, Mobiltelefon *25*
model Muster, Vorbild *32*
monitor Monitor *40*
to monitor überwachen, kontrollieren *50*
moonlit im Mondschein *25*
to mop (auf)wischen *17*
moped Moped *93*
T **motorway** Autobahn *120*
move, on the ~ in Bewegung, unterwegs *38*
to move umziehen *86;* **to move on (to sth)** weitergehen, (zu etw) übergehen *81*
to murder ermorden *78*
murder mystery Krimi *78*
T **muscle** Muskel(n) *72*
musical instrument Musikinstrument *61*
musician Musiker/in *30*
mystery Rätsel, Geheimnis *18;* **mystery shopper** Testkäufer/in *62*

N

to name benennen, nennen *21*
napkin *(AE)* Serviette *44*
nappy Windel *92*
narrow eng *84*
nasty gemein *62*
natural natürlich *95*
nearby in der Nähe *30*
necessary nötig, notwendig *63*
to neglect vernachlässigen *101*
nervous nervös *101*
network Netzwerk *53*
to network vernetzen, Kontakte knüpfen *57*
nickname Spitzname *26*
nightmare Albtraum *6*
T **noisy** laut, lärmend *37*
noodle Nudel *42*
F **nose** Nase *72*
not ... either auch nicht, auch kein/e/n *46*
not ... yet noch nicht *8*
to note down notieren, aufschreiben *50*

A–Z word list

noticeboard Pinnwand *55*
nowadays heutzutage, jetzt *94*
number plate Nummernschild *73*
numerical numerisch, digital *65*
nurse Krankenschwester, Krankenpfleger *103*
nursing home Pflegeheim *50*
nut Nuss *93*

O

object Gegenstand, Objekt *10*
to observe beobachten *97*
occasionally gelegentlich, hin und wieder *54*
odd jobs die anfallenden Arbeiten *17*
to offend beleidigen *56*
official language Amtssprache *109*
oil Öl *93*
once einmal *11*
onion Zwiebel *94*
to operate bedienen *65*
operation Operation *116*
opinion Meinung *15*
opposite Gegenteil *38*
optimist Optimist/in *45*
optimistic optimistisch *45*
option Option, Wahlmöglichkeit *34*
optional optional *79*
order Reihenfolge *55;* Auftrag, Bestellung *98;* **to fill an order** einen Auftrag ausführen *103*
T **order processing** Auftragsabwicklung, -bearbeitung *98*
to order bestellen *44*
organic Bio- *93*
to organize organisieren *50*
organized (gut) organisiert *38*
organizer Organisator/in, Veranstalter/in *34*
originally ursprünglich *126*
out of date überholt, veraltet *65*
to overcook verbrennen *42*
to overdo übertreiben *56*
overtime, to work ~ Überstunden machen *85*
overweight übergewichtig *15*
ownership Besitz *87*

P

to pack packen, einpacken *82*
package Paket *92*
packing list Packliste, Versandliste *98*
pain Schmerz *117;* **painkiller** Schmerzmittel, -tabletten *117*
painting Malen *61*
pan Pfanne, Topf *42*
to pan (Kamera:) schwenken *106*
panel Gremium *67*
panic attack Panikattacke *123*
paramedic Sanitäter/in *34*
to paraphrase umschreiben *114*
parent company Muttergesellschaft *86*
part, to take ~ in sth an etw teilnehmen *16*
part-time Teilzeit- *62*
particular besondere/r/s, spezielle/r/s *54;* **particularly** besonders *50*
pass Pass *33*
to pass reichen, geben *116;* **to pass sth** an etw vobeigehen/-fahren *81;* **to pass a test** eine Prüfung bestehen *122*
passenger Passagier- *26;* Passagier/in, Fahrgast *118*
passion Leidenschaft *102*
patch (of land) Stück (Land) *99*
patience Geduld *124*
patient Patient/in *116;* geduldig *50*
T **pay** Lohn, Gehalt *64*
to pay sich auszahlen *74;* **to pay attention** aufpassen, achtgeben *20*
payment Zahlung *30*
peaceful friedlich *94*
peacekeeping soldier Soldat/in einer UN-Friedenstruppe *22*
to peel schälen *42*
pensioner Rentner/in *49*
pepper Paprika *25*
percentage Anteil, Prozentsatz *77*
to perform aufführen, spielen *76*
performer Mitwirkende/r *33*
performing arts darstellende Künste *61*
personnel officer Personalreferent/in, Personalchef/in *52*
to persuade sb jdn überzeugen, überreden *110*
pessimist Pessimist/in *45*
pesticide Schädlingsbekämpfungsmittel *97*
pharmaceutical Pharma-, pharmazeutisch *103*
pharmacy Apotheke *37*
PhD Doktortitel *102*
phew! puh! *46*
photograph Foto(grafie) *25*
to photograph fotografieren *28*
phrase Formulierung, Satzteil *11*
physical körperlich, physisch *23*
piano Klavier *34*
to pick pflücken, ernten *94*
pickaxe Pickel *94*
pie Kuchen, Pastete *33*
pile Haufen, Stapel *94*
place, to take ~ stattfinden *16*
to plant pflanzen *94*
plant nursery Gärtnerei *98*
plantation Plantage *128*
plaster Pflaster *117*
T **platform** Bahnsteig *37*
pleased froh, erfreut *33*
T **to plug sth** in etw anschließen, einstecken *80*
point, There isn't any ~ in ... Es hat gar keinen Sinn ... *45*
to point zeigen *82*
to polish polieren *17*
pollution (Umwelt-)Verschmutzung *46*
popular (with sb) beliebt (bei jdm) *8*
population Bevölkerung *39*
pork Schweinefleisch *43*
port operative Hafenarbeiter/in *130*
position Stelle, Position *63*
possession Besitz *69*
possibility Möglichkeit *17*
poster Plakat *30*
pot Kanne *25;* Topf *98*
potential Potential *57;* potenziell *126*
power Energie, Strom *46;* Macht *126;* **power failure** Stromausfall *117;* **power generation** Stromerzeugung *65;* **power tool** Elektrowerkzeug *61*
powerful mächtig *126*
practical praktisch *9*
practice Praxis *116*
precision Präzision, Präzisions- *103*
to predict voraussagen, vorhersehen *65*
prediction Voraussage *46*
preparation Vorbereitung *42*
to prepare (sich) vorbereiten *42;* zubereiten *42*
to present vorstellen, präsentieren *84*
presentation Präsentation, Vortrag *81*
press Presse *50*
to pretend vorgeben, sich ausgeben als *76*
to prevent verhüten, verhindern *97*
primary school Grundschule *32*
printer Drucker *18*
printout Ausdruck *54*
prison Gefängnis *69;* **prison officer** Gefängniswärter/in *69*
prize Preis *78*
probation Bewährung *69;* **probation officer** Bewährungshelfer/in *69*
to process bearbeiten *98*
to produce produzieren, herstellen *40*
producer Produzent/in, Hersteller/in *87*
product Produkt *9*
production Produktion, Herstellung *87*
profession Beruf *102*
professional Berufs-, professionell, berufsmäßig *9*
profile Profil *50*
profit Gewinn, Profit *129*
to program programmieren *9*
programme Sendung *48*
programmer Programmierer/in *9*
to promise versprechen *24*
T **promotion** Beförderung, Aufstieg *64*
properly richtig *60*
property Eigentum *69;* **property developer** Immobilienfirma *94*
to protect schützen *97*
protest Protest *129*
to publish verlegen, veröffentlichen *86*

A–Z word list

publisher Verleger/in, Verlag *86*
to pull sb/sth out jdn/etw herausziehen *76*
pulse Puls *120*
punishment Bestrafung, Strafe *76*
T **to put out (a fire)** (ein Feuer) löschen *119;* **to put sb through** (Telefon:) jdn durchstellen *88;* **to put up** aufstellen *17*
puzzle Rätsel *92*

Q
qualification Qualifikation, Abschluss *45*
quality Qualität *106;* Eigenschaft *116*
questionnaire Fragebogen *45*
to quit aufhören, aussteigen *56;* **to quit school** die Schule schmeißen *102*
quotation Zitat *69*

R
race (Wett-)Rennen *12*
to race um die Wette fahren *12*
to raise money Geld aufbringen, hier: sammeln *50*
ram Widder *108*
rand Rand (südafrikanische Währung) *38*
range Reihe, Auswahl *65;* Spannbreite, Umfang *110*
ranger Förster/in, Waldhüter/in *97*
rare (Steak:) blutig *44*
rather eher *111;* **rather than** statt *94*
reaction Reaktion *61*
to read out (laut) vorlesen *15*
to realise bemerken *114;* **to realise sth** etw verwirklichen, umsetzen *86*
realistic realistisch, wirklichkeitsnah *46*
reality Wirklichkeit *14*
T **reason** Grund, Begründung *48*
rebellious rebellisch *108*
to receive erhalten *54*
reception Empfang, Rezeption *88*
receptionist Empfangsmitarbeiter/in *87*
recipient Empfänger/in *56*
to recognize erkennen, wiedererkennen *55*
to recommend empfehlen *78*
record Aufzeichnung, Dokumentation *97*
recording Aufnahme *98*
to recruit einstellen *50*
recyclable recyclebar *93*
to reduce verringern, mindern, reduzieren *106*
referee Schiedsrichter/in *14*
reference Referenz *32;* **reference number** Referenz *130*
to reject ablehnen *67*
relationship Verhältnis, Beziehung *14*
relative Verwandte/r *126*
to relax sich entspannen, sich erholen *96*
relaxed locker, entspannt *38*
T **relevant** wichtig, relevant *64*
relief Hilfe *22*
to remove entfernen *97*
to repair reparieren *9*
to repeat wiederholen *70*
to replace ersetzen, austauschen *60*
replacement Ersatz *110*
to report berichten *16*
report Bericht *43*
to represent repräsentieren *42*
request, on ~ auf Anfrage *32*
to require erfordern, brauchen *65;* verlangen *116*
to rescue retten *118*
T **rescue squad** Rettungskommando, -trupp *119*
rescuer Retter/in *119*
research Forschung, Recherche *16*
to research recherchieren *81*
T **reservation** Reservierung *37*
resident Bewohner *50*
resort Urlaubsort, Ferienanlage *86*
resource Mittel, Ressource *110*
respect Respekt *49*
to respect achten, respektieren *56*
responsible verantwortungsbewusst *50;* **to be responsible for sth** für etw zuständig sein *17;* für etw verantwortlich sein *50*
to restore wiederherstellen *118*
result Ergebnis *45*
retail Einzelhandel *30*
to return zurückkehren *111*
to rewrite umformulieren *75*
rickshaw Rikscha *38*
rid, to get ~ of sth etw loswerden *90*
riddle Rätsel *82*
ride Fahrt *119*
to ride reiten *13;* **to ride sth** etw fahren *38*
ridiculous lächerlich, lachhaft *121*
risk Risiko *45*
(the) Roaring Twenties die Wilden Zwanziger *78*
to roast braten *121*
to rob rauben, berauben, ausrauben *69*
robbery Raub, Raubüberfall *117*
robot Roboter *6*
rock Stein, Fels *6*
role-playing game Rollenspiel *78*
romance Romanze *108*
roof Dach *96*
rope Seil *118*
rose Rose *92*
routine Routine *16*
royal königlich *110*
rubbish Müll, Abfall *94*
T **rude** unverschämt, unhöflich *54*
to run sth etw betreiben, leiten, führen *17;* **to run out of sth** etw nicht mehr haben *112;* **to run out of time** keine Zeit mehr haben *66*
runner Läufer/in *15*
running Laufen *13*
rural ländlich *120*
T **to rush into doing sth** etw überstürzt tun *64*

S
sack Sack *131*
safe sicher *17*
safety Sicherheit *17*
to sail segeln, (mit dem Schiff) fahren *24*
sale, on ~ im Verkauf; zu kaufen *45*
sales Verkauf, Vertrieb *30;* **sales assistant** Verkäufer/in *62;* **salespeople** Verkaufspersonal, Vertriebsmitarbeiter *9*
sample Probe *116*
sandal Sandale *11*
satisfying befriedigend, zufriedenstellend *62*
to save sb jdn retten *104*
scale Maßstab *40;* **scales** Waage *108*
to scan absuchen, überfliegen *22*
to scare sb jdn erschrecken, jdm Angst machen *101*
school leaver Schulabgänger/in *63*
scientist (Natur-)Wissenschaftler/in *40*
scissors Schere *117*
score Ergebnis, Punktestand *61*
scorpion Skorpion *108*
to scrape kratzen *121*
to scream schreien *80*
screen Bildschirm *40*
sea, by ~ auf dem Seeweg *130*
seafood Meeresfrüchte *43*
to seal zukleben *98*
to search for sth nach etw suchen *110*
secondary school weiterführende Schule *32*
secretary Sekretär/in *92*
security officer Sicherheitsbedienstete/r *33*
seed Samen *98*
to seek suchen *28*
to select wählen, auswählen *98*
self-confident selbstbewusst *47*
seller Verkäufer/in *58*
semi- halb-, semi- *40*
to send sth out etw verschicken *17*
senior leitende/r (Angestellte/r) *52;* **senior staff** Führungskräfte, leitende Angestellte *110*
sensation Sensation *86*
sense Sinn *56;* **to make sense** Sinn haben/ergeben, einleuchten *56*
sensitive sensibel *108*
separate getrennt *44*
to separate (sich) trennen *102*
serious ernst, ernsthaft *50*
to serve servieren *25*
service Dienstleistung *77*
to service warten *60*
to settle down sesshaft werden, eine Familie gründen *110;*
T **to settle in** sich eingewöhnen *52*

A–Z word list

several mehrere *14*
to sew nähen *76;*
to sew sth up etw zunähen *76*
shame, a ~ schade, ein Jammer *46*
shelf, shelves Regal, Regale *89*
shellfish Schalentier *42*
F **shelter** Unterkunft *67*
to shine scheinen *131*
shock Schock *22*
shocked schockiert *90*
to shoot (Film:) drehen; fotografieren *106*
to shop einkaufen *83*
to shoplift Ladendiebstahl begehen *74*
shoplifting Ladendiebstahl *69*
shopping trolley Einkaufswagen *94*
short, to be/go ~ of sth nicht genug von etw haben *110*
shot (Film:) Einstellung, Szene *106*
to show sb around jdn herumführen *52*
shy schüchtern *54*
side dish Beilage *42*
sight Anblick, Blick *24;* **at first sight** auf den ersten Blick *24*
sign Schild *17*
to sign unterschreiben, signieren *34;*
to sign up sich anmelden *58*
similar ähnlich *27*
Sincerely yours, *(AE)* Mit freundlichen Grüßen *70*
T **single room** Einzelzimmer *37*
F **to sink** sinken, untergehen *67*
to sit around herumsitzen *17*
situation Situation *31*
size Größe *82*
skiing Skifahren *13*
skill Fähigkeit, Fertigkeit *11*
to skim (Text) überfliegen *14*
skin Haut *72*
slave Sklave/Sklavin *128*
slavery Sklaverei *128*
to slow sth down etw verlangsamen, bremsen *106*
smart schick, elegant *14*
smoothly glatt *33*
Snow White Schneewittchen *86*
soccer Fußball *14*
social sozial *50*
soil Erde, Boden *94*
solar Sonnen- *46*
sold out ausverkauft *45*
soldier Soldat/in *22*
to solve lösen *33*
someday irgendwann *8*
to sort sortieren *85;* **to sort through sth** etw durchsehen *61*
to sound klingen *12*
(the) southern seas die Südsee *24*
to sow säen, aussäen *99*
space (Brettspiel:) Feld *24;* Platz *96*
spacecraft Raumschiff *65*
spade Spaten *94*
speaker Lautsprecher *80*
Speaking. Am Apparat. *18*
special besonders, Spezial- *21*
to specialize in sth sich auf etw spezialisieren *91*
specific bestimmt, spezifisch *22*
speech Rede; gesprochene Sprache *47;* **speech bubble** Sprechblase *63*
speed Geschwindigkeit *56*
spell checker Rechtschreibüberprüfung *56*
springer spaniel Englischer Springer Spaniel (Hunderasse) *24*
square Quadrat, Feld, Platz *24*
stadium Stadion *37*
staff Personal, Belegschaft, Angestellte *17*
stage Bühne *33*
star Stern *109*
statement Aussage, Behauptung *9*
to steal stehlen *69*
stereotype Klischee *124*
to sterilise sterilisieren *116*
stevedore Hafenarbeiter/in *130*
steward Ordner/in *30*
to stick kleben *54;* **to stick sth out** etw hinausstecken *81*
stinky stinkend *124*
stone Stein *76*
T **to store** speichern *80*
strange seltsam, komisch *25*
strawberry Erdbeere *11*
street light Straßenlaterne *94*
strength Stärke, Kraft *7*
stressed out gestresst *38*
strict streng *42*
to strike schlagen, zuschlagen *99;* treffen *104*
striker Stürmer/in *15*
to study lernen, studieren *102*
stuff Zeug, Kram *33*
style Stil *30*
subject Thema *22*
substance Substanz, Stoff *69*
subway *(AE)* U-Bahn *40*
to succeed gelingen, Erfolg haben *61*
success Erfolg *86*
successful erfolgreich *86*
such (a) so, solch (eine/r/s) *38*
to suggest vorschlagen *67*
suggestion Vorschlag *67*
suicide Selbstmord *70*
suit Anzug, Kostüm *126*
to suit passen *19;*
T **to suit sb** (Kleider:) jdm stehen *82*
suitable passend *55*
suitcase Koffer *82*
sunglasses Sonnenbrille *82*
sunrise Sonnenaufgang *124*
sunset Sonnenuntergang *124*
to supervise beaufsichtigen, kontrollieren *17*
supplier Lieferant, Anbieter *98*
support Unterstützung, Betreuung *60;* **after-sales support** Nachverkaufsunterstützung, Kundendienst, Support *60*
to support unterstützen *16*
sure sicher(lich), (na) klar *12;* sicher *22;* **to make sure** sicherstellen, gewährleisten *17*
surface Oberfläche *116*
surgeon Chirurg/in *97*
surgery Arztpraxis *116*
surgical chirurgisch *103*
to surprise sb jdn überraschen *12*
surprising überraschend *127*
surroundings Umgebung *96*
survey Umfrage, Erhebung *30;*
survey-taker Befragte/r *101*
to survive überleben *76*
to sweep kehren, putzen *54*
sweets Süßigkeiten *93*
swelling Schwellung *117*
to swipe (a chip card) (eine Chipkarte) durchziehen *116*

T

tails (Münze:) Zahl *24*
to take a test eine Prüfung ablegen *122;* **to take part in sth** an etw teilnehmen *16;* **to take place** stattfinden *16;* **to take sb on** jdn einstellen *62;* **to take sb's temperature** bei jdm Fieber messen *104;* **to take turns** sich abwechseln *16*
talented talentiert *8*
talk Vortrag *128;* **to give a talk** einen Vortrag halten *128*
tall groß (Körpergröße) *15*
tank Tank *96*
tap Wasserhahn *74*
to tape a bandage einen Verband anlegen *117*
target group Zielgruppe *84*
to target sb auf jdn zielen, es auf jdn absehen *70*
task Aufgabe *17*
taste Geschmack *128*
to taste schmecken *43*
tasteless geschmacklos *84*
to teach beibringen, lehren *9*
technician Techniker/in *26*
T **technique** Methode, Technik *64*
technology Technik, Technologie *9*
telephone harassment Telefonterror *69*
temperature Temperatur *39;* Fieber *104;* **to take sb's temperature** bei jdm Fieber messen *104*
tent Zelt *30*
terrible furchtbar, schrecklich *22*
test, to take a ~ eine Prüfung ablegen *122*
text message SMS *53*
therapy Therapie *62*
therefore deshalb, daher *102*
thief Dieb/in *74*
thoroughness Gründlichkeit *116*

A–Z word list

though aber, allerdings *18*
thought Gedanke *49;* **thought-provoking** zum Nachdenken anregend *49*
to throw werfen *14;* **to throw sth away** etw wegwerfen *42*
thumb Daumen *98*
to tick off abhaken *59*
tidy sauber *97*
tight eng *83*
time, to have a hard ~ doing sth es schwer haben *38*
to time den richtigen Zeitpunkt abpassen *42*
timetable Stundenplan *16*
tiny winzig, klein *40*
title Titel *28*
together, to go ~ (well) (gut) zueinander passen *61*
tone Ton *56*
tool Werkzeug *6;* **toolbox** Werkzeugkasten *18*
tooth, teeth Zahn, Zähne *116*
top, to keep on ~ of things den Überblick haben/behalten *59*
to toss werfen *24*
total, in ~ insgesamt *14*
touch, to get in ~ with sb sich mit jdm in Verbindung setzen *16;* **to keep in touch** in Kontakt bleiben *57*
trade Handel, Gewerbe, Branche *18*
traffic Verkehr *39*
tragedy Tragödie *119*
to train eine Ausbildung machen *42*
trainee Auszubildende/r *16*
traineeship Ausbildungsplatz *62*
trainers Turnschuhe *125*
training Ausbildung *9*
to translate übersetzen *7*
translation Übersetzung *27*
transparent durchsichtig *40*
transport Verkehrswesen *61*
to trap sb jdn einschließen *118*
trapped, to be ~ in der Falle sitzen *104*
traumatized traumatisiert *76*
tray Wanne *98*
to treat sb jdn behandeln *70*
treatment Behandlung *116*
trespasser Eindringling, Unbefugte/r *94*
trial Gerichtsverhandlung, Prozess *76*
trip Ausflug *50*
trivia wissenswerte Kleinigkeiten *78*
trophy Trophäe, Pokal *16*
trouble Ärger, Schwierigkeiten *76;* **to get in trouble** Ärger bekommen, in Schwierigkeiten geraten *70*
truck Lastwagen *33*
to try sth on etw anprobieren *82*
turkey Truthahn *121*
turn, to be one's ~ dran/an der Reihe sein *24;* **to take turns** sich abwechseln *16*
to turn sich drehen *40;* **to turn sth off** etw ausschalten *113;* **to turn sth on** etw anschalten *80;* **to turn out** ausgehen, sich herausstellen *47;* **to turn right/left** rechts/links abbiegen *41;* T **to turn up** auftauchen, erscheinen *130*
Tuscan toskanisch *25*
tweezers Pinzette *117*
twins Zwillinge *108*
two-stroke engine Zweitaktmotor *93*
T **to type (in)** (ein)tippen *80*
tyre Reifen *38;* **flat tyre** platter Reifen *38*

U

unappetizing unappetitlich *84*
underground *(BE)* U-Bahn *37*
underwater unter Wasser *6*
unemployment Arbeitslosigkeit *50*
unfair ungerecht *126*
unfortunately leider, unglücklicherweise *55*
unfriendly unfreundlich *23*
unit Einheit, Gerät, Element *80*
United Nations Vereinte Nationen *22*
unlikely unwahrscheinlich *65*
to unload abladen *33*
unnecessary unnötig *47*
unpredictable unberechenbar *108*
to unscramble entwirren *37*
unused ungenutzt *94*
to update aktualisieren, auf den neusten Stand bringen *59*
upset aufgeregt, verärgert *56*
T **upstairs** oben *37*
urban städtisch, urban, Stadt- *94*
urgent dringend *33*
use Gebrauch *80*
F **useless, to be ~ at doing sth** zu etw nicht zu gebrauchen sein *67*
user Nutzer/in, Benutzer/in *17*

V

to vacuum staubsaugen *17*
vacuum cleaner Staubsauger *18*
valid gültig *33*
to value schätzen *94*
vampire Vampir/in *80*
vandalism Vandalismus *69*
to vandalize verwüsten *94*
vandals Vandalen *94*
varied abwechslungsreich *62*
variety Abwechslung *42*
vegetarian Vegetarier/in *25*
vehicle Fahrzeug *65*
via über, mittels *118*
victim Opfer *69*
view Ansicht *48*
viewer Zuschauer/in *106*
virgin Jungfrau *108*
visible sichtbar *57*
vision Sehvermögen, Blickfeld *40*
to visualize bildlich umsetzen, visualisieren *94*
voice Stimme *56*
voicemail Anrufbeantworter, Voicemail *59*
volume Lautstärke *80*
voluntary freiwillig, ehrenamtlich, unentgeltlich *29*
volunteer ehrenamtliche/r Helfer/in, Freiwillige/r *30*
to volunteer ehrenamtlich tätig sein *30*
T **to vomit** sich erbrechen *119*
vote Abstimmung *76*

W

wage Lohn *128*
T **waist** Taille *82*
waiting room Wartezimmer *116*
to wake up aufwachen *94*
walk Spaziergang *25*
walking trail Wanderweg *97*
wall Wand, Mauer *96*
ward (Kranken-)Station *110*
warehouse Lager *98*
waste Verschwendung *46*
wasteful verschwenderisch *47*
wasteland Ödland, unbebautes Gelände *94*
watch (Armband)uhr *125*
waterproof wasserdicht *45*
to wave winken *34*
wealthy wohlhabend, reich *50*
wedding Hochzeit *25*
T **welcome, You're ~.** Bitte sehr. Gern geschehen. *18*
welfare Wohl *50*
well, to be ~ off gut dran sein *126*
well-being Wohlbefinden *23*
well-done (Steak:) durch *44*
wheel Rad, hier: Lenkrad *69*
wheelbarrow Schubkarre *97*
wide breit, weit, groß *107*
wide shot Totale *107*
width Breite, Stärke *40*
wildlife Tierwelt *97*
wine Wein *126*
witness Zeuge/Zeugin *69*
woodsman Waldarbeiter *76*
work: to work out herausfinden *61;* **to work overtime** Überstunden machen *85*
work placement Praktikum *32*
workstation Arbeitsplatz *52*
worldwide weltweit *86*
worth wert, im Wert von *30*
wound Wunde *117*
to wrap einwickeln, hier: verbinden *117*
to wreck zerstören *94*

XYZ

X-ray Röntgen *116*
T **You're welcome.** Bitte sehr. Gern geschehen. *18*
youth Jugend, Jugendlicher *69*
yummy lecker *128*
T **zone** Bereich *80*

Unregelmäßige Verben

be – was/were – been	*sein*
beat – beat – beaten	*schlagen, besiegen*
become – became – become	*werden*
begin – began – begun	*anfangen, beginnen*
bleed – bled – bled	*bluten*
break – broke – broken	*brechen*
bring – brought – brought	*bringen*
build – built – built	*bauen*
burn – burn – burn	*(ver)brennen*
buy – bought – bought	*kaufen*
catch – caught – caught	*fangen*
choose – chose – chosen	*wählen*
come – came – come	*kommen*
cost – cost – cost	*kosten*
cut – cut – cut	*schneiden*
do – did – done	*tun, machen*
draw – drew – drawn	*zeichnen*
dream – dreamt – dreamt	*träumen*
drink – drank – drunk	*trinken*
drive – drove – driven	*fahren*
eat – ate – eaten	*essen*
fall – fell – fallen	*fallen*
feed – fed – fed	*füttern, ernähren*
feel – felt – felt	*(sich) fühlen, empfinden*
fight – fought – fought	*kämpfen*
find – found – found	*finden*
fit – fit/fitted – fit/fitted	*passen*
fly – flew – flown	*fliegen*
forget – forgot – forgotten	*vergessen*
get – got – got (*AE* gotten)	*bekommen*
give – gave – given	*geben*
go – went – gone	*gehen, fahren*
grow – grew – grown	*wachsen*
hang – hung – hung	*hängen*
have – had – had	*haben*
hear – heard – heard	*hören*
hide – hid – hidden	*(sich) verstecken*
hit – hit – hit	*schlagen*
hold – held – held	*halten, festhalten*
keep – kept – kept	*behalten*
know – knew – known	*kennen, wissen*
lay – laid – laid	*legen*
lean – leant/leaned – leant/leaned	*(sich) lehnen, neigen*
learn – learnt/learned – learnt/learned	*lernen*
leave – left – left	*verlassen, weggehen*
let – let – let	*lassen*
lie – lay – lain	*liegen*
light – lit – lit	*anzünden, beleuchten*
lose – lost – lost	*verlieren*
make – made – made	*machen*
mean – meant – meant	*meinen, bedeuten*
meet – met – met	*treffen*
pay – paid – paid	*bezahlen*
put – put – put	*setzen, stellen, legen*
quit – quit/quitted – quit/quitted	*verlassen, aufhören*
read – read – read	*lesen*
ride – rode – ridden	*reiten, fahren*
rise – rose – risen	*(an)steigen*
run – ran – run	*laufen, rennen*
say – said – said	*sagen*
see – saw – seen	*sehen*
seek – sought – sought	*suchen*
sell – sold – sold	*verkaufen*
send – sent – sent	*senden, schicken*
set – set – set	*setzen, stellen*
show – showed – shown	*zeigen*
shut – shut – shut	*schließen*
sing – sang – sung	*singen*
sit – sat – sat	*sitzen*
sleep – slept – slept	*schlafen*
smell – smelt/smelled – smelt/smelled	*riechen*
speak – spoke – spoken	*sprechen*
spell – spelt/spelled – spelt/spelled	*buchstabieren*
spend – spent – spent	*ausgeben, verbringen*
stand – stood – stood	*stehen*
steal – stole – stolen	*stehlen*
swim – swam – swum	*schwimmen*
take – took – taken	*nehmen*
teach – taught – taught	*unterrichten, beibringen*
tear – tore – torn	*zerreißen*
tell – told – told	*sagen, erzählen*
think – thought – thought	*denken*
throw – threw – thrown	*werfen*
understand – understood – understood	*verstehen*
wake – woke – woken	*aufwachen, wecken*
wear – wore – worn	*tragen (Kleidung)*
win – won – won	*gewinnen*
write – wrote – written	*schreiben*

Lösungen zu den Tests

In den allermeisten Fällen gibt es mehrere richtige Antworten. Hier sind unsere Vorschläge, aber Sie können sich bestimmt auch andere ausdenken:

Test 1 (S. 36)

1 I get up at a quarter to seven. / The first lesson begins at five past eight. / I eat lunch at half past twelve. / I go home at three o'clock.	**4** a You can play tennis or do karate. b You can listen to music or go clubbing. c You can go to the shops / go shopping or to the cinema.
2 a How can I help you? b What was your name (again), please? c Can I have your phone number, please?	**5** a date of birth b primary school c work experience
3 On Saturday I went to a football match. / Then I went clubbing. / On Sunday I played a computer game.	**6** a I'm waiting in front of the cinema. b It's raining. c The film is (just) starting.

Test 2 (S. 68)

1 Siam Thai is the best restaurant. / Mumbai Curry is the cheapest restaurant. / Pronto Pizza is cheaper than Siam Thai, but it isn't as good.	**4** a Dear Mrs Barker b Thank you for your email. c I look forward to hearing from you.
2 a Can I just say something? b I don't agree with you there. c What do you think, Sarah?	**5** I've replied to the email from Mr Schmidt. / I haven't translated the company brochure (into German) yet. / I've photocopied the applications (for the new job).
3 Will I be rich one day? / Will I have a good job? / Will I have a nice boyfriend/girlfriend?	**6** I'm going to ... / buy new clothes. / look at the company website. / do a practice interview with a friend.

Test 3 (S. 100)

1 She's got light skin. / She's got long hair. / She wears glasses.	**4** a May I speak to Mr Francis, please? b This is (your name). c I'll call back (later).
2 We have to be at the railway station at half-past seven. / We have to take warm clothes. / We don't have to take lunch.	**5** Six of: chair, computer, drawers, envelopes, files, keyboard, mouse, pencils, pens, photocopier, plants, shelves, telephone
3 a If the monkey eats a banana, you lose a point. b If the tiger eats a monkey, you get ten points. c If/When you don't have any points, the game ends.	**6** a The plant is put in a box. b A barcode is stuck on the box. c The barcode is scanned

Test 4 (S. 132)

1 I'm interested in childcare. / I enjoy playing with children. / I'm good at looking after babies. / I've decided to become a nursery nurse.	**4** a Sorry, I didn't quite catch that. b I must have used the wrong word. c You're speaking a bit fast for me.
2 Lots of people were dancing. / Some people were drinking beer. / Two boys were arguing.	**5** Hello, there has been a robbery. / A person has been hurt. / We need an ambulance and the police.
3 a I would phone my father and he would take me to work in his car. b I would use my mobile phone to read and write emails. c I would do extra work and then ask for some free time later.	**6** Without globalization: There wouldn't be the Internet, so I wouldn't be able to play computer games or download music. There wouldn't be as many different goods in the shops, so shopping would be less fun. English wouldn't be so important, so I wouldn't have to learn it.

Bildquellenverzeichnis

RF-Fotos:

Alamy: S.12 / Radius Images, S.17 / Gamut Stock Images, S.18 / Gamut Stock Images, S.18 / 4 oben, S.38 / 2 / Radius Images, S.38 / 3 / FancyVeerSet8, S.72 / 1 / ImageSource, S.72 / 2 / ImageSource, S.72 / 6, S.77 / 2 / Radius Images, S.85 / 1 / D. Baker, S.85 / 2 / image100 Business J, S.85 / 8 / IE055, S.117 / 1 / canadabrian, S.117 / 5 / Radius Image, S.117 / 6 / IS545, S.119 / 5 / Huntstock, S.119 / 6 / moodboard, S.125 / oben / K. Wood, S.126/1 / graficart.net;

S. Ashdown: S.106 / 2 / 3 / 4 / 6

Corbis: S.85 / 4;

Fairtrade.net: S.128;

IStockphoto: S.6, S.17 / 1, 2, 3, 4, 6, S.19, S.21 / oben, S.21 / 1, 3, 5, 6, S.29 / oben, S.29 / 4, 5, 8, S.29 / unten (1–33), S.34, S.37, S.39 / 3, S.41 / 1 / 2, S.45 / oben, S.45 / 1, 3, 4, 5, S.51, S.53 / oben, S.54, S.55 / 1, 2, S.77 / oben, S.77 / 1, S.83, S.85 / 3, S.88, S.100, S.101 / 1–3, S.103 / 1–4, S.104, S.106 / 1, S.109 / oben, S.110 / 1–3, S.116 / 1–3, S.117 / oben, S.117 / 2 / 3 / 4, S.119 / 1 / 2 / 3 / 7, S.125 / 1 / 3 / 4 / 6, S.128, S.130 / 2 / 4;

Y. Thron: S.29;

Shutterstock: S.8, S.9 (1–3), S.13, S.18 (1, 2, 3, 5, 6, 7 oben), S.22 (6), S.29 / 3, 9, S.32, S.39 / 1, 2, S.45 / 2, S.48 (2), S.53 / 1, 3, 6, 9, S.58, S.60 (1–3), S.78, S.81 / 1–4, S.82 / 1–5, S.84 / 1–6, S.85 / oben, S.85 / 4, 6, 9, S.93 / oben, S.93 / unten, S.94, S. 97 (1–10), S.107, S.106 / 5 / 7, S.109, S.113, S.125 / 2 / 5, S.126/ 3, S.130

RM-Fotos:

Alamy: S.21 / 2 / Image Broker / J. Tack, S.4 / A. Segre, S.29 / 1 / J. Greenberg, S.29 / 2 / viennaphoto, S.29 / 6 / Image Source Black, S.30 / A. Flahive, S.30 / K.deWitt, S.31 / S. Kujawa, S.38 / E. Lacoste, S.41 / blickwinkel, S.46 / SouthBeach Production, S.50 / moodboard, S.53 / 10 / B. Mason, S.61 / M. Campbell, S.67 / Stockbroker, S.69 oben / A. Copson, S.69 / 1 / A. Hampton, S.69 / 2 / Beyond, S.69 / 3 / M. Heitner, S.69 / 4 / Kreutzer, S.69 / 5 / Acestock, S.70 / A. Hampton, S.72 / D. Plewka, S.72 / 4 / IndiaImages, S.72 / 5 / BlueMoonStock, S.77 /3 / Real-image, S.85 / 7 / S. May, S.96 / R. Levine, S.102 / M. Weber, S.103 / 9 / whitefoxphoto, S.110 oben / Baily-Cooper Photography3, S.114 / C. Howes, S.119 /4 / Ian Miles Flashpoint-Pictures, S.120 / Shout, S.122 / S.123 / I. Schulz (1 Foto), S.126 / Kai-Otto Melau;

Fotofinder: S.14 (re) / VISUM, S. 23 / VISUM, S.26 / 1 / photothek, S.53 / 8 / VISUM, S.103 / 5 / Vario, S.103 / 6, S.103 / 8 / Blickwinkel, S.118 / Blickwinkel, S.130 / 1 / Keystone / J. Zick, S.130 / 5 / Jalens / J. Affeldt;

PictureAlliance: S.14 (li) / epa / J. Smith, S.16 / epa / J. Castro, S.26 / 2 / C. Hager, S.86 / 1 / dpa, S.86 / 2 / AKGimages, S.90 / C. Dernbach;

Ullsteinbild: S.90 / 1